Total Quality in
PURCHASING
& SUPPLIER
MANAGEMENT

The St. Lucie Press
Total Quality Series™

BOOKS IN THE SERIES:

Total Quality in HIGHER EDUCATION

Total Quality in PURCHASING and SUPPLIER MANAGEMENT

Total Quality in INFORMATION SYSTEMS

Total Quality in RESEARCH and DEVELOPMENT

Total Quality in GOVERNMENT

Total Quality in HUMAN RESOURCES

Total Quality in TRANSPORTATION

Total Quality in MAINTENANCE

Total Quality in ORGANIZATIONAL DEVELOPMENT

Total Quality in PROJECT MANAGEMENT

Total Quality in MARKETING

Total Quality and ISO 9000

MACROLOGISTICS STRATEGY MANAGEMENT

For more information about these books call St. Lucie Press at (407) 274-9906

Series Editor • *Frank Voehl*
Series Development Editor • *Sandy Pearlman*

Total Quality in

PURCHASING & SUPPLIER MANAGEMENT

P.E., C.P.M., C.P.P.
Senior Partner
Advent Group, Inc.
Miami, Florida

S^t_L

St. Lucie Press
Delray Beach, Florida

Library of Congress Cataloging-in-Publication Data

Fernandez, Ricardo R.
    Total quality in purchasing and supplier management / by Ricardo R. Fernandez.
        p.   cm. — (Total quality series)
    Includes bibliographical references and index.
    ISBN 1-884015-00-X (alk. paper)
    1. Industrial procurement—Management.   2. Total quality management.   I. Title.   II. Series.
    HD39.5.F46   1995
    658.7'2—dc20   94-9069
                                                             CIP

Direct all inquiries to St. Lucie Press, Inc., 100 E. Linton Blvd., Suite 403B, Delray Beach, Florida 33483.

Phone: (407) 274-9906
Fax: (407) 274-9927

S^t_L

Published by
St. Lucie Press
100 E. Linton Blvd., Suite 403B
Delray Beach, FL 33483

CONTENTS

Foreword ix

Series Preface xi

Author Preface xiii

**1 The Need for Purchasing/Supplier Quality Management:
The Missing Link** 1
When Suppliers Are Not Involved 1
The Extended Organization 4
The Missing Link 6
Impact of Procurement on the Bottom Line 7
Factors Affecting Purchasing Decisions 9
Abstracts 11

2 Overview of Total Quality 15
What Is Total Quality 15
Total Quality as a System 20
Abstracts 27
Article: *The Deming Prize vs. The Baldrige Award* 30

**3 The Total Purchasing/Supplier Quality
Management Model** 45
The Supplier within Total Quality Management 45
Purchasing/Supplier Quality Management System 48
TQM vs. PSQM 50
The Organization as a System 51
Purchasing/Supplier Quality Management Flow 55
Exercises 57
Abstracts 62

4 Customer–Supplier Relationship 65
Customer Focus and Orientation 65
Hierarchy of Customer Needs 66
The Japanese Model of Customer–Supplier Relationships 68
Exercises 75
Abstracts 76
Article: *The Buyer–Supplier Relationship in*
    Total Quality Management 80

5 Linking Suppliers through Policy Deployment 95
Objectives of Linking 95
The Supplier within Policy Deployment 97
Steps in Supplier Policy Deployment 100
Exercises 115
Abstracts 121

6 Supplier Certification 127
Objectives of Supplier Certification 127
Certification Paradigms 128
The Supplier Audit 128
Types of Certification 132
Abstracts 137

7 ISO 9000 and Purchasing/Supplier Quality
    Management: A View to the Future 139
Prologue: The Coming of the Global Marketplace 139
Overview 140
Getting Started with ISO 9000 146
Implementing ISO 9000 158
Epilogue: The Driving Force Behind TQM 160

8 Supplier Continuous Improvement 165
Improvement Strategies 166
Systematic Improvement Method 171
Use of Quality Tools 177
Improvement Case Study 178
Variability Reduction 184
Abstracts 185

9 Supplier Measurement and Feedback 187
Closing the Loop 187
Factors to Consider 189
Feedback Methods 189
Statistical Process Control 191
Supplier Report Card 202
Supplier Scoring Methods 203
Supplier Selection 205
Abstracts 206
Article: *Building the Supplier-Focused*
ISO 9000 Quality Measurement System 208

10 Strategy for Implementation 213
Management Commitment 213
Establish a Design and Implementation Team 215
PSQM Implementation Planning 218
PSQM Structure 221
PSQM Training of Internal Staff 224
Supplier Policy Deployment 226
Supplier Symposia 227
Supplier and Project Selection and Planning 228
Quality Improvement Activities 229
Continuous Improvement 229
Project Results and Monitoring 230
Certification 231
Review of Certification 232
Review of the PSQM System 233
Abstracts 234

11 Conclusions and Future Expectations 235
Organizational Success Factors 235
The Business Environment Today and Tomorrow 239
Getting On With It 244
Abstracts 245

Case Study: Michigan Consolidated Gas Company 247
Applying the Quality Process to an MRO Environment 247
MichCon Quality Supplier's Manual (Goods and Services) ... 252

Appendix: Filling in the Gaps with a
History of Total Quality 285
  In the Beginning 285
  Introduction of Interchangeable Parts and
  Division of Labor 286
  The First Control Limits 287
  Defective Parts Inspection 287
  Statistical Theory 288
  Scientific Management and Taylorism 289
  Walter Shewhart—The Founding Father 292
  Origins of Deming 297
  Post-World War II 299
  The Other "Gurus" Arrive 301
  ISO 9000 and the Quality Movement 306

Glossary 311

Index 319

FOREWORD

There are four groups who could benefit from reading this book: those in purchasing and materials management, those in operations management, those in internal auditing, and those in business schools taking a sequence of courses in purchasing and materials management. It is equally appropriate for newcomers to purchasing who have some experience in this arena. It is also filled with great ideas for moving a purchasing agent or executive to a higher level of understanding and performance.

Rick Fernandez has brought together the great ideas of today that will help in the field not only now, but into the future as well. Included are concepts in Total Quality Management, ISO 9000 standards, the Malcolm Baldrige National Quality Award, and Quality Functional Deployment, which are of importance to leading professionals in procurement.

The book is well-written; it is easy at times but challenging at others. The wide variety of mini-case studies that cover a broad range of business applications help enliven the book. Finally, the large case study near the end of the book provides superb insight on how Michigan Consolidated Gas Company brought the concepts of quality into their supplier program. The philosophy and methods can be applied to any purchasing organization.

This is not a book to be read straight through. Take notes as you read, and write down the ideas that you can convert into action.

Having done that, I hope that you will join me in thanking Rick Fernandez for the effort and results in providing a needed and valuable book.

William A. Golomski

SERIES PREFACE

The St. Lucie Press Series on Total Quality originated when some of us realized that the rapidly expanding field of Total Quality Management was neither well defined nor well focused. This realization, coupled with the current hunger for specific, how-to examples, led to the formulation of a plan to publish a series of subject-specific books on total quality, a new direction for books in the field to follow.

The essence of this series consists of a core nucleus of seven titles, around which the remaining fifteen or so books will revolve:

- Education Transformation: *Total Quality in Higher Education*
- Respect for People: *Total Quality in Human Resources*
- Speak with Facts: *Total Quality in R&D*
- Customer Satisfaction: *Total Quality in Marketing*
- Continuous Improvement: *Total Quality in Information Systems*
- Supplier Partnerships: *Total Quality in Purchasing and Supplier Management*

As we move toward the mid-1990s, we at St. Lucie Press are pleased to witness a true convergence of the philosophy and underlying principles of total quality, leading to a common set of assumptions. One of the most important deals with the challenges facing the purchasing and supplier quality management functions of many organizations.

This book introduces the reader to the relevance of total quality for these areas. The objective is to provide managers and practitioners with a ready guide to implementation issues as they relate to quality management techniques and practices, as well as to the broader themes presented in the planning, organizational sciences, and systems technology fields.

What this means to the enterprise is that total quality is a means of assuring quality and standards by providing a philosophy as well as a set of tools. The premise is that excellence can be achieved through a singular focus on customers and their interests as the number one priority, a focus which requires a high degree of commitment, flexibility, and resolve. However, no book can tell an organization how to achieve total quality; only the customers and stakeholders can.

As Series Editor, I am pleased with the manner in which the series is developing and am pleased to contribute in various ways. Of particular interest to me has been the production of the abstracts contained in the books, as well as the preparation of the case studies, exercises, and ISO 9000 material. The chapter on the history of total quality, which will appear in each book, was a fascinating journey for me, and I hope that each of you will feel the same way after reading it. I am indebted to my son, Chris Voehl, for all his help in the research and writing of certain abstracts.

In the area of abstracts, we are also indebted to Richard Frantzreb, President of Advanced Personnel Systems, who has granted permission to incorporate selected abstracts from their collection, which they independently publish in a quarterly magazine called *Quality Abstracts*. This feature is a sister publication to *Training and Development Alert*. These journals are designed to keep readers abreast of literature in the field of quality and to help readers benefit from the insights and experience of experts and practitioners who are implementing total quality in their organizations. Each journal runs between 28 and 36 pages and contains about 100 carefully selected abstracts of articles and books in the field. For further information, contact Richard Frantzreb (916-781-2900).

We trust that you will find this book both usable and beneficial and wish you maximum success on the quality journey. If it in some way makes a contribution, then we can say, as Dr. Deming often did at the end of his seminars, "I have done my best."

Frank Voehl
Series Editor

AUTHOR PREFACE

With the many different books that have been published on Total Quality Management, it is hard to come up with a topic that has not been addressed, yet some areas have been given more emphasis than others. Although Purchasing and Supplier Management in an organization really accounts for the majority of the variability within the products and services being delivered to the customer, little has been written that provides an integrated management approach to this very important function. This, I believe, is the "missing link" in many quality systems. Many different approaches to supplier management have been published and have been implemented in the last few years, ranging from JIT and supplier audits to EDI among others, yet these approaches seem to be disconnected from the overall strategic direction of the organization.

This book provides an integrated systematic approach that links the needs of the organization and its customers to its suppliers. It does so by understanding and linking the overall quality objectives of the organization to those of the Purchasing Department and the supplier organizations. This approach emphasizes the concepts of policy deployment as applied to the strategic planning and integration of the Purchasing and Supplier Management function. The approach is additive in nature. You don't necessarily have to throw away what you have done to start the system; instead, you can actually build on existing structures and systems to implement this Purchasing and Supplier Management System. A Systematic Improvement Method developed by Advent Group, Inc. that can be used to work with supplier process improvements is also featured. A customer–supplier relationship is utilized as an umbrella that defines the culture within which a Purchasing and Supplier Quality Management System can succeed in the long run. An implementation approach is suggested that motivates all the interested and affected parties in the organization to participate in the design of the system and therefore helps to gain overall buy-in. The book also looks at current and future issues that affect the development of the Purchasing and Supplier Quality Management System, including ISO 9000, education, and developing technologies. Finally, selected articles and abstracts and a complete case study are included to complement the concepts being studied. These articles can be the starting point for further research in order to gain a deeper understanding of the subject.

None of the accomplishments of an individual can be attributed to that individual alone, and the development of this book is no exception. Not only do I need to acknowledge the people who specifically assisted with the book, but also the many other people in my life who have made it possible for me to have the background, desire, and drive necessary to write this book. Many people have influenced me during my years, but some stand out. The first are my parents, Ricardo and Maria. As immigrants from communist Cuba, they exemplified the concepts of work, ethics, and the need for education. They had lost everything and had to start a new life in a foreign land that provided great opportunity for those who were willing to work for it. Another very important influence was my first mentor, William W. Swart. Bill helped me put it all together at the University of Miami and for many years to come. Now as I have matured in the professional arena, I am very honored to be considered a good friend and associate of Bill Golomski, who has provided me with many opportunities to learn. Last, but not least, is my wife, Mari. She has always been there to share my successes and to support me when I have felt down or pessimistic. We are so different that we complement each other beautifully. Her strengths are my weaknesses and her weaknesses my strengths. She has provided great inspiration and motivation to finish this book. Of course, you can't leave out my boys, Ricky and Danny, who understood when we had to sacrifice some of our "family days" so that this book could be completed. Together we make the perfect team.

Thanks should also go to my many co-workers at Florida Power & Light who together gave it all they had during the development of the Quality System at FPL and the preparation for the Deming Prize audit. That was truly a historical effort that will go down in the management books so that everyone can learn what to do and what not to do when implementing a Total Quality Management System. I also want to thank all the people who have directly or indirectly assisted in this project, especially Frank Voehl for always having faith in my abilities and making publication of this book possible, Jorge Fernández for his contributions and reviews of the original manuscript, my fellow examiners and other members of the Sterling Quality Award for their comradeship, Jorge Ros and Angel Alonso for their interest in the completion of this book, and to our clients for providing the environment in which these concepts can be applied.

Although this book is intended to fill some of the voids that currently exist in the area of Purchasing and Supplier Quality Management, it still leaves some voids to be filled by others within their own corporate environments. The book explains some of the approaches that have been successful at particular companies in their own corporate cultures, but these approaches should not be taken as a prescription to be applied universally. Each company needs to consider the particular nature of its business, and the associated benefits and risks, before deciding to adopt or adapt any of the approaches explained in this book to its own environment. The book provides a conceptual structure which needs to be further developed within each organization. This is the job of the Design and Implementation Team and the PSQM Council, whose roles are discussed in Chapter 10. They, along with their consultant, must make the transition from the general concepts in the book to application at their company. Only if this is done successfully can the system have a reasonable chance to meet the goals that have been designated for it by the PSQM Council.

Ricardo R. Fernandez
Author

DEDICATION

To Ricardo, Maria, and Mari
who have been the greatest influences in my life

And to Ricky and Danny
who I love dearly

CHAPTER 1

The NEED for PURCHASING/ SUPPLIER QUALITY MANAGEMENT: The MISSING LINK

WHEN SUPPLIERS ARE NOT INVOLVED

In order to understand the benefits of a Purchasing/Supplier Quality Management System, it is necessary to first understand the types of problems that could be encountered in the absence of such a system. One of the best ways to illustrate these problems is to examine some case studies. The two that follow provide a good indication of the types of problems that are created when the supplier is not involved and how the same problems might be avoided with the involvement of the supplier.

Case Study: The New Avensis (Automotive)

A new hypothetical automobile, the Avensis, was recently developed by an American manufacturer to directly compete with the Japanese and German high-quality imports. The Avensis was based on some currently successful models that this manufacturer had recently redesigned. The R&D department along with the marketing department conducted extensive market research in preparation for this design. In addition, they joined forces with the engineering and manufacturing departments to develop a design that was customer oriented, easy to manufacture, and price competitive. Once a prototype of this new car was built, a few customer focus groups were invited to review the car and to provide feedback on its strengths and weaknesses. Overwhelmingly, the customer groups indicated that the quality of the dashboard must be improved.

The dashboard had been designed just like every other part on the new car, with input from the R&D, marketing, engineering, and manufacturing departments. All of this information was considered in developing the new dashboard. Why was the response so negative? The design was not European or Japanese in concept; it simply followed the current design trends in American cars. The customer groups that had been assembled were buyers from the target market. These individuals had seen the dashboards of some of the new Japanese and German imports and were not at all impressed with the dashboard on the Avensis.

The concurrent engineering team was in a quandary. How could they improve this design? One of the team members had an idea. He went on to explain that their current supplier of dashboards had suggested that they reconsider the dashboard design, but the team had thought that it would not be in their best interest to change the design. They believed that they had come up with an excellent design that would be very pleasing to their customers. They were so wrong.

The team member persisted. He believed that the team should bring in the supplier to talk to the members about their ideas. Maybe the supplier could offer some good suggestions as to how to improve the design of the dashboard. The other team members were very concerned about this possibility. They would have to be very careful because the original design had been sent out for bid and the lowest bid had been selected. They did not know if the purchasing department would allow them talk to the supplier about this issue. Because the contract had already been awarded, a new design would have to be rebid; if a supplier was assisting in the design of the new dashboard, that supplier would have an unfair advantage in the bidding process. This might be viewed as unethical. What should they do? How did they get into this situation? Should they have included a supplier or various suppliers in the original design meetings? Could they trust the suppliers not to divulge their trade secrets to other automobile manufacturers?

Case Study: The Host Hospital (Healthcare/Service)

After a few years of trying to create a total quality culture at a hypothetical hospital called The Host Hospital, the administration noticed that although most areas of patient care had reduced the number of complaints per admission, the number of complaints about pharmacy services was increasing. They wondered why. They knew that pharmacy services were currently provided by an outside supplier to the hospital. This firm was very well known in the industry and had a good reputation. Each year the hospital requested bids from the various suppliers that provide this kind of service. The current pharmacy supplier was selected based on the lowest bid and had only been with the hospital for the past six months. When the original total quality management (TQM) training took place at the hospital, another supplier had the contract. Since then, various other suppliers had been awarded the contract. In fact, the supplier had changed almost every year, because the suppliers became more competitive and undercut each others' prices. Administration was very pleased with the reduced costs for pharmacy services, but doctors, nurses, and patients were now complaining about these services.

A quality improvement team had been working on this issue for about four months, but with few results. The team was composed of doctors, nurses, and administrators. They claimed that the only possible solution seemed to be to terminate the current supplier and get a new one or to start an in-house pharmacy service where the situation could be better managed and the quality control of the pharmacy process improved. They hit two major barriers. First, there was no money in the budget to be able to take over the pharmacy process. Money was not available for the equipment, systems, inventory, and fixtures necessary to develop a new pharmacy department within the hospital. A facilitator of the quality improvement process visited one of the team meetings and asked whether the team had talked to the current supplier to determine why the quality standards of the hospital were not being met. Team members replied that they had met with the supplier, but because they had no data about the complaints, the supplier felt that the dissatisfaction was unfounded.

The supplier had already heard rumors that the team was trying to get rid of him. He felt that he had been doing a good job and did not understand the accusations. He kept track of the amount of time his employees took to deliver drugs once they were requested. He maintained an adequate inventory of all drugs normally utilized by the hospital staff for patient care. In addition, he kept track of inventory stock-outs, number of requests not met, number of backorders, and other indicators. All the indicators were within the thresholds. He had set these thresholds himself based on his extensive experience in this area.

One of the team members asked why the supplier had not been included as part of the team. How could this service be improved without involving the supplier? Instead of just replacing the supplier, the team considered improving the relationship with the supplier and providing better feedback. If the supplier knew the extent of the complaints, perhaps he could improve. Why was feedback not provided by the hospital to this supplier and other suppliers as well? Did it make sense to discuss the hospital's needs with potential suppliers, rather than just requesting bids and then awarding a contract based on the lowest bid?

In this book we will discuss many ways that an organization can better work with suppliers by bringing them into the extended organization, by making them part of the overall process of designing new products and services, and by promoting their participation for the long-term future benefit of both organizations.

THE EXTENDED ORGANIZATION

What is normally included in the traditional organization? Most traditional organizations are made up of departments such as R&D, marketing, procurement, engineering, planning, finance, sales, service, manufacturing, and distribution among others. Other organizations are not organized by major function, but instead organize according to business unit or product group. These organizations usually consider their employees to be one of the most important parts of the organization. As many managers have noted, an organization is only as good as its employees. Today, most companies also include their customers as part of the organization. Most successful companies have found that it is crucial to involve their customers in the organization. They need constant input from their customers in order to identify their requirements and develop better and more innovative ways to meet those requirements.

These companies have learned that the boundaries of the organization must include more than just their own employees. They have included other stakeholders as part of the organization. The stakeholders should include the customers, employees, and stockholders of the organization, government agencies that regulate the industry, and suppliers.

Today's most successful companies have become successful by integrating the supplier into the corporate organization. These forward-thinking organizations have adopted the concept of the **extended organization**, which is depicted in Figure 1.1 This type of organization incorporates all suppliers and subsuppliers into the supply chain of the organization. The extended organization considers suppliers to be

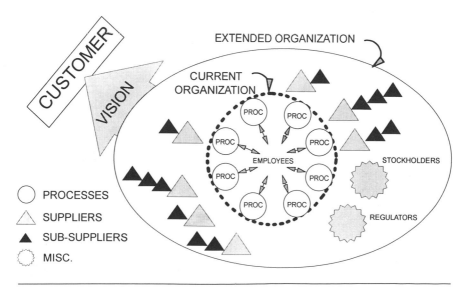

Figure 1.1 The Extended Organization.

partners in the future of the organization. The good of the organization becomes the good of the suppliers and vice versa.

Another somewhat similar concept is the **virtual organization**. This type of organization has a very limited corporate staff and few or no line personnel. All manufacturing is done by world-class suppliers that are very good at what they do. These suppliers are better able to respond rapidly to changes in customer requirements for quality, functionality, reliability, and quantity. Because of their world-class nature, they can also provide the product at a lower overall cost. These suppliers work on large economies of scale, the benefits of which they can pass on to their customers. Organizations that buy from them can therefore provide the ultimate consumer with a higher quality product at a lower cost. These suppliers can also change designs more easily, with a lower changeover cost for equipment, plant, and other fixed overhead costs.

For additional information, see Abstract 1.1 at the end of this chapter.

THE MISSING LINK

Many companies leave their suppliers out of the loop and treat them as outsiders. They consider their suppliers to be servants who must meet their requirements as stated, and they underutilize the creative talents of their suppliers by alienating them.

The supplier is one of the most critical links to profit, market share, and survival of most firms. World-class companies know that the quality of their products and services is directly related to the quality of their suppliers and the products and services that they provide. A chain of factors that affect the overall attainment of improved market share, profit, and viability is depicted in Figure 1.2.

A customer-focused firm first works with its customer groups to better define their needs and to negotiate their customer requirements. This information, along with information about the economy, competitors, the market, benchmarks, technology, and government regulations, as well as the visionary ideas of the leadership of the organization, is utilized to develop the **vision, mission,** and **values** of the organization. These are integrated throughout the organization at different levels through the development and deployment of quality strategies and goals. These strategies and goals are deployed at differ-

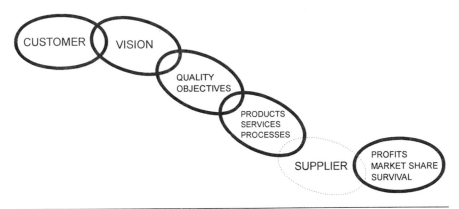

Figure 1.2   The Missing Link.

ent organizational levels (i.e., different divisions, departments, and functional areas) and align the different products and services that the organization provides to ensure that they are all focused in the same direction.

The problem is that many companies believe that this is sufficient. They believe that by performing the functions mentioned above, automatically market share is increased, profits go up, and the company survives. The missing link in this chain as described is the supplier. When the supplier is not totally integrated in this chain, the chances of success are drastically diminished. Internal processes cannot be adequately improved without considering the effect of incoming materials or services. These become a major source of variation which must be dealt with in order to improve overall variability and to gain control of the overall process.

For additional information, see Abstract 1.2 at the end of this chapter.

IMPACT OF PROCUREMENT ON THE BOTTOM LINE

Many companies stress the need to sell in order to increase profits. These companies have grown basically because of their emphasis on marketing and sales. Let's compare an increase in sales versus a reduction in the cost of products and services purchased.

Assume that a company has a profit margin of 10 percent and the cost of goods purchased is 50 percent of sales. This means that if the company sold $1 million a year, the following breakdown would represent costs and profits:

Sales	$1,000,000
Manufacturing and overhead costs (40 percent of sales)	$400,000
Cost of products and services purchased (50 percent of sales)	$500,000
Total costs	$900,000
Profit (10 percent profit margin)	$100,000

Now let's examine at the effect of a 10 percent decrease in cost of products and services purchased for the same company, assuming that both sales and the sales price remain the same:

Sales	$1,000,000
Manufacturing and overhead costs (40 percent of sales)	$400,000
Cost of products and services purchased (45 percent of sales)	$450,000
Total costs	$ 850,000
Profit (15 percent profit margin)	$150,000

This analysis shows that reducing the cost of goods and services purchased by only 10 percent actually represents a 50 percent increase in profit, assuming that the sales prices and total sales do not change. This same effect would require a 50 percent increase in sales with the original 10 percent profit margin and no reduction in cost of products and services purchased:

Sales	$1,500,000
Manufacturing and overhead costs (40 percent of sales)	$600,000
Cost of products and services purchased (50 percent of sales)	$750,000
Total costs	$1,350,000
Profit (10 percent profit margin)	$150,000

One can conclude from this analysis that the effect of reducing the cost of products and services purchased is equal to a much larger percentage increase in sales. Which is preferable: to work with suppliers to reduce costs by 10 percent or to spend time and energy trying to increase sales? In some companies with limited markets, this may not even be a valid question. Companies in mature industries find it very difficult to improve marketing significantly. They are at the top of the S curve of the product or service development cycle, and the only way that they can improve profit is through significant cost reduction. An excellent example of this is the electric utility industry, in which the market is limited and regulated. The only to improve profit is to reduce costs. One of the most efficient ways to reduce costs is to integrate suppliers into the organization as part of the extended organization.

FACTORS AFFECTING PURCHÁSING DECISIONS

Which factors are considered the most important in determining purchasing decisions? Until recently, most companies still used price as the key determining factor. As a matter of fact, the American Society for Quality Control recently published a survey of "Factors Affecting

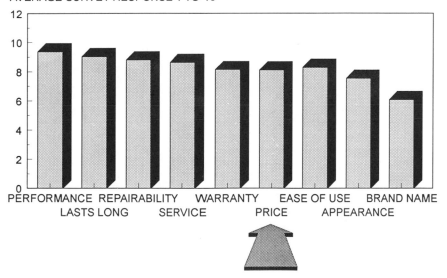

Figure 1.3 Factors in Consumer Purchasing Decisions. (Source: *Quality Progress.*)

Consumer Purchasing Decisions" (Figure 1.3). According to this survey, price was not the factor that received the highest score. Five out of nine factors actually scored higher than price: performance, lasts long, repairability, service, and warranty. Price ranked sixth out of nine factors. A graph of the results from this survey is provided in Figure 1.3.

What does this mean to organizations? It means that organizations need to reassess their buying practices. Do they buy based on price alone or do they take into account the other factors that affect buying decisions. These factors will be discussed in greater depth later in this book, to indicate how they can be utilized and combined with the overall objectives of the organization for the selection of suppliers.

For additional information, see Abstracts 1.3 and 1.4 at the end of this chapter.

ENDNOTES

1.   Figures 1.1 and 1.2 ©Advent Group, Inc.

ABSTRACTS

ABSTRACT 1.1
DEBUNKING THE *KEIRETSU* MYTH

Ota, Fusae
Quality Digest, March 1992, pp. 73–76

"Instead of whining and pressuring Tokyo," says the author, director of research at Japan's Ministry of International Trade and Industry Research Institute, "U.S. parts suppliers should beef up their technical development capability and quality control." He contends that the Japanese auto industry's pyramids of suppliers and subcontractors serving a manufacturer—called a *keiretsu*—are a far cry from the incestuous, exclusive groupings U.S. executives assume them to be. Actually, the author claims, "Japan's automotive *keiretsu* are overlapping networks built on cooperation and infused with a healthy dose of competition." Japanese automakers, he notes, get 70 percent of their parts from outside sources compared with about 40 percent for Detroit's Big Three. The same supplier in Japan often will have contracts with each of Japan's Top Four auto manufacturers (Toyota, Nissan, Honda, and Mazda). "In effect, automakers and their primary suppliers are simultaneously partners and competitors. Where several makers share a supplier, cross-holding of stocks is obviously not the glue binding these partnerships." While emphasis on long-term cooperation and joint development surely put newcomers at a disadvantage, the author suggests that U.S. companies start at the ground level, teaming up with one of the Japanese makers' U.S. transplants at the development stage of a new component.

ABSTRACT 1.2
COLLABORATION, COOPERATION, AND CELEBRATION

Severson, David
Quality Progress, September 1992, pp. 63–65

Collaborating, cooperating, and celebrating successes of front-line people are earmarks of successful companies, says the author. He gives three illustrations of these principles from companies which sought to reduce product changeover times:

- Eli Lilly's Tippecanoe, Indiana plant worked with suppliers to develop one-turn cam clamps needed for solvent changes with toxic chemicals.
- Cherry-Burrell Corp., of Cedar Rapids, Iowa, developed a cross-functional problem-solving group to study how to reduce the time it took on a particular machine to convert production from one part to another. Recognition of participating shop-floor workers increased morale.
- Procter & Gamble's Mehoopany, Pennsylvania plant developed teams to study ways to reduce changeover times. When a worker substituted a derailleur mechanism to replace a gearing system—reducing changeover time from an hour to a couple of seconds—the company videotaped him telling about it and circulated the inspiring tape to every P&G plant.

Most important ideas cost less than $500 to implement, says one P&G engineer. Finding the money to experiment and supporting the employee until he or she gets it right pays off handsomely for the company.   (©*Quality Abstracts*)

ABSTRACT 1.3
THE COPYING MACHINE PAPER CAPER:
WHERE LOWEST PRICE DID NOT WORK

Hammons, Charles
Business Horizons, March–April 1992, pp. 68–70

This is the true story of an organization that was instructed by upper management to cut costs across the board. The author relates how a purchaser, prompted by a memo on this initiative, bought lower-priced copy machine paper from an unknown supplier. Then he outlines the disastrous consequences for the entire organization when the copy machines got jammed, and the remaining paper was left sitting useless in the company's warehouse. The author, who had been called in after these events to study the situation, interviewed the three people closest to the problem—the purchaser, the purchasing department manager, and the plant manager—and he quotes each at length on their perspective of the situation and on what they learned. The author briefly enumerates the mistakes made, and he concludes by urging what sounds like participative management: "Employees should be encouraged to continually look for ways to increase the quality of the organization's activities. In this way, the costs of doing business will decrease while the quality increases. (©*Quality Abstracts*)

ABSTRACT 1.4
CUSTOMER–SUPPLIER INTEGRATION:
WHY BEING AN EXCELLENT CUSTOMER COUNTS

Moody, Patricia E.
Business Horizons, July–August 1992, pp. 52–57

What does it take to be a good supplier? The author uses a supplier survey and the experiences of several companies to provide an answer. First of all, she found that suppliers need enlightened customers in order to do their best. Suppliers want a relationship with customers that includes early supplier involvement in decisions, commitment to partnership, crisis management, and mutual trust. The common practice of buying by price rather than total value is a trust destroyer. Furthermore, partnership is crucial in an environment where suppliers are being overwhelmed by various quality audits and certification exercises, according to the author. Unfortunately, benchmark data on customer/supplier integration is readily available for only certain areas of operations and certain industries. The author describes various ways in which companies have obtained feedback from suppliers to improve partnership. The article also includes the complete Motorola Supplier Survey, as well as a five-stage model of customer–supplier partnership development.

CHAPTER 2

OVERVIEW of
TOTAL QUALITY

Frank Voehl

WHAT IS TOTAL QUALITY

Introduction

During the past five years, there has been an explosion of books in the field of Total Quality. Yet in all of the thousands of books and billions of words written on the subject, there is an absence of three essential ingredients: a good working definition, a comprehensive yet concise history, and a clear and simple systems model of total quality. This overview of total quality is intended to fill this void and provide some interesting reading at the same time.

Understanding the Concept of Total

Total quality is total in three senses: it covers every process, every job, and every person. First, it covers *every process*, rather than just manufacturing or production. Design, construction, R&D, accounting, marketing, repair, and every other function must also be involved in quality improvement. Second, total quality is total in that it covers *every job,* as opposed to only those involved in making the product. Secretaries are expected not to make typing errors, accountants not to make posting errors, and presidents not to make strategic errors. Third, total quality recognizes that *each person* is responsible for the quality of his or her work and for the work of the group.

Total quality also goes beyond the traditional idea of quality, which has been expressed as the degree of conformance to a standard or the product of workmanship. Enlightened organizations accept and apply the concept that quality is the degree of user satisfaction or the fitness of the product for use. In other words, *the customer determines whether or not quality has been achieved in its totality.*

This same measure—total customer satisfaction—applies throughout the entire operation of an organization. Only the outer edges of the company actually have contact with customers in the traditional sense, but each department can treat the other departments as its customer. The main judge of the quality of work is the customer, for if the customer is not satisfied, the work does not have quality. This, coupled with the achievement of corporate objectives, is the bottom line of total quality.

In that regard, it is important, as the Japanese say, to "talk with facts and data." Total quality emphasizes the use of fact-oriented discussions and statistical quality control techniques by everyone in the company. Everyone in the company is exposed to basic quality control ideas and techniques and is expected to use them. Thus, total quality becomes a common language and improves "objective" communication.

Total quality also radically alters the nature and basic operating philosophy of organizations. The specialized, separated system developed early in the twentieth century is replaced by a system of *mutual feedback and close interaction of departments.* Engineers, for example, work closely with construction crews and storekeepers to ensure that their knowledge is passed on to workers. Workers, in turn, feed their practical experience directly back to the engineers. The information interchange and shared commitment to product quality is what makes total quality work. Teaching all employees how to apply process control and improvement techniques makes them party to their own destiny and enables them to achieve their fullest potential.

However, total quality is more than an attempt to make better products; it is also a search for better ways to make better products. Adopting the total quality philosophy commits the company to the belief that there is always a better way of doing things, a way to make better use of the company's resources, and a way to be more productive. In this sense, total quality relies heavily upon value analysis as a method of developing better products and operations in order to maximize value to the stakeholder, whether customers, employees, or shareholders.

Total quality also implies a different type of worker and a different attitude toward the worker from management. Under total quality, workers are generalists, rather than specialists. *Both workers and managers are expected to move from job to job, gaining experience in many areas of the company.*

Defining Total Quality

First and foremost, total quality is a set of philosophies by which management systems can direct the efficient achievement of the objectives of the organization to ensure customer satisfaction and maximize stakeholder value. This is accomplished through the continuous improvement of the quality system, which consists of the social system, the technical system, and the management system. Thus, it becomes a way of life for doing business for the entire organization.

Central to the concept is the idea that a company should *design quality into its products,* rather than inspect for it afterward. Only by a devotion to quality throughout the organization can the best possible products be made. Or, as stated by Noriaki Kano, "Quality is too important to be left to inspectors."[1]

Total quality is too important to take second place to any other company goals. Specifically, it should not be subsidiary to profit or productivity. Concentrating on quality will ultimately build and improve both profitability and productivity. Failure to concentrate on quality will quickly erode profits, as customers resent paying for products they perceive as low quality.

The main focus of total quality is on *why*. It goes beyond the *how to* to include the *why to*. It is an attempt to identify the causes of defects in order to eliminate them. It is a continuous cycle of detecting defects, identifying their causes, and improving the process so as to totally eliminate the causes of defects.

Accepting the idea that the customer of a process can be defined as the next process is essential to the real practice of total quality. According to total quality, control charts should be developed for each process, and any errors identified within a process should be disclosed to those involved in the next process in order to raise quality. However, it has been said that it seems contrary to human nature to seek out one's own mistakes. People tend to find the errors caused by others and to neglect their own. Unfortunately, exactly that kind of self-disclosure is what is really needed.[2]

Instead, management too often tends to blame and then take punitive action. This attitude prevails from frontline supervisors all the way up to top management. In effect, we are encouraged to hide the real problems we cause, and instead of looking for the real causes of problems, as required by total quality, we look the other way.

The Concept of Control

The Japanese notion of *control* differs radically from the American; that difference of meaning does much to explain the failure of U.S. management to adopt total quality. In the United States, control connotes someone or something that limits an operation, process, or person. It has overtones of a "police force" in the industrial engineering setting and is often resented.

In Japan, as pointed by the Union of Japanese Scientists and Engineers counselor and Japanese quality control scholar Noriaki Kano, *control* means "all necessary activities for achieving objectives in the long-term, efficiently and economically. Control, therefore, is doing whatever is needed to accomplish what we want to do as an organization."[1]

The difference can be seen very graphically in the Plan, Do, Check, Act (P-D-C-A) continuous improvement chart, which is widely used in

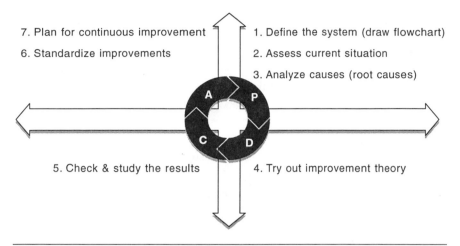

7. Plan for continuous improvement   1. Define the system (draw flowchart)

6. Standardize improvements   2. Assess current situation

    3. Analyze causes (root causes)

5. Check & study the results   4. Try out improvement theory

Figure 2.1 P-D-C-A Chart. System improvement is the application of the Plan-Do-Check-Act cycle on an improvement project.

Japan to describe the cycle of control (Figure 2.1). Proper control starts with planning, does what is planned, checks the results, and then applies any necessary corrective action. The cycle represents these four stages—Plan, Do, Check, Act—arranged in circular fashion to show that they are continuous.

In the United States, where specialization and division of labor are emphasized, the cycle is more likely to look like Fight, Plan, Do, Check. Instead of working together to solve any deviations from the plan, time is spent arguing about who is responsible for the deviations.

This sectionalism, as the Japanese refer to it, in the United States hinders collective efforts to improve the way things are done and lowers national productivity and the standard of living. *There need be nothing threatening about control if it is perceived as exercised in order to gather the facts necessary to make plans and take action toward making improvements.*

Total quality includes the control principle as part of the set of philosophies directed toward the efficient achievement of the objectives of the organization. Many of the individual components of total quality are practiced by American companies, but few practice total quality as a whole.

For additional information, see Abstract 2.1 at the end of this chapter.

TOTAL QUALITY AS A SYSTEM

Introduction

Total quality begins with the redefinition of management, inspired by W. Edwards Deming:

> *The people work in a system. The job of the manager is to work on the system, to improve it continuously, with their help.*

One of the most frequent reasons for failed total quality efforts is that many managers are unable to carry out their responsibilities because they have not been trained in how to improve the quality system. They do not have a well-defined process to follow—a process founded on the principles of customer satisfaction, respect for people, continuous improvement, and speaking with facts. Deming's teachings, as amplified by Tribus,[3] focus on the following ten management actions:

1. Recognize quality improvement as a system.
2. Define it so that others can recognize it too.
3. Analyze its behavior.
4. Work with subordinates in improving the system.
5. Measure the quality of the system.
6. Develop improvements in the quality of the system.
7. Measure the gains in quality, if any, and link them to customer delight and quality improvement.
8. Take steps to guarantee holding the gains.
9. Attempt to replicate the improvements inother areas of the system.
10. Tell others about the lessons learned.

Discussions with Tribus to cross-examine these points have revealed that the manager must deal with total quality as *three* separate systems: a social system, a technical system, and a management system. These systems are depicted as three interlocking circles of a ballantine,[4] as shown in Figure 2.2.

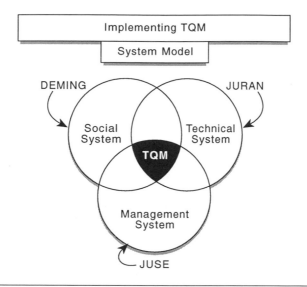

Figure 2.2   Implementing TQM—System Model.

Overview of the Social System

Management is solely responsible for the transformation of the social system, which is basically the culture of the organization. It is the social system that has the greatest impact on teamwork, motivation, creativity, and risk taking. How people react to one another and to the work depends on how they are managed. If they enter the organization with poor attitudes, managers have to re-educate, redirect, or remove them. The social system includes the reward structure, the symbols of power, the relationships between people and among groups, the privileges, the skills and style, the politics, the power structure, the shaping of the norms and values, and the "human side of enterprise," as defined by Douglas McGregor.

If a lasting culture is to be achieved, where continuous improvement and customer focus are a natural pattern, the social system must be redesigned so as to be consistent with the vision and values of the organization. Unfortunately, the social system is always in a state of flux due to pressure from ever-changing influences from the external political and technological environments. The situation in most orga-

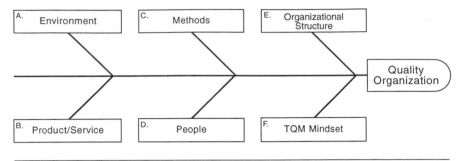

Figure 2.3 Strategic Areas for Cultural Transformation.

nizations is that the impact of total quality is not thought through in any organized manner. Change occurs when the pain of remaining as the same dysfunctional unit becomes too great and a remedy for relief is sought.

As shown in Figure 2.3, six areas of strategy must be addressed in order to change and transform the culture to that of a quality organization:

- Environment
- Product/service
- Methods
- People
- Organizational structure
- Total quality management mindset

Each of these areas will be covered in some detail in the chapters in this book. Of the six, however, structure is key in that total quality is about empowerment and making decisions at lower levels in the organization. Self-managing teams are a way to bring this about quickly.

The Technical System

According to Tribus,[5] "The technical system includes all the tools and machinery, the practice of quality science and the quantitative aspects of quality. If you can measure it, you can probably describe and perhaps improve it using the technical systems approach." The technical system thus is concerned with the flow of work through the organization to the ultimate customer. Included are all the work steps performed, whether by equipment, computers, or people; whether manual labor or decision making; or whether factory worker or office worker.

The technical system in most organizations contains the following core elements:

- Scientific accumulation of technology
- Pursuit of standardization
- Workflow, materials, and specifications
- Job definitions and responsibility
- Machine/person interface
- Number and type of work steps
- Availability and use of information
- Decision-making processes
- Problem-solving tools and process
- Physical arrangement of equipment, tools, and people

The expected benefits from analyzing and improving the technical system are to (1) improve customer satisfaction, (2) eliminate waste and rework, (3) eliminate variation, (4) increase learning, (5) save time and money, (6) increase employee control, (7) reduce bottlenecks and frustration, (8) eliminate interruptions and idle time, (9) increase speed and responsiveness, and (10) improve safety and quality of work life.

The three basic elements of every system are (1) suppliers who input, (2) work processes which add value, and (3) output to the customer. High-performing units and teams eliminate the barriers and walls between these three elements. A standard problem-solving process is often used by teams, such as the Quality Control Story, Business Process Analysis, etc.[6]

The Management System

The third system is the managerial system, which becomes the integrator. Only senior managers can authorize changes to this system. This is the system by which the other two systems are influenced. It is the way that practices, procedures, protocols, and policies are established and maintained. It is the leadership system of the organization, and it is the measurement system of indicators that tell management and the employees how things are going.

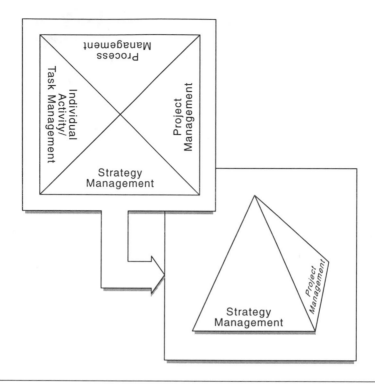

Figure 2.4   Management System Pyramid.

The actual deployment of the management system can be visualized in the shape of a pyramid. As shown in Figure 2.4, there are four aspects or intervention points of deployment: strategy management, process management, project management, and individual activity management. (Abstract 2.2, "Scientifically Selecting Suppliers" [see end of this chapter], describes the vertical integration of these management systems in the Japanese hierarchy.) A brief overview of these four aspects is as follows.

- **Strategy Management:**   Purpose is to establish the mission, vision, and guiding principles and deployment infrastructure which encourage all employees to focus on and move in a common direction. Objectives, strategies, and actions are considered on a three- to five-year time line.
- **Process Management:**   Purpose is to assure that all key processes are working in harmony to guarantee customer satisfaction and

maximize operational effectiveness. Continuous improvement/ problem-solving efforts are often cross-functional, so that process owners and indicator owners need to be assigned.

- **Project Management:** Purpose is to establish a system to effectively plan, organize, implement, and control all the resources and activities needed for successful completion of the project. Various types of project teams are often formed to solve and implement both process-related as well as policy-related initiatives. Team activities should be linked to business objectives and improvement targets.
- **Individual Activity Management:** Purpose is to provide all employees with a method of implementing continuous improvement of processes and systems within each employee's work function and control. Flowcharting key processes and individual mission statements are important linkages with which all employees can identify. A quality journal is often used to identify and document improvements.

Various types of assessment surveys are used to "audit" the quality management system. Examples include the Malcolm Baldrige assessment, the Deming Prize audit, and the ISO 9000 audit, among others. Basic core elements are common to all of these assessments. Their usefulness is as a yardstick and benchmark by which to measure improvement and focus the problem-solving effort. Recent efforts using integrated quality and productivity systems have met with some success.[7]

The House of Total Quality

The House of Total Quality is a model which depicts the integration of all of these concepts in a logical fashion. Supporting the three systems of total quality described in the preceding section are the four principles of total quality: customer satisfaction, continuous improvement, speaking with facts, and respect for people. These four principles are interrelated, with customer satisfaction at the core or the hub.

As with any house, the model and plans must first be drawn, usually with some outside help. Once the design has been approved, construction can begin. It usually begins with the mission, vision, values, and objectives which form the cornerstones upon which to build for the future. The pillars representing the four principles must be carefully constructed, well-positioned, and thoroughly understood, because the success of the total quality system is in the balance. As previously mentioned, many of the individual components of total quality are practiced by American companies, but few practice total quality as a whole.

ENDNOTES

1. During the course of the Deming Prize examination at Florida Power & Light in 1988 and 1989, Dr. Kano consistently emphasized this point during site visits to various power plants and district customer service operations. The concept of worker self-inspection, while new in the United States, has been a practiced art in Japan over the past twenty years.
2. Whethan, C. D. (1980). *A History of Science.* 4th edition, New York: Macmillan.
3. Tribus, Myron (1990). *The Systems of Total Quality.* published by the author.
4. The total quality ballantine was developed by Frank Voehl to illustrate the three-dimensional and interlocking aspects of the quality system. It is loosely based on the military concept of three interlocking bullet holes representing a perfect hit.
5. Tribus, Myron (1990). *The Three Systems of Total Quality.* published by the author; referenced in Voehl, Frank (1992). *Total Quality: Principles and Practices within Organizations.* Coral Springs, Fla.: Strategy Associates, pp. IV, 20.
6. The use of a storyboard to document the various phases of project development was introduced by Dr. Kume in his work on total quality control and was pioneered in the United States by Disney Studios, where it was used to bring new movies to production sooner.
7. For details, see Voehl, F. W. (1992). *The Integrated Quality System.* Coral Springs, Fla.: Strategy Associates.
8. Figures 2.2 and 2.3 ©1992 Strategy Associates, Inc.

ABSTRACTS

ABSTRACT 2.1
SCIENTIFICALLY SELECTING SUPPLIERS

Pang, Vera K.
Quality Progress, February 1992, pp. 43–45

Rejecting the definition of "supplier quality" as simple conformance to specifications, the author argues that it should be thought of as the supplier's ability to meet customer expectations—which are by nature dynamic. She shows how a better understanding of customer expectations (on the part of both customer and supplier) can be a win–win situation for both parties. One systematic approach to enhancing long-term customer–supplier relationships, she continues, is the supplier certification plan, which should be based on a "scientific" means for supplier evaluation. She proposes such a means—one which has been implemented in her firm, the Cummins/ Onan Corporation of Minneapolis, Minnesota. The author explains that the firm decided to collect information on supplier performance from six departments: purchasing, material control, design engineering, receiving, inspection, and quality assurance. These departments brainstormed evaluation criteria, and those selected were used to build a matrix of suppliers/ parts against performance criteria. Several representatives of each department were then asked to rate suppliers on each criterion on a five-point scale (though decimal ratings were accepted). The ratings from each department were averaged, and then the departments' ratings were averaged together (with equal weighting) to give an overall supplier rating. Much of this article is devoted to (1) a lengthy selection from the matrix that illustrates some of the criteria used and (2) a sample of the summary rating report. The author concludes by suggesting several ways in which these ratings can be used to improve supplier–vendor relationships and provide useful feedback for suppliers.   (©*Quality Abstracts*)

ABSTRACT 2.2
KEIRETSU IN AMERICA

Kinni, Theodore B.
Quality Digest, December 1992, pp. 24–31

The author is a well-known business writer who presents a concise and intriguing look at one of the key features of Japan's purchasing/supplier quality management system: *keiretsu.* The opening frame sets the stage with a simple well-directed statement: "Corporate Communism? Industrial war machines? As U.S. business comes to terms with dealing with Japan Inc. on home turf, it's time we understood how our neighbors do business." The reason, according to Kinni, is that Japanese business interests hold a sizeable stake in over 1500 U.S. factories, a fact that is confirmed by the Japan External Trade Organization.

Keiretsu is the Japanese system of conglomerates that trade heavily with one another, dating back to the Meiji Restoration of 1868. The author quotes Robert Kearns in describing how an American *keiretsu* structured along the lines of the Mitsubishi or Sumitomo group might operate: "Such a group would be worth close to a trillion dollars. Each of the 30 or so lead companies would own a piece of each other, would do business among themselves and meet once a month for lunch and discuss matters." *Keiretsu* members share in the economies of large-scale operation, says the author, such as low-cost capital at rates of 0.5 to 1.5 percent interest. Membership in a *keiretsu* virtually guarantees a market for one's goods, since other member companies own large stakes in each other's companies and the value of their investments depends on the long-term success and growth of the member firms. According to Kinni, "the *keiretsu* system is an ideal structure for rapid and secure economic growth and a major reason for Japan's economic success since World War II." After describing how the system operates, the author turns to examples of the *keiretsu* way, which means allowing a foreign group to eventually own about 30 percent of one's company stock and, to some extent, dictate the organization's future. Some U.S. companies, like Timken Co., are building structures reminiscent of the *keiretsu* on their own, such as the "supplier city" in Perry Township, Ohio, which will bring its suppliers within arm's reach. What does the future hold?

Is this an invasion or an evolution? The author uses observers and "experts" to sum up the final arguments. "As the Japanese investments in this country mature, their plants and equipment will age, their employees will grow more expensive, and the playing field will level. Perhaps the *keiretsu* will learn a new respect for the individual and will begin to temper its authoritarian structures." On the other hand, he believes that U.S.

corporations can learn much from the business practices of the *keiretsu*, with its efficient supplier relationships. The best way to come to terms with *keiretsu*, he concludes, is to think of it as an immigrant, not an invader, with gifts to offer and lessons to learn—for those wise and gracious enough to know how to use them. Illustrations and models are provided, although the citations are from 1978 and 1986 material. Overall, this is a most worthwhile article on an often misunderstood topic.

ARTICLES

THE DEMING PRIZE VS. THE BALDRIGE AWARD*

Joseph F. Duffy

The Deming Prize and the Baldrige Award. They're both named after Americans, both very prestigious to win, both standing for a cry for quality in business, both engaged by their share of critics. One is 40 years old; the other a mere four. One resides in an alluring, foreign land; the other on American soil. One is awarded to the paradigm of Japanese business, individuals and international companies; the other to the best of U.S. business. One has grown in what a psychologist might call a mostly safe, nurturing environment; the other amongst a sometimes sour, sometimes sweet, bipolar parental image of government officials, academia and business gurus who seem to critically tug every way possible. One represents a country hailed as the world leader in quality; the other is trying to catch up—trying very hard.

A battle between Japan's Deming Prize and the Malcolm Baldrige National Quality Award would be as good a making for a movie as *Rocky* ever was: You have the older, wiser Japanese, who emanates a wisdom that withstands time, against the younger, quickly maturing American who has an outstanding reputation for being a victorious underdog. Who would win? We took the two awards to center ring, made them don their gloves and have a go.

ROUND 1: HISTORY

Although residing almost half a world apart, the Deming Prize and the Malcolm Baldrige National Quality Award are bonded by influence. After the ravages unleashed during World War II took a ruinous toll on Japan,

---

*This article is reproduced from *Quality Digest*, pp. 33–53, August 1991. In it, the author interviewed four individuals representing organizations with a reputation for being involved in the formation of the Baldrige Award. While no conclusions are drawn, the topics are central to total quality and worthy of debate.

W. Edwards Deming came to aid this seemingly hopeless land. With his expertise in statistical quality control (SQC), Deming helped lift Japan out of the rubble and into the limelight by having Japanese businesses apply SQC techniques.

In 1951, the Union of Japanese Scientists and Engineers (JUSE) created an accolade to award companies that successfully apply companywide quality control (CWQC) based on statistical quality control. In honor of their American quality champion, JUSE named the award the Deming Prize.

Not until 31 years later did a similar prize take root in the United States, mainly due to the efforts of Frank C. Collins, who served as executive director of quality assurance for the Defense Logistics Agency and has formed Frank Collins Associates, Survival Twenty-One—a quality consulting firm; he also serves on the board of directors of the Malcolm Baldrige National Quality Award Consortium.

Collins, after many trips to Japan, based his U.S. quality award idea on the Deming Prize. "That's where I got the idea for the Malcolm Baldrige Award," he explains, "although I never in my wildest dreams expected it to be connected to Malcolm Baldrige."

Malcolm Baldrige, Secretary of Commerce in the Reagan administration, was killed in a rodeo accident in 1987. Reagan chose to honor Baldrige by naming the newly created award after him.

"The original concept was that it would be the National Quality Award," says Collins. "It would be strictly a private sector affair. The government would have no part in it other than the president being the awarder of the recognition."

ROUND 2: PROCESS

The Deming Prize has several categories: the Deming Prize for Individual Person, the Deming Application Prize and the Quality Control Award for Factory. Under the Deming Application Prize and the Deming Application Prize for Small Enterprise and the Deming Application Prize for Division. In 1984, another category was added: The Deming Application Prize to Oversea Companies, which is awarded to non-Japanese companies.

The Deming Application Prize has 10 examination items and is based on CWQC—the Prize's main objective.

A company or division begins the Deming Prize process by submitting an application form to the Deming Prize Committee, along with other pertinent information. Prospective applicants are advised to hold preliminary consultations with the secretariat of the Deming Prize Committee before completing and submitting the application.

After acceptance and notification, applicants must submit a description of quality control practices and a company business prospectus, *in Japanese*. If successful, the applicant will then be subject to a site visit. If the applicant passes, the Deming Prize is awarded.

Sound easy? Sometimes the applicant's information can fill up to 1,000 pages, and the examination process for U.S. companies is expensive.

The Baldrige Award applicant must first submit an Eligibility Determination Form, supporting documents and $50. Upon approval, the applicant must then submit an application package—running up to 50 pages for small business, 75 pages for a manufacturing or service company—and another fee. Among seven categories, 1,000 points are awarded. No particular score guarantees a site visit.

Each of the three categories—manufacturing, service and small company—are allowed up to two winners only.

ROUND 3: PURPOSE

The American obsession for winning is enormous. From Watergate to Iran-Contra, the American Revolution to Desert Storm, Americans have shown that they love to win no matter what the cost. So it's no wonder that as soon as quality awards and prizes have an impact, they fall under scrutiny. But most critics of these two world-class quality awards think these coveted prizes are mostly pristine in purpose.

Frank Voehl, *Quality Digest* columnist and corporate vice president and general manager of Qualtec Inc., a Florida Power & Light Group company, oversees the implementation of the total quality management programs within Qualtec's client companies. In 1987, Florida Power & Light (FPL) became the first and only U.S. company to win the Deming Prize. Through his work with hundreds of Japanese and U.S. companies, Voehl feels that there are seven reasons why companies quest for the Deming Prize or the Baldrige Award.

"The first general comment that a number of companies that I've talked to in Japan that have applied for the Deming Prize said was, 'We did not apply for the Deming Prize to win but to drive us toward better quality control,' says Voehl. "Second is applying for and receiving the examination had more meaning than did winning the Prize." Voehl's other five reasons are:

- The audit or the exam itself helped point out many areas of deficiencies and continuous improvement activities that they hadn't noticed.
- Since the Deming Prize dictates a clear goal and time limit, quality control advanced at an extremely rapid rate.

- The company going for the quality award was able to accomplish in one or two years what would normally have taken five or 10 years.
- There was a unification of a majority of the employees.
- They were able to communicate with a common language to the whole company. This is where the cultural change takes place.

Robert Peach, who was project manager of the Malcolm Baldrige National Quality Award Consortium for three years and now serves as a senior technical advisor to the administrator, feels the Baldrige Award "is not an award for the sake of the award—it is the 200,000 guidelines and applications that go out that matter, not the handful that actually apply."

And the companies that experiment with and implement the Baldrige criteria, as well as the Deming criteria, can only learn from their endeavor. However, for the companies taking it a step further and committing to win the prize, it isn't Little League, where the profits extracted from learning and having fun are supposed to outweigh the benefits of scoring more points than the other team. The Deming and the Baldrige are the Majors, where going for the award may mean 80-hour work weeks, quick hellos and goodbyes to spouses and missing your child's Little League games.

ROUND 4: GOING TO WAR

So your boss comes up to you and says, "Get ready—we're going for it." How you react may depend on the attitude of your senior-level management and the present quality state of your company. Ken Leach, a senior examiner for the Baldrige Award and founder of Leach Quality Inc., implemented the quality system at Globe Metallurgical—1988 winner of the Baldrige Award's small company category. He says winning the Baldrige was easy because its quality system was in place well before the birth of the Baldrige Award criteria.

"We got into it before Baldrige was even heard of, and we got into it at the impetus of our customers—Ford and General Motors in particular," explains Leach. "So we implemented a number of specific things to satisfy the customer, and you don't have a choice with them—you have to go through their audit system. We did that and did it very well. So that gave us the base to apply for the Baldrige and win it the very first year without trying to redo what we were already doing."

Leach says that because Globe was in such a readied state before the inception of the Baldrige Award, the company did not add any people or spend large sums of money on the implementation of a quality system. In fact, Globe was so advanced in its quality system that Leach claims he took the Baldrige Award application home after work on a Friday and returned it complete by the following Monday.

But even Leach agrees that Globe was exceptional and that not all companies can implement the Baldrige criteria as smoothly as Globe did.

Yokogawa-Hewlett-Packard (YHP) won the Deming Prize in 1982. Unlike Globe and its easy conquest of the Baldrige, YHP claims the quest for the Deming was no Sunday stroll. The company released the following statement in *Measure* magazine:

"Japanese companies compete fiercely to win a Deming Prize. Members of a management team typically work several hundred extra hours each month to organize the statistical charts, reports and exhibits for judging."[1] YHP also says that "audits had all the tension of a championship sports event."[2]

Voehl calls these extra hours and added stresses "pain levels and downside effects" and found that they were typical of most companies going for the Deming Prize. And because the Baldrige Award is a "second generation" of the Deming Prize, Voehl says the Baldrige Award is no exception to possible disruption. He explains that the quest for winning becoming greater than the quest for quality is a "natural thing that occurs within these organizations that you can't really prevent. Senior management focuses in on the journey and the overall effects that will happen as a result of going for the examination and the prize."

Voehl adds, "Getting ready for the examination and the site exams brings a tremendous amount of pressure upon the organizations, whether it's the Deming or the Baldrige, because of the implications that you should be the one department that results in the prize not being brought home."

William Golomski, who is the American Society for Quality Control's representative to JUSE, says deadline time for the award may be a time of pressure.

In the case of the Baldrige, there have been a few companies that hired consultants to help them get ready for a site visit after they've gone through an evaluation by examiners and senior examiners," recalls Golomski. "So I can understand that people who are still being asked to go through role playing for a site visit might get to the point where they'll say, 'Gosh, I don't know if I'm interested as I once was.' "

Collins looks at customers in a dual sense: your internal customers—employees or associates—and your external customers—the people who pay the freight to keep you in business.

"To me," Collins says forcefully, "when you *squeeze* your internal customer to win an award, you're really making a mockery of the whole thing."

But for the companies that take the Baldrige application guidelines and implement them without competing, Peach says the quality goal remains the biggest motivator.

"In my exposure both to applicants and other companies that are using the practice and guidelines independent of applying, I feel that they have the right perspective, that companies identify this as a pretty good practice of what quality practice should be," expounds Peach. "And they're using it that way. That's healthy; that's good."

Deming says it best: "I never said it would be easy; I only said it would work." And this piece of wisdom can pertain to the implementation and competing processes of both the Baldrige Award and the Deming Prize. But although sometimes not easy to pursue, these awards spark many companies to the awareness and benefits of a quality system. But as more companies win the Baldrige, more critics are discussing which accolade— the Baldrige or the Deming—holds more advantages over the other.

ROUND 5: ADVANTAGES VS. DISADVANTAGES

With a U.S. company capturing the Deming Prize, U.S. businesses are no longer without a choice of which world-class quality award to pursue. Motorola, before it went for the Baldrige Award, contemplated which award would improve Motorola's quality best, according to Stewart Clifford, president of Enterprise Media, a documentary film company that specializes in management topics. In a recent interview with Motorola's quality staff, Clifford asked if Motorola was interested in questing for the Deming Prize.

"I asked them the question about if they were looking at applying and going for the Deming," remembers Clifford. "And they said that they felt frankly that while the Deming Prize had some valuable points for them, the reason why they liked the Baldrige Award better was because of its much more intense focus on the customer."

But Voehl claims this is a misconception and that both approaches focus heavily on the customer. "Florida Power & Light really got a lot of negatives from our counselors that we weren't zeroing in on the external and internal customers enough," recalls Voehl. "We had to demonstrate how our quality improvement process was a means of planning and achieving customer satisfaction through TQC."

Section Seven of the Baldrige Award covers total customer satisfaction, and it's worth more points than any other section. In the Deming criteria, total customer satisfaction may seem lost among the need for applicants to document, document, document and use statistical approaches.

One reason Collins says he would compete for the Baldrige instead of the Deming is the Deming's unbending demand to have everything documented. "If you say something, you have to have a piece of paper that covers it," he jokes. "Having worked for the government for 33 years, I see that as a bureaucratic way of doing things. And the Japanese are extremely bureaucratic."

And in an open letter to employees from James L. Broadhead, FPL's chairman and CEO, printed in *Training* magazine, his employees confirm Collins' beliefs: "At the same time, however, the vast majority of the employees with whom I spoke expressed the belief that the mechanics of the QI [quality improvement] process have been overemphasized. They felt that we place too great an emphasis on indicators, charts, graphs, reports and meetings in which documents are presented and indicators reviewed."[3]

However, Collins says that what he likes about the Deming Prize criteria that's missing in the Baldrige Award criteria is the first two examination items of the Deming Prize: policy organization and its operation.

If you want people to understand what you mean by quality, you have to spell it out, you have to define it as policy, explains Collins. As far as objectives go, he remembers asking a Japanese firm what their objectives were. The president of this company said, "First to provide jobs to our company." "How many American firms would say that?" asks Collins. Organization and understanding its operation is extremely important. He says, "Those two criteria are the bedrock foundation of the Deming Prize that makes it somewhat stronger and of greater value than the Malcolm Baldrige National Quality Award."

Another point that may persuade a U.S. company to compete for one of the two awards is cost. All things considered, U.S. companies going for the Deming Application Prize to Oversea Companies seems more costly than U.S. companies competing for the Baldrige Award. Leach describes Globe's venture as very inexpensive: "It doesn't have to cost an arm and a leg for the Baldrige. You don't have to reinvent the wheel of what you're already doing." Peach worked with a small-category company that spent $6,000 on its Baldrige Award venture, and that included the application fee and retaining a technical writer for $1,000.

But these are small companies with 500 employees or fewer. FPL, on the other hand, with about 15,000 employees, spent $1.5 million on its quest for the Deming Prize, according to Neil DeCarlo of FPL's corporate communications. And there are some Baldrige applicants that have spent hundreds of thousands or even millions of dollars on their quality quest, according to *Fortune* magazine.[4]

But no matter how much the Baldrige applicant pays, whether it be $6,000 or millions, it still receives a feedback report as part of the application cost. In comparison, those companies not making it past the first level of the Deming Prize criteria may pay JUSE for counselors, who will come into the company and do a diagnostic evaluation.

Because FPL was a pioneer in the oversea competition, many of the costs that would have otherwise been associated with this award for an overseas company had been waived by JUSE, according to Voehl. But still, FPL dished out $850,000 of that million-and-a-half for counselor fees, says DeCarlo—an amount Voehl claims would be three or four times more if FPL had to hire a U.S. consulting firm.

One of FPL's reasons to go for the Deming award was because in 1986 when it decided to go for a quality award, the Baldrige Award did not yet exist. In fact, what many people, including some FPL critics, don't know is that the company heavily funded the activities leading to the Baldrige Award. FPL agreed not to try for the Baldrige Award for five years to deter any conflict of interest, says Voehl. Also, FPL had an excellent benchmarking company in Japan's Kansai Electric, which had already won the Deming Prize.'

The Deming Prize puts no cap on the number of winners; the Baldrige allows a maximum of two winners for each of the three categories. Leach contests that by putting a limit on the winners, you make the Baldrige Award a more precious thing to win. Peach agrees. "I think there should be a limit," he says. "You just don't want scores of winners to dilute this."

Voehl disagrees. "We should take the caps off," he argues. "I think we'd do a lot more for the award, for the process if we didn't have a win-lose mentality toward it."

ROUND 6: CONTROVERSY

"The Baldrige is having such an impact," asserts Peach, "that now people will take a look at it and challenge. That will always happen—that's our American way." And at four years old, the Baldrige Award has already received a fair share of controversy. One of the most disturbing criticisms aimed at the Baldrige Award comes from Deming himself. Deming called the Baldrige Award "a terrible thing, a waste of industry" in a recent issue of *Automotive News*. The article states: "Among the reasons Deming denounces the award is its measurement of performance and the effects of training with numerical goals, which he cites as 'horrible things.'

" 'It's a lot of nonsense,' he said. 'The guidelines for 1991 (make that) very obvious.' "[5]

Golomski says that Deming is unhappy with two parts of the Baldrige guidelines. One is the concept of numerical goals, which Deming believes can cause aberrations within companies. "I don't take quite as strong a stand as Deming does," Golomski explains. "He makes another statement about goals and that far too often, goals are set in the absence of any way of knowing how you're going to achieve these goals."

Deming Prize Application Checklist: Items and Their Particulars

1. Policy

- Policies pursued for management, quality and quality control
- Methods of establishing policies
- Justifiability and consistency of policies
- Utilization of statistical methods
- Transmission and diffusion of policies
- Review of policies and the results achieved
- Relationship between policies and long- and short-term planning

2. Organization and Its Management

- Explicitness of the scopes of authority and responsibility
- Appropriateness of delegations of authority
- Interdivisional cooperation
- Committees and their activities
- Utilization of staff
- Utilization of quality circle activities
- Quality control diagnosis

3. Education and Dissemination

- Education programs and results
- Quality-and-control consciousness, degrees of understanding of quality control
- Teaching of statistical concepts and methods and the extent of their dissemination
- Grasp of the effectiveness of quality control
- Education of related company (particularly those in the same group, subcontractors, consignees and distributors)
- Quality circle activities
- System of suggesting ways of improvements and its actual conditions

4. Collection, Dissemination and Use of Information on Quality

- Collection of external information
- Transmission of information between divisions
- Speed of information transmission (use of computers)
- Data processing, statistical analysis of information and utilization of the results

5. Analysis

- Selection of key problems and themes
- Propriety of the analytical approach
- Utilization of statistical methods
- Linkage with proper technology
- Quality analysis, process analysis
- Utilization of analytical results
- Assertiveness of improvement suggestions

6. Standardization

- Systematization of standards
- Method of establishing, revising and abolishing standards
- Outcome of the establishment, revision or abolition of standards
- Contents of the standards
- Utilization of the statistical methods
- Accumulation of technology
- Utilization of standards

7. Control

- Systems for the control of quality and such related matters as cost and quantity
- Control items and control points
- Utilization of such statistical control methods as control charts and other statistical concepts
- Contribution to performance of quality circle activity
- Actual conditions of control activities
- State of matters under control

8. Quality Assurance

- Procedure for the development of new products and services (analysis and upgrading of quality, checking of design, reliability and other properties)
- Safety and immunity from product liability
- Process design, process analysis and process control and improvement
- Process capability
- Instrumentation, gauging, testing and inspecting
- Equipment maintenance and control of subcontracting, purchasing and services
- Quality assurance system and its audit
- Utilization of statistical methods
- Evaluation and audit of quality
- Actual state of quality assurance

9. Results

- Measurement of results
- Substantive results in quality, services, delivery, time, cost, profits, safety, environment, etc.
- Intangible results
- Measuring for overcoming defects

10. Planning for the Future

- Grasp of the present state of affairs and the concreteness of the plan
- Measures for overcoming defects
- Plans for further advances
- Linkage with long-term plans

Leach does not know what to think of "Deming's non-supportive or active disregard for the Baldrige Award." He finds it ironic that "a company could very much have a Deming-type philosophy or a Deming-oriented kind of company and could do quite well in the Baldrige application. I'm sure that Cadillac [1990 Baldrige Award winner] must have had a number of Deming philosophies in place."

Even if Deming is trying to be the burr under the saddle and spark U.S. companies into a quality quest, Leach doesn't think that Deming's "serving the pursuit of quality in general or himself very well by making public statements like that."

But Voehl agrees with some of Deming's points. "Cadillac got severely criticized by the board of trustees of the Baldrige because Cadillac took the Baldrige Award and General Motors tried to use it as a marketing tool," he says. "And that's not the intention. Those sort of things do not do the Baldrige Award any good because it seems like all you're interested in is public relations.

Cadillac has fallen under scrutiny from many critics for taking home the Baldrige Award.

After returning from consulting in Israel, Collins heard that Cadillac had won the Baldrige Award. "I couldn't believe my eyes," Collins exclaims. "Cadillac has gotten so much bad press over the last decade—transmission problems, difficulty with their diesel engines, their service record—a whole number of things that to me when they said Cadillac won it, I said, 'Impossible. They couldn't win it. Somebody's pulling a cruel joke.'"

Deming is not the only quality guru criticizing the Baldrige Award. Philip Crosby says in *Quality Digest* (February 1991) that customers should nominate the companies that compete for the Baldrige, not the companies themselves.

It is difficult to come by harsh criticism about the Deming Prize since few Americans are familiar with it. However, Collins questions FPL's quest for winning as superseding their quest for quality.

"There's no question in my mind that Florida Power & Light's John Hudiburg was intent on leading Florida Power & Light in a blaze of glory," insists Collins. "And money was absolutely no consideration as far as winning the Deming Prize. I don't know what the final tab on it was, but he bought the prize—there's no question about it."

Collins' comments do not go without backing. A number of articles on FPL's quest contain complaints from disgruntled employees who worked long hours to win the Deming Prize.

"If the goal is to win an award then the cost of winning the award is not worth the award itself," Voehl admits. "The focus needs to be on the outcomes for the organization." And Voehl feels that FPL's quality outcomes very much outweigh the cost put forth.

ROUND 7: CONSULTANTS

With the two awards, there's a big difference in the use of consultants or counselors, as they're called in Japan. In the case of the Deming Prize, a successful applicant uses counselors trained by JUSE throughout the examination, explains Golomski. "For the Baldrige, you're on your own or you use whomever you wish to help you—if you think it's worth it."

"Considering the tremendous number of brochures I get every day," says Collins, "it appears that everybody and his brother is an expert on the Malcolm Baldrige National Quality Award. And my experience tells me that there *ain't* that many experts on the Malcolm Baldrige National Quality Award."

So, are some consultants or counselors using the Baldrige Award to prey on aspiring companies? Voehl says he sees it happening all over and calls it "absolutely preposterous and absurd and unethical."

Voehl compares it to just like everybody jumping on the TQC bandwagon. "Everybody from a one-man or two-man mom-and-pop consulting company to a 1,000-employee consulting arm of the Big 8 seems to be an expert in TQM," he says. "It's like a dog with a rag: They're shaking it and shaking it, and they won't let it go because they see it can mean money to their bottom line. It's giving the consulting field a terrible black eye. It's giving the people who bring in these consultants the expectations clearly that they are going to win the award. These are false expectations, false hopes and false starts. They shouldn't even be looking at winning the award; they should be looking at implementing a quality system that can ensure customer satisfaction."

But there are good reasons to have consultants help you through the Baldrige quest. Leach points out that if a CEO of a company needs to change his or her approach on something, an employee will probably be intimidated to approach the CEO; instead, a consultant can do this. Also a consultant may carry in an objective view that brings different ideas to the company.

Deming Prize counselors, however, have a reputation to guard. That's why Golomski feels FPL had no chance to "buy the Prize."

"The counselor simply wouldn't agree with them that they [FPL] were ready," Golomski argues. "The counselors help an organization improve itself, but if they don't think the company is ready for the big leagues, they simply won't recommend it."

ROUND 8: MODIFICATIONS

The Baldrige Award criteria are constantly modified to meet changing expectations. This is how it grows stronger, becomes more mature. When awarded the Baldrige Award, recipients must share their knowledge of total quality, but Golomski wants to see better ways of technology transfer.

Collins thinks we will probably have a follow-up award similar to the Japan Quality Control Prize—which is awarded to Deming Prize winners if they have improved their quality standards five years after winning the Deming Prize and pass rigorous examination—but not until the Baldrige Award can be further improved.

Peach feels the Baldrige criteria are at a position where modifications will be in smaller increments. He says cycle time might become important enough to be emphasized more.

The possible modifications of the Deming Prize are hard to predict. However, modifications of the Baldrige Award may be based on the Deming Prize's influence.

ROUND 9: SAVING FACE

Junji Noguchi, executive director of JUSE, was contacted for an interview for this article. When he learned of the subject matter—comparing the two world-class quality awards—he declined to answer. He said, "I am sorry I have to reply that I cannot answer your interviews. That is because the contents were not preferable and that they are not what I was expecting."

Noguchi continued, "Awards or prizes in the country have been established under the most suitable standards and methods considering their own background of industries, societies and cultures. We do not understand the meaning of comparing awards in different countries that have different backgrounds."

Noguchi is displaying some of that ancient wisdom and showing a difference in our cultures that even Americans find difficult to explain. Is this why their award has been going strong for 40 years and why the Baldrige Award is a 4-year-old child growing much too fast thanks to our intrinsic desire to slice it up, examine it and try to put it back together more completely than before? Maybe. But as a result, our U.S. quality award will always remain provocative and exciting and keep the people talking. And this is good.

REFERENCES

1. *"YHP Teamwork Takes the Prize,"* Measure *(January-February 1983), 3000 Hanover St., Palo Alto, CA 94304, pg. 6.*
2. Measures, *pg. 6.*
3. *James L. Broadhead, "The Post-Deming Diet: Dismantling a Quality Bureaucracy,"* Training, *Lakewood Building, 50 S. Ninth St., Minneapolis, MN 55402, pg. 41.*
4. *Jeremy Main, "Is the Baldrige Overblown?"* Fortune *(July 1, 1991), Time & Life Building, Rockefeller Center, New York, NY 10020-1393, pg. 62.*
5. *Karen Passino, "Deming Calls Baldrige Prize 'Nonsense,' "* Automotive News *(April 1, 1991), 1400 E. Woodbridge, Detroit, MI, 48207.*

CHAPTER 3

THE TOTAL PURCHASING/ SUPPLIER QUALITY MANAGEMENT MODEL

THE SUPPLIER WITHIN TOTAL QUALITY MANAGEMENT

One of the best ways to depict a total quality management (TQM) system was developed as part of the Malcolm Baldrige National Quality Award for the United States. This system is illustrated in Figure 3.1. The TQM system as depicted encompasses a **driver** that determines and manages the direction of various **systems** whose actions toward predetermined **goals** can be gauged by utilizing specific **measures**. These four major components of the overall system are further broken down by the Malcolm Baldrige criteria into a total of seven categories used to rate companies that apply for the award.

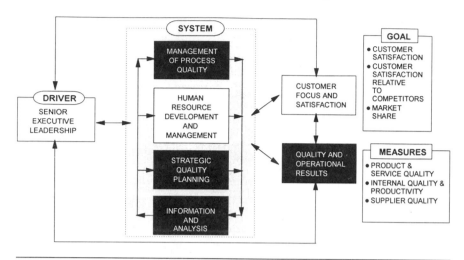

Figure 3.1 Total Quality System. (*Source:* Excerpted from the 1994 Malcolm Baldrige Award handbook.)

It is interesting to note how the supplier relationships, supplier inputs, supplier results, and supplier feedback are integrated into four of the seven categories:

- **Management of process quality:** Current capabilities of a supplier and future requirements of the organization are considered very important parts of the criteria. This includes determining how well a current supplier is meeting the requirements of the organization today and its potential for meeting future requirements.
- **Strategic quality planning:** In this category, the award criteria define the need to consider supplier capabilities in the development of business plans.
- **Information and analysis:** In Section 2.1.a, for example, the criteria include supplier performance data as part of the scope and management of quality and performance data and information. Specifically, the organization must explain how the data were gathered and utilized to improve the products or services provided or how the data were used in the selection process.
- **Quality and operational results:** In Section 6.4 (Supplier Quality Results), the award criteria call for monitoring and reporting qual-

ity of and improvements in supplier-related quality. The criteria require tracking the most important quality characteristics and the improvement of overall quality from suppliers either through improvements made to the products and services provided to the organization by its suppliers or through improvements that are gained from better selection processes.

The important role played by the supplier in the overall quality process is therefore obvious. This connection can be viewed from another perspective, similar to the way Frank Voehl describes the three major systems that form the basis of a TQM system (a more detailed explanation of these systems is provided in Chapter 2 of this book). Voehl, along with others such as Jay Spechler[1] and Myron Tribus,[2] stratifies the overall TQM system as follows:

- **Social (cultural) system:** This system is the summation of the cultural values—the interrelationships between different groups of people inside the *extended organization.* This would include relationships with suppliers, as well as the behavioral patterns between all members of the extended enterprise. It is the social system that has the greatest impact on such factors as motivation, creativity, innovative behavior, and teamwork. Managers have a major responsibility for the nature and character of the social system. A diagram of the social system characteristics that constitute a total quality enterprise is presented in Figure 3.2.
- **Technical system:** This second part of the TQM system is composed of core elements such as technology, specifications, ergonomics, analysis and improvement tools and process, equipment, and layout, among others.
- **Management system:** This system includes the leadership system, policy deployment, strategic quality planning, process management, management of daily processes, cross-functional management, and the concepts of the House of Quality.

These different systems can easily be correlated with the different aspects of purchasing and supplier quality management, but first it is necessary to understand some of the basic concepts of purchasing and supplier quality management.

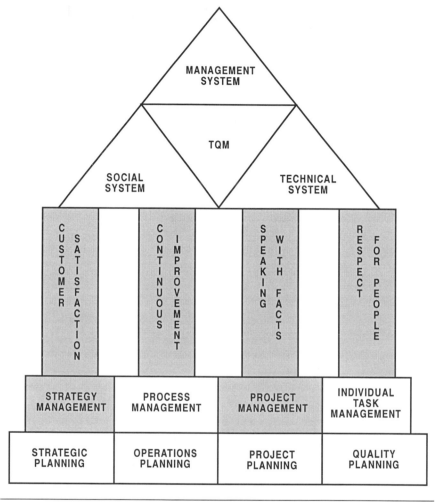

Figure 3.2 Social System Characteristics of a Total Quality Organization (Fishbone Diagram).

PURCHASING/SUPPLIER QUALITY MANAGEMENT SYSTEM

A purchasing/supplier quality management (PSQM) system (Figure 3.3) must define the various components of a supplier system along with their interrelationships; furthermore, it should also explain how to achieve these relationships. At this point, the major components will be briefly discussed; each component will be considered in much greater depth in the chapters that follow.

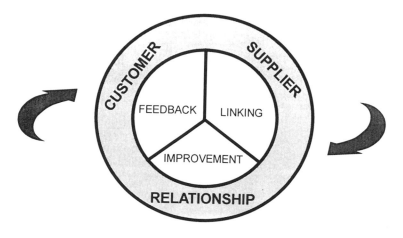

Figure 3.3 Purchasing/Supplier Quality Management.

Customer–Supplier Relationships: This is part of the social or *cultural system* as described earlier. An organization must try to establish long-term relationships with its suppliers. A strong sense of trust must be created and developed over many years. A win–win constancy of purpose must be established whereby the relationship is always to the benefit of both parties.

Linking: This part of the PSQM system provides for the integration of the supplier into the overall vision, values, and objectives of the organization. This is very much a part of the *management system* described earlier. Both the supplier and the organization must consider the needs of the ultimate consumer. Suppliers with the strongest links or ties to the plans and objectives of the organization, and whose own organization is in alignment with the same, will inevitably provide products and services that better meet the overall needs of the organization.

Improvement: The supplier and the organization must be willing to constantly improve their respective products, processes, and services to better mesh with each other. This part of PSQM is directly tied to the *technical system* of TQM described earlier. The organization wants an innovative supplier who is constantly improving the product being delivered for use. The results are mutually beneficial: the supplier can gain market share for its product and the buying organization can improve its processes and ultimately its products or services.

Feedback: This last part of the PSQM system is critical to its success. This component addresses the need to report information on the supplier's performance so that the supplier can assess and improve the product or service provided and the buying organization can better manage the process. This component is also tied to the *technical system* described earlier.

TQM VS. PSQM

The relationships among the three-component TQM system and the PSQM system is depicted in Figure 3.4. First, as indicated, the customer–supplier relationship becomes a part of the social system of TQM. The relationships and culture that are developed as part of TQM must involve the suppliers in order to be completely successful. The same values and rules of conduct that apply to interdepartmental relationships and interemployee relationships must also apply to relationships with suppliers. Second, the management system includes the strategic direction and objectives of the organization which a supplier must link into in order to provide products and services that are aligned with the direction of the organization. Third, the technical system is tied into two of the major components of PSQM: improve-

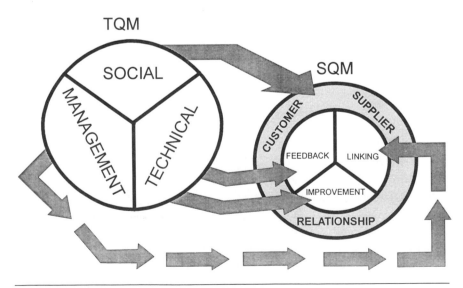

Figure 3.4 TQM vs. PSQM.

ment and feedback. Both of these components deal with such issues as measurement of performance, communication of expectations, use of systematic improvement methods, and use of quality improvement tools and statistical techniques. The technical system encompasses both of these components to varying degrees.

For additional information, see Abstract 3.1 at the end of this chapter.

THE ORGANIZATION AS A SYSTEM

Each organization can be represented as a system. Before examining the organization as a system, it is appropriate at this point to first review the components of a system. Every system is composed of five main elements (Figure 3.5):

- **Process:** This is usually referred to as the *system,* with the steps of the process as the boundaries. These are the functions, services, or value-added activities that are performed on the incoming materials, products, or customers (services).
- **Outputs:** Every system has certain goals to be achieved. These are the specific reasons why the system exists. These reasons can usually be defined by the expected output of the system. This output

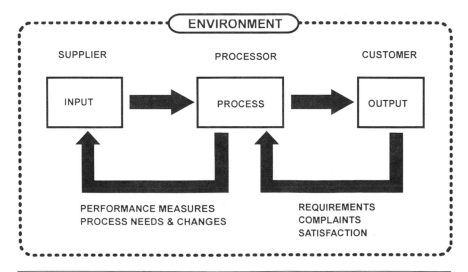

Figure 3.5 Standard System Diagram.

can be in the form of a desired result or change in the input or a specific effect.

- **Inputs:** This is one of the most critical parts of the system because it determines the starting point. The quality of the inputs determines the starting condition of materials or services entering the system and directly affects the steps in the process. Inputs that are more geared to the steps in the process are more likely to assist in achieving the expected output.

- **Feedback:** A closed loop system usually provides for the delivery of information about the functioning of downstream subsystems back into upstream subsystems. This information allows for the adjustment of the upstream subsystems in order to better achieve the needs and requirements of downstream subsystems.

- **Environment:** Every system works within a given environment. This environment can either modify the behavior of the system or could potentially be affected by the system itself. The environment usually includes the sources of inputs and the destinations of the outputs from a system. It also includes all the stakeholders in the system.

This is very similar to the concept of the extended organization presented earlier. The overall environment includes the stakeholders in the system, including the customers, suppliers, and others involved with the organization.

Juran[3] discusses the concept of a processor team in very similar terms. He explains the roles of different parts of a processor team, i.e., as the supplier, the processor, and the customer. As can be seen from Figure 3.5, this is very similar to the input, process, and output components of a system. Let's examine these roles in closer detail:

- **Customer:** The customer of every process has certain expectations of the process. These are referred to as quality characteristics of the products or services being provided. An organization must understand these characteristics and, to a certain extent, must be able to determine and often predict their requirements.

- **Processor:** Once the quality characteristics are known, processes must be designed to meet and exceed them. This can only be accomplished by translating these requirements into the process steps and methods that will provide the appropriate output to meet or exceed customer requirements.

• **Supplier:** These processes are very dependent on the materials or services that are being provided by the suppliers to the process. These inputs to the process greatly affect the potential variability and capability of the process. The quality of the inputs must be controlled in order to control the process itself.

If these concepts were applied to a manufacturer, the result would be as depicted in Figure 3.6. This figure is an adaptation of Deming's "production as a system," which he used in one of his first lectures in Japan. As can be seen from this figure, a manufacturer can be viewed as a system with various subsystems such as market research, product design and development, process management, a complaint process, and most importantly, the customers, suppliers, and other stakeholders in the overall system. This figure obviously is a very simple representation of the real complexities in a manufacturing organization. These complexities can be further developed by looking at each of the subsystems and breaking them down even further into processes and subprocesses within each subsystem. These can be stratified down to the most detailed steps of each employee on a daily basis.

Any type of organization can be viewed at as a system. For example, a hospital and a utility are depicted as systems in Figures 3.7 and 3.8, respectively.

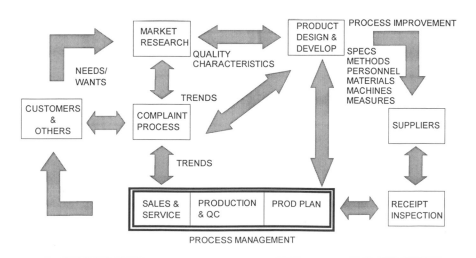

Figure 3.6 The Manufacturing System. (Adapted from Deming.)

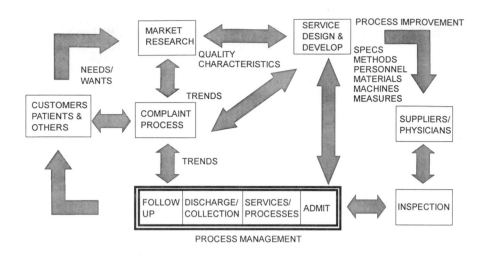

Figure 3.7 The Hospital System. (Adapted from Deming.)

The interrelationships between the subsystems are most important. What one subsystem produces would most likely be utilized by some other subsystem within the overall organization. The requirements of each subsystem must be met by the subsystem that is its supplier. In viewing this concept at an organization level, the supplier must meet the requirements of those subsystems within the organization that use its products or services.

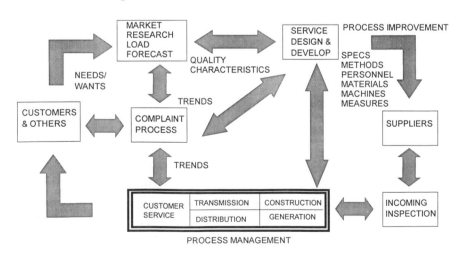

Figure 3.8 The Utility System. (Adapted from Deming.)

PURCHASING/SUPPLIER QUALITY MANAGEMENT FLOW

The PSQM system introduced in this chapter can be implemented in many different ways. One set of steps that has been successful is described in Figure 3.9. This figure shows that the first step in the process is to develop a corporate strategic quality plan with input from suppliers. Next, the processes that are of highest priority should be determined. Beyond these processes are the commodities that are of highest priority and in turn the products and services that are also of highest priority. This links the efforts in the purchasing/supplier quality area with the overall objectives of the organization. In order for TQM to be considered fully implemented, the strategic quality areas should be completely deployed throughout all areas of the organization. The last step in the linking subsystem is the selection of suppliers to provide these high-priority products and services.

The second major subsystem is the improvement subsystem. Here the intent is to work with the suppliers that were selected to increase their awareness of quality improvement and to improve their processes, thereby improving the quality of the products and services they

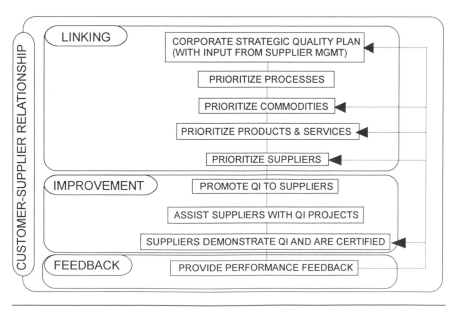

Figure 3.9 Purchasing/Supplier Quality Management Flow.

provide to the organization. This subsystem would also assist the suppliers in becoming certified.

The next subsystem includes providing feedback in the form of information and results to the suppliers about their performance. This is a very effective way to help establish the customer–supplier relationships needed for the long-term success of this management system. These customer–supplier relationships are built as the process continues, based on mutual trust and common goals.

For additional information, see Abstract 3.2 at the end of this chapter.

ENDNOTES

1. Spechler, Jay (1993). *Managing Quality in America's Most Admired Companies.* Norcross, Ga.: Industrial Engineering and Management Press, p. 12.
2. Tribus, Myron (1992). "Ten Management Practices." In: Voehl, Frank (1992). *Total Quality: Principles and Practices within Organizations.* Coral Springs, Fla.: Strategy Associates, pp. IV, 20.
3. Juran, Joseph M. (1989). *Quality Control Handbook.* New York: McGraw-Hill, section 9-42 to 9-45.
4. Exercises 3.1, 3.2, and 3.3 and Figure 3.2 ©Strategy Associates, Inc.
5. Figures 3.3, 3.4, 3.5, and 3.9 ©Advent Group, Inc.

EXERCISES

EXERCISE 3.1
LEADERSHIP SELF-ASSESSMENT

This instrument is designed to provide an individual with insight concerning the degree to which she or he holds views that are consistent, or inconsistent, with total quality improvement principles. It may be used entirely for self-diagnosis or the results may be used to stimulate group discussions when the possibility of total quality improvement efforts is being explored. Responses to the questionnaire may be yes or no or a rating system such as 1 = strong agreement, 2 = agreement, 3 = undecided, 4 = disagreement, 5 = strong disagreement.

Agreement with the statements indicates a belief system consistent with the general principles of total quality improvement. When you complete the exercise, if you have not answered yes to most of the questions, you probably should not attempt to implement quality improvement efforts at any level, let alone try to intervene in terms of strategy management.

Please indicate your agreement or disagreement with the following statements.

1. I recognize all work (activities) as processes that involve inputs, transforming activities, outputs, and outcomes.

2. I believe that quality improvement requires building quality in (the prevention of errors and defects, the avoidance of rework) rather than merely the detection of defects.

3. I believe in a problem-solving approach that emphasizes systematic problem identification based on data developed through the use of feedback systems, understanding the causes of problems (both common and special), and statistical thinking.

4. I believe in a problem-solving approach that emphasizes experimental efforts to find the right solution through the use of data and feedback systems. This ultimately is reflected in the use of the Shewhart model: Plan, Do, Check, Act (PDCA).

5. I believe that it is the primary function of management to facilitate quality performance, particularly the elimination of barriers that prevent individuals from achieving quality performance.

6. I believe that most problems (errors, defects) are the result of existing processes (common causes), not special causes—including workers. Thus, I first look for ways to improve the process.

7. I believe that the people closest to the operational activities (the process) have substantial knowledge about the process and how to improve it.

8. I believe that most people are motivated toward quality performance.

9. I believe that the people closest to the process must be empowered to improve the quality of the process.

EXERCISE 3.2
QUALITY READINESS ASSESSMENT

This exercise provides examples of the type of questions that should be asked about the college or university during exploratory discussions concerning the possibility of becoming involved in a total quality improvement effort. One approach to its use would be for all key managers to answer the Quality Readiness Assessment questions.[a] If a Quality Council has already been established, its members should answer the questionnaire. In either case, the answers should be shared and discussed.

It is probably best if the synthesis of the results is done by a single individual and a written document provided to the entire group. The use of a written report is suggested because it allows individuals an opportunity to review all of the responses and to develop a holistic interpretation of the results before becoming involved in the discussion of details. Ultimately, the results should be used to make decisions concerning the need for becoming involved in a total quality improvement effort.

Please answer the following questions concerning current conditions in your organization relative to the status of your quality system.[b] Your answers may be brief but they should be specific enough to be understood when they are presented in the report on the responses of the group.

1. *Top Management:* How (to what degree) does top management make planning an integrated part of the culture of the enterprise?

2. *Customer Satisfaction:* How (to what degree) does the enterprise use customer feedback to identify problems and design and plan improvements?

3. *Design:* How (to what degree) does the enterprise attempt to improve operations by finding and solving potential problems while products and services are being designed?

4. *Purchasing:* How (to what degree) do individuals responsible for purchasing make suppliers an integral part of the planning process and team?

5. *Production:* How (to what degree) does the strategic plan of the enterprise emphasize that productivity and quality have a common goal as partners in productivity?

6. *Education and Training:* How (to what degree) does the enterprise provide every member with the knowledge and skills needed to do his or her job and to take part in the total quality improvement process?

7. *Speaking with Facts:* How (to what degree/how well) does the enterprise use data as the basis for identifying problems and reaching decisions?

---

[a] Voehl, Frank (1992). *Total Quality: Principles and Practices within Organizations.* Coral Springs, Fla.: Strategy Associates, pp. III, 25–31.

[b] The questions in this readiness survey are a loosely based adaptation of the general elements contained in the ASQC-based Quality System elements.

8. *Technology:* How (to what degree) does the enterprise build quality into automated processes, rather than attempting to automate a mess?

9. *Teams, Teamwork, and Synergy:* How (to what degree) does the enterprise develop and train teams and encourage teamwork?

10. *Quality Costs:* How (to what degree) does the enterprise attempt to identify the costs of nonquality? How (to what degree) is this information used to identify targets for future quality improvement efforts?

11. *Internal Auditing:* How (to what degree) does the enterprise conduct audits of major internal processes such as the Strategic Planning System?

12. *Continuous Improvement:* How (to what degree) does the enterprise set planning teams that bridge departmental boundaries.

13. *People:* To what degree does the enterprise demand good planning from everyone?

14. *Integrated Vision:* To what degree does the enterprise have an integrated vision of a desired future?

EXERCISE 3.3
TOTAL QUALITY CULTURE ASSESSMENT FORM

Please rate your organization on the following criteria. (1 = definitely applies, 2 = somewhat applies, 3 = neutral, 4 = does not apply, 5 = definitely does not apply.)

A. ENVIRONMENT

1. Constancy of purpose clearly exists	1 2 3 4 5
2. High degree of democratization achieved	1 2 3 4 5
3. Accepts responsibility to all stakeholders	1 2 3 4 5
4. Organization demonstrates long-term focus	1 2 3 4 5
5. Quality performance measures in place	1 2 3 4 5
6. Human rights and diversity accepted	1 2 3 4 5
7. Workers enabled to do their jobs	1 2 3 4 5
8. Workers empowered	1 2 3 4 5
9. Workers supported by management	1 2 3 4 5
10. Quality profiles established	1 2 3 4 5
11. A shared common vision exists	1 2 3 4 5

Environmental Total _____

B. PRODUCTS AND SERVICES

12. Products and services based on customer need	1 2 3 4 5
13. Customers "sell" other customers	1 2 3 4 5

14. Satisfy customer needs and expectations	1	2	3	4	5
15. Reflect added value	1	2	3	4	5
16. Customer input to product and service development	1	2	3	4	5
17. Partnership with customers and suppliers	1	2	3	4	5
18. Measure customer satisfaction proactively	1	2	3	4	5

Products and Services Total _____

C. METHODS

19. Study/learn from successes and failures	1	2	3	4	5
20. Establish operational definitions of quality for key processes	1	2	3	4	5
21. Obtain constant feedback	1	2	3	4	5
22. Hear voices of employees	1	2	3	4	5
23. Study/learn from others	1	2	3	4	5
24. Work effectively with suppliers	1	2	3	4	5
25. Manage processes and stabilize through Statistical Process Control	1	2	3	4	5
26. Communicate using data	1	2	3	4	5
27. Hear voice of customer	1	2	3	4	5
28. Hear voice of process	1	2	3	4	5
29. Follow PDCA discipline (Plan, Do, Check, Act)	1	2	3	4	5
30. Use consensus	1	2	3	4	5

Methods Total _____

D. PEOPLE

31. Feel "I belong"	1	2	3	4	5
32. Recognize contribution	1	2	3	4	5
33. Train in job	1	2	3	4	5
34. Feel pride in work	1	2	3	4	5
35. Learn continuously	1	2	3	4	5
36. Committed to team	1	2	3	4	5
37. Share customer vision	1	2	3	4	5
38. "Connected" to customer	1	2	3	4	5
39. Trained in process improvement methods	1	2	3	4	5
40. Use people's ideas	1	2	3	4	5
41. Included in strategic planning	1	2	3	4	5
42. Work to potential	1	2	3	4	5

People Total _____

E. ORGANIZATIONAL STRUCTURE

43. Managers literally lead	1 2 3 4 5
44. Cooperate at all levels	1 2 3 4 5
45. Inverted through customer/supplier relationships	1 2 3 4 5
46. Pay any bonus based on overall effectiveness	1 2 3 4 5
47. Operate all systems/processes using total quality	1 2 3 4 5
48. Align process management with strategic business	1 2 3 4 5
49. Function defines form	1 2 3 4 5
50. Understand roles/responsibilities	1 2 3 4 5
51. Respond like small organizations	1 2 3 4 5
52. Members share in ownership of structure and processes	1 2 3 4 5
53. Encourage creativity and innovation	1 2 3 4 5
54. Operate effectively cross-functionally	1 2 3 4 5
55. Delegate responsibility and authority	1 2 3 4 5

Organizational Structure Total _____

F. TOTAL QUALITY MINDSET

56. Practice win–win strategies	1 2 3 4 5
57. Improved quality increases	1 2 3 4 5
58. Recognize that variation is normal	1 2 3 4 5
59. All members learn continuously	1 2 3 4 5
60. Teamwork is encouraged	1 2 3 4 5
61. Added value to customer	1 2 3 4 5
62. All employees use data	1 2 3 4 5
63. Employ the PDCA cycle	1 2 3 4 5
64. Measure and track results	1 2 3 4 5
65. Recognize that all outcomes result from a process	1 2 3 4 5
66. Recognize that all quality means continuous improvement	1 2 3 4 5
67. Recognize that all workers want to do their best	1 2 3 4 5
68. Recognize that managers control (are responsible for) the work process	1 2 3 4 5
69. Practice systems thinking	1 2 3 4 5
70. Move from enumerative to analytical approach	1 2 3 4 5
71. Customer needs define quality	1 2 3 4 5

Total Quality Mindset _____

ABSTRACTS

ABSTRACT 3.1
BUILDING SUPPLIER PARTNERSHIPS

Johnson, John G.
Journal for Quality and Participation, January–February 1992, pp. 18–22

Harris Corporation, an aerospace and defense contractor, began its journey towards strategic supplier partnerships using their vision statement of 1988 which reads in part: *"Suppliers are a vital part of our resources...Our relationship with suppliers will be sincere, ethical, and embrace the highest principles of purchasing practice."* In order to reach their goal, they established a senior-level team whose main objective was to create and empower a smaller supplier base. Starting with an initial 5000-supplier base, they were able to reduce it by half. The next step was to establish supplier criteria. After 4 months, the team was able to agree on 4 categories of "authorized suppliers" based on 14 attributes tailored for 2 groups: manufacturers and distributors. Commodity teams were also established and empowered to select the suppliers they felt were best suited for a long-term relationship with Harris. They were also charged with making sure that small and socially disadvantaged businesses were not unfairly treated. The author identifies the following results of these initiatives:

- By January 1990, the number of suppliers had dropped 88 percent.
- By the end of 1991, most commodity teams had advanced their suppliers to "preferred" or "best-in-class" status.
- Harris' reject rate for incoming supplies has decreased by 70 percent.
- Its delivery performance to its customers has improved by 50 percent.

There were problems that surfaced along the way. For example, the tasks imposed on the commodity teams took most of their time, thus hurting their everyday activities. Accurate information was a problem due to the many codes used to identify the suppliers' materials. Wrong commodity codes became a significant problem, since component technology is constantly changing. Sometimes the supplier partnership process was inadvertently defeated by engineering decisions that dictated purchase from nonauthorized suppliers. Most of all, the traditional competitive price model was found to detract from the ideal quality and partnership goals. To combat this, Harris has been trying to establish shared goals between buyer and supplier. They also encourage their suppliers to continually benchmark themselves against their competitors and against best practices. The author concludes that "supplier partnership strategies are easier to articulate than to implement." (©*Quality Abstracts*)

ABSTRACT 3.2
THE IMPACT OF JUST-IN-TIME INVENTORY SYSTEMS
ON SMALL BUSINESSES

Sadhwani, A.T. and Sarhan, M.
Journal of Accountancy, January 1987, pp. 118–132

Although written in 1987, this article by Sadhwani and Sarhan is as timely today as the day it was written. The key notion is that just-in-time (JIT) inventory management systems, used to reduce inventories and improve quality and productivity, are being adopted more frequently by large manufacturing corporations, thus presenting new challenges for small businesses as well. JIT, a "pull" system (the assembly line triggers withdrawal of parts from preceding work centers), has two aspects that are heavily emphasized by manufacturers: JIT purchasing and JIT delivery and transportation. JIT purchasing, which relies heavily on a dependable supplier network, calls for manufacturers to deal with fewer suppliers, small lot sizes, and statistical quality control (SQC) techniques.

In addition to using fewer suppliers and signing larger contracts (with suppliers), JIT manufacturers are working with smaller lot sizes, thereby reducing unnecessary inventories and freeing storage areas to reduce cost and improve quality. SQC is a powerful problem-solving tool that pinpoints variations and their causes and eliminates after-the-fact inspection—an expensive, wasteful procedure that rarely detects the causes of poor quality.

More recently, JIT manufacturers have encouraged their suppliers to form "focused factory" arrangements, which enable the supplier to focus on a limited number of products and become a specialized maker to a major manufacturer. This usually leads to suppliers relocating closer to their respective manufacturer, one of the tenets of JIT delivery and transportation. In addition to elimination of centralized loading docks and staging areas, another benefit is the use of information sharing and microcomputers, which expose small businesses to computerized information systems.

The implications of JIT for businesses are profound, such as better customer relationships and stable product demand. Not all the benefits come easy, though. For example, suppliers must institute statistical process control and understand freight economics, but the benefits of long-term contracts, smooth production, improved quality, and reduced scrap and rework greatly enhance the success of small businesses. Good graphs are provided in the article, but no references are given.

CHAPTER 4

CUSTOMER– SUPPLIER RELATIONSHIP

CUSTOMER FOCUS AND ORIENTATION

One of the fundamental principles of total quality management (TQM) is the concept of customer focus. Without customers, there is no reason for the organization to exist. Every organization should be able to define its external customers. In addition, it should be able to define the "next process" that is the customer for every process within the organization. The latter are the internal customers. For each of these customers, whether internal or external, there is at least one supplier. These suppliers can also be internal or external. Just as it is important to break down the internal barriers between departments within the organization, it is also important to break down the barriers between an organization and its suppliers.

Quality Characteristics

Let's first examine this relationship from the perspective of the organization. The organization is looking for a supplier that will meet or exceed its requirements. These customer requirements can be referred to as quality characteristics of the products and services being provided by the supplier. These quality characteristics can be divided into the following types:

- **Quality:** These are the functional aspects of the product or service. Does it do the right thing? Does it look right? Does it feel good? Does it accomplish what I want it to?
- **Cost:** These are the value aspects of the product or service. Is there a value to what I am buying? Is the cost reasonable? Is the quality comparable to other products or services on the market in terms of functionality and reliability? Is it within the budget? Does it minimize total life cycle or ownership cost of the product or service that I am buying?
- **Safety:** This is one of the most important characteristics of a product or service. If a product or service will increase my exposure to certain potential risk factors, including but not limited to employee safety, then I probably should consider modifications to either the supplier's design or process or our organization's processes or products.
- **Delivery:** These are the timeliness and location or logistics issues of the product or service. If I need it tomorrow, but it cannot be delivered for two months, then I need to either readdress my delivery requirements or work with the supplier to somehow improve the delivery schedule.

HIERARCHY OF CUSTOMER NEEDS

The needs of the organization as a customer can be broken down into different levels. For example, a company may be very interested in on-time delivery of its products because it is trying to start a just-in-time (JIT) manufacturing system. The subcharacteristics into which on-time delivery can be broken down are depicted in Figure 4.1.

It is important to recognize that some needs are more important

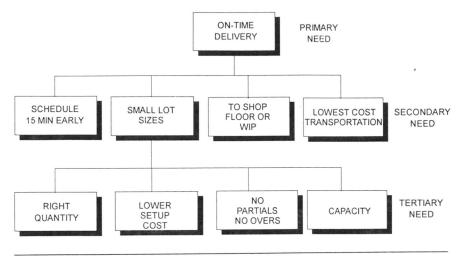

Figure 4.1 Hierarchy of Needs in a JIT Environment.

than others and that some are really only a component of others, as shown in Figure 4.1. For example, if setup costs are reduced, then smaller lot sizes become more economical and on-time delivery becomes more likely.

This type of analysis should be done for the different processes within the organization, and this should be communicated to the supplier. Suppliers may add some processes that the organization did not recognize. These should also be included in the overall process and negotiated with the supplier. The supplier should then translate these needs into the quality characteristics of the process. This ensures that the customer requirements are being satisfied.

For additional information, see Abstract 4.1 at the end of this chapter.

We All Wear Two Hats

Most people consider themselves to be either a supplier or a customer and do not realize that at different times they may be both. This is not to say that simply buying something makes one a customer or selling something makes one a supplier. This means that even during the same transaction, for example purchasing a piece of equipment, at some point in the negotiation the customer is a supplier and the supplier is a customer. Let's consider this scenario in further detail.

You are in the market for a new laptop computer. You call a dealer and ask for a good, reliable machine. At this point you are acting as the customer in the negotiation. The dealer asks you questions to further define your specifications for this computer. Do you want a 386 or a 486? How large a hard drive do you want? How much memory? How fast? Color or monochrome? This continues for a few minutes, with few answers from you because you just started looking. You do not know much about computers and were just told that the president of your organization wanted a laptop. You then hang up with the dealer and do some research. Think about how the situation changed from your being a customer to your being a supplier. In order for the dealer to properly determine which laptop would help you do what you want to do, he or she must receive answers to the questions posed. When you are providing those answers, you are a supplier of information.

This may be similar to other situations commonly encountered in the workplace. At times, the supplier must be treated as a customer in order to obtain the product that is needed. A long-term teamwork-based relationship must be developed with suppliers so that over time they can come to understand the processes of the customer and how to best meet these needs. A partnership based on trust must be developed in order to create a strong bridge between the two organizations so that they are linked together for the common good.

For additional information, see Abstract 4.2 at the end of this chapter.

THE JAPANESE MODEL OF CUSTOMER–SUPPLIER RELATIONSHIPS

In one of his books on TQM, Dr. Kaoru Ishikawa[1] developed a comprehensive list of values and principles for customer–supplier relationships (Table 4.1). If followed, these values and principles can assist in the development of long-term partnerships with suppliers. Dr. Ishikawa's basic values and his ten principles are considered to be comprehensive and are examined in greater depth here.

First, Dr. Ishikawa refers to some basic values under which these relationships must exist:

Table 4.1 Dr. Kaoru Ishikawa's[1] Ten Quality Control Principles
for Customer–Supplier Relationships

Both customer and supplier should have mutual confidence, cooperation, and the high resolve of live and let live…and should practice the following ten principles:

1. Both customer and supplier are fully responsible for the application of quality control with mutual understanding and cooperation between their quality control systems.

2. Both customer and supplier should be independent of each other and esteem the independence of the other party.

3. The customer is responsible for bringing clear and adequate information and requirements to the supplier so that the supplier can know precisely what he should manufacture.

4. Both customer and supplier, before entering into business, should conclude a rational contract in respect to quality, price, delivery terms, and method of payment.

5. Supplier is responsible for the assurance of quality that will give satisfaction to the customer and is also responsible for submitting necessary and actual data upon customer's request.

6. Both supplier and customer should decide on the evaluation method of various items beforehand, which will be admitted as satisfactory to both parties.

7. Both customer and supplier should establish in their contract the systems and procedures through which they can reach amicable settlement of disputes whenever any problems occur.

8. Both customer and supplier, taking into consideration the other party's standing, should exchange information necessary to carry out better quality control.

9. Both customer and supplier should always perform control business activities sufficiently, such as ordering, production and inventory planning, clerical work, and systems, so that their relationship is maintained on an amicable and satisfactory basis.

10. Both customer and supplier, when dealing with business transactions, should always take full account of the ultimate consumer's interest.

- **Mutual confidence:** This is the most critical of all the values that he mentions. One of the objectives of this customer–supplier relationship is to build a long-term partnership with specific suppliers of the most important materials or services. In order for this partnership to work, both parties must develop a strong sense of trust in each other. There will be many cases where the parties may have to divulge trade secrets to the each other in order to better integrate their objectives and processes. They may even need to better understand each other's finances in order to determine fair prices.

- **Cooperation:** Both parties must be willing to work together for mutual benefit. The relationship cannot be antagonistic. It must be a win–win situation. Each party must understand the benefits they will realize. Decisions should not be one sided or simply ruled in favor of the more powerful party; instead, cooperation in all aspects of the relationship is required.

- **Live and let live:** One of the objectives will be to develop very strong relationships with a limited number of suppliers. This must be a sound endeavor for both sides. Each must respect the other's existence and not try to win concessions that will jeopardize the other party's business. The viability of both parties should be an objective of both sides.

Expansion of the Ishikawa Model into Purchasing/Supplier Quality Management

The preceding three values work together to create an atmosphere of mutual respect and continuity which allows for the long-term strengthening of the relationship. Although mostly self-explanatory, the ten principles warrant some further explanation.

1. **Both customer and supplier are fully responsible for the application of quality control with mutual understanding and cooperation between their quality control systems.**
   Each party in the relationship must be responsible for its own quality control system. Both systems, however, must interact with trust and cooperation to develop an understanding of each other's requirements. Both parties must use the same measurement techniques (e.g., statistical process control, process capability studies, etc.); otherwise, measurements of quality for the same materials or services may differ.

2. **Both customer and supplier should be independent of each other and esteem the independence of the other party.**
   This principle expands on the more general value of live and let live discussed earlier.

3. **The customer is responsible for bringing clear and adequate information and requirements to the supplier so that the supplier can know precisely what he should manufacture.**
    This is the "two hats" principle. Recall, the importance of a customer understanding his or her role as a supplier of information to the supplier of the goods or services being purchased so that the correct goods or services may be delivered.

4. **Both customer and supplier, before entering into business, should conclude a rational contract in respect to quality, price, delivery terms, and method of payment.**
    A contract should be agreed upon prior to conducting business. If this is to be a long-term agreement, then it should be stated as such, so that business can be conducted based on this premise. The conduct of the two parties would likely differ under this premise as opposed to a one-time purchase; therefore, this needs to be made clear. In addition, the more general commercial terms such as price, quantity, delivery, and payment terms must be specified.

5. **Supplier is responsible for the assurance of quality that will give satisfaction to the customer and is responsible for submitting necessary and actual data upon customer's request.**
    In addition to responsibility for the quality system at his or her site, the supplier is also responsible for meeting or exceeding the quality levels agreed upon with the customer, thereby satisfying the customer. In order to build trust and show proof of quality to the customer, the supplier should respond to the customer's request for actual data on key quality characteristics of the product or service. This could be in the form of control charts, capability studies, reliability studies, etc.

6. **Both supplier and customer should decide on the evaluation method of various items beforehand, which will be admitted as satisfactory to both parties.**
    When evaluating quality levels, a good operational definition of the quality characteristics must be determined beforehand. This must be negotiated between the supplier and the customer so that there is no ambiguity in the expectations of either party. If these characteristics are well defined, there will be little ground for future disputes and a stronger relationship can be built.

7. **Both customer and supplier should establish in their contract the systems and procedures through which they can reach amicable settlement of disputes whenever any problems occur.**

   Disputes can easily destroy a long-term customer–supplier relationship, especially if no agreement has been reached on the methods to be used to resolve these disputes. For example, today many contracts refer disputes to binding arbitration. This keeps disputes more amicable and makes them less costly to resolve for all involved. Other methods could be utilized, such as predetermined, mutually agreed upon outcomes for different standard types of disputes.

8. **Both customer and supplier, taking into consideration the other party's standing, should exchange information necessary to carry out better quality control.**

   This principle is similar to Principles 1, 3, and 5. It is more general and explains the need for good communication and the exchange of information in order to perform better quality control.

9. **Both customer and supplier should always perform control business activities sufficiently, such as ordering, production and inventory planning, clerical work, and systems, so that their relationship is maintained on an amicable and satisfactory basis.**

   Continuity and repetition are key to this principle. Basically, a good long-term relationship benefits from frequent contact; therefore, it is of mutual interest that both parties conduct many transactions on a continuous basis. This promotes trust and facilitates understanding of each other's systems and processes.

10. **Both customer and supplier, when dealing with business transactions, should always take full account of the ultimate consumer's interest.**

    Last, but certainly not least, is the need to keep the ultimate consumer in mind. Without that ultimate consumer's purchases, neither party can survive. When making decisions in this relationship, both parties must maintain the highest emphasis on the needs of that ultimate consumer. For example, a very high-quality product with a very high price may not be in the best interest of the ultimate consumer, who wants value for his or her money. The ultimate consumer believes that the manufacturer or service provider is being as efficient as possible to provide the best value for the money.

These values and principles must be followed over a long period of time in order to be successful. A culture cannot be changed overnight, and a relationship with a supplier is a culture of its own. Change occurs over time and only with a concerted effort.

Many companies that have not implemented a purchasing/supplier quality management system have a very large number of suppliers with whom they deal on a constant basis. This sometimes includes literally thousands of suppliers. How many people are needed to properly deal with all of these suppliers? In the most common way of dealing with suppliers (on the basis of the lowest bid), the commitment of time for each transaction is minor. Transactions become almost automatic. A specification is sent out with a request for a quote. Bids are then compared in terms of price, and the purchase is awarded to the lowest bidder. Little attention is devoted to comparing the supplier's product to the specifications or to determining the usability of the product within the customer's processes. There may be some negotiation of terms for high-priced items, but the great majority of transactions are performed automatically and are virtually clerical in nature. Even though the effort per transaction may be minor, the overall commitment of time is significant because so many different suppliers are involved.

The true potential of procurement personnel is not being utilized in these organizations. Procurement professionals have been trained in negotiation skills, contract development, purchasing law, materials management, some business law, materials requirements, planning, etc., yet in these organizations procurement personnel perform mostly repetitive clerical functions. What a waste! These organizations would be well advised to develop long-term partnerships with a more limited supplier base. These relationships will require more time to establish in the short term; however, in the long run, as the relationships are developed and the number of suppliers is decreased, the overall commitment of time will decrease significantly. At the same time, the jobs of procurement personnel are enriched and they can provide more value-added services to their internal customers. They can become a key part of the customer–supplier team that manages the quality being provided by the supplier to the customer.

These relationships help to eliminate those non-value-added steps in the procurement process. For example, inspection of incoming materials can be significantly reduced as trust is built and the two quality control systems are better integrated. Both parties can benefit from improvements to each other's processes. These improvements can increase the quality level that is delivered to the ultimate consumer, thereby ultimately improving the market share of both the manufacturer and the supplier.

For additional information, see Abstract 4.3 at the end of this chapter.

ENDNOTES

1. Ishikawa, Kaoru (1985). *What Is Total Quality Control? The Japanese Way.* London: Prentice-Hall International, pp. 159–160.
2. Figure 4.1 ©Advent Group, Inc.
3. Exercise 4.1 ©Strategy Associates, Inc.

EXERCISES

EXERCISE 4.1
CREATING SUCCESSFUL SUPPLIER RELATIONSHIPS

This exercise provides examples of the types of questions that should be asked about the customer–supplier relationships at work within your organization. These questions should be asked as if you owned the company. They should first be answered individually and then by small groups of six to seven persons.

1. If you were in charge of your company, what would be your official mission statement regarding external suppliers? (Use the Mission Statement Guideline Form provided in Exercise 4.3.)

2. How could you improve the relationships that currently exist?

3. In what ways is money being wasted, as far as your suppliers are concerned?

4. Describe the "two hats" that you often wear as a customer and a supplier.

5. It is said that "word-of-mouth" is the best kind of advertising. What are the words that are probably coming out of the mouths of your suppliers as far as your company is concerned?

6. To improve supplier relationships, many firms are organizing supplier conferences. Assuming that you are in charge of such a conference for your organization, what would the agenda for that conference include?

7. For most of us, the internal supplier is a more immediate source of improvement than the external supplier. What changes would make your relationships with your internal suppliers even more effective than they currently are?

ABSTRACTS

ABSTRACT 4.1
JIT AND THE MANAGEMENT ACCOUNTANT

Cobb, Ian
Management Accounting–London (MAC), Vol. 70, Issue 2, February 1992, pp. 42–44

A noble philosophy, this just-in-time (JIT), or, as author Cobb calls it, "Just Intelligent Thinking." Eliminate waste from *all* parts of the manufacturing process through the use of the continuous improvement cycle is the author's basic definition of JIT. Like all things noble in England, however, JIT has been subjected to intense scrutiny and has been met with some skepticism. These are a few of the things discovered in a recent survey of 211 senior Chartered Institute of Management Accountants (CIMA) members from 205 companies across the United Kingdom. The survey based its questions upon E.J. Hays' seven aspects of JIT. However, the author is probably more accurate to say that these seven aspects are the engine or mechanism of JIT rather than the "seven immovable pillars" of JIT.

The first aspect, JIT purchasing, requires smaller, more frequent delivery of raw materials. The second, machine cells, is where workers and machines are grouped in order of production. The third is set-up time reduction, hopefully eliminating time-consuming set-ups. The fourth aspect is uniform loading, which matches production to the rate at which the product is needed by the customer (internal and external). The fifth is the use of a pull system or *kanban*, which eliminates backstock. The sixth aspect incorporates total quality to eliminate inspection. The seventh is employee involvement at all levels of the company.

These elements allow for a wide range of applications, and as seen by Cobb in the survey, most companies have embraced at least some of the aspects of JIT. The survey points out a lack of understanding of some of these aspects and underscores the need for better education of future CIMA members in the aspects and applications of JIT. Many benefits of introducing JIT were seen by Cobb in the survey, such as reduction of accounting transactions, increased manufacturing flexibility, and improved customer service. However, reasons for not introducing JIT, such as lack of knowledge about JIT and reluctance to face challenges posed by JIT, point out the need for better education. Overall, 33 management accounting system companies reported a total of 50 changes in the areas of accounting for work-in-process, direct labor, and manufacturing overhead. As JIT is worked into more companies every day, one thing is clear: the management accounting systems of the past are going to change and the criteria for evaluating management accountants will change with them. References and graphs are provided.

ABSTRACT 4.2
PARTNERING: A PATH TO TOTAL QUALITY

Hutchins, Greg
National Productivity Review (NLP), Vol. 11, Issue 2, Spring 1992, pp. 213–230

The recent integration of the world's economic activities has led to markets becoming more specialized and customers becoming more astute regarding price, quality, and the products and services themselves. Global competition, high customer expectations, and product development costs have encouraged companies to form alliances and begin partnering—a process in which two or more companies with complementary objectives combine to satisfy customers in different markets.

However, before this can be accomplished, executives must organize for partnering by demonstrating their commitment to partnering, eliminating organizational obstacles to quality, and enhancing communication between the partners. Top management commitment to continuous improvement starts with education, training, and deployment of organizational development principles, such as encouraging risk taking. Purchasing personnel must have knowledge of quality management and statistical techniques, just-in-time process manufacturing, and engineering.

Regardless of how a company gets a partnership under way, all continuous improvement efforts usually involve the following steps: (1) establish a team, (2) develop an action plan, (3) develop specifications and standards, (4) prioritize product attributes, (5) determine process control and capability, (6) measure performance, (7) improve continuously, (8) take ownership, and (9) audit performance. When choosing a partner, suppliers are periodically evaluated on their quality, service, cost, and technology, as well as past performance history, location, R&D, and their production facilities.

Throughout the different strategies and techniques for developing and then assessing partners, there will conceivably be hurdles to overcome, such as contractual disputes, nonconforming products, or poor service. These disputes can be resolved through acceptance, negotiation, litigation, or corrective action. When this fails, it is time to either manufacture the product in-house or find new suppliers. As supplier partnering becomes an economic necessity, many companies are securing supplier partners through intensive evaluation processes that emphasize quality, cost competitiveness, advanced technology, and excellent service. No references are given, but good graphs are provided.

ABSTRACT 4.3
QUALITY MANAGEMENT SYSTEMS: ALTERNATIVE APPROACHES TO INTEGRATING QUALITY FACTORS IN PURCHASING AND MATERIAL MANAGEMENT DECISION MAKING

Perkins, Charles and Perry, James Jr.
Production and Inventory Management Journal, 3rd Quarter 1992, pp. 58–62

During the development of a quality-oriented purchasing system, the benefits of quick results should be balanced against an approach that yields long-term improvement. A case study of two competing, independent business units, Rabbit and Turtle, is presented to illustrate this dichotomy. While developing its quality purchasing system, Rabbit collected a great deal of quality and purchasing information, but it was neither integrated nor retrievable in a timely form. They chose to focus on one objectively established, familiar measure (similar to the low hanging fruit from *The Fox and The Grapes*), ignoring other information.

On the other hand, Turtle developed its quality purchasing system in a step-by-step fashion by forming a team of quality and purchasing professionals who incorporated information from all parts of the quality information cycle. Seeking to improve the performance of their suppliers (rather than punish them), Turtle provided their suppliers with a report card emphasizing Turtle's commitment to hold suppliers accountable and also be fair.

Although integration of the data took longer than planned, Turtle's system was accepted by the vast majority of their suppliers because of the continuous updating and feedback. The most significant impediment to the implementation of a quality-oriented purchasing system is the lack of an integrating database system. Another impediment is the invisible line between the quality and purchasing organizations because acceptance by suppliers is so important.

Meanwhile, when trying to accurately assess bid factors, several questions must be asked: How much does a one-week delivery delay cost your firm? What is the cost of rework caused by a defective part? What is the cost of a finished product being returned by a customer? The best strategy seems to be to integrate all available measures into something resembling a composite quality rating system, for excellent suppliers will welcome such systems because of the increase in their customer base. Limited references and graphs are provided.

ARTICLES

THE BUYER–SUPPLIER RELATIONSHIP IN TOTAL QUALITY MANAGEMENT

D. M. Lascelles and B. G. Dale

The quality of purchased materials is critical to the quality of a company's finished products. Philip Crosby estimates that 50 percent of a company's quality nonconformances are caused by defective purchased material. Writers such as Deming and Ishikawa agree as to the culpability of purchasing organizations in allowing this to happen. Ishikawa claims that at least 70 percent of the blame for defective purchased material lies with the purchasing organization, and Deming's view is that buyers have new responsibilities to fulfill, one of which is to end the practice of awarding business solely on the basis of price. Louis DeRose notes that many buyers have recognized this and are experimenting with various new approaches, such as supplier base reduction, single or limited sourcing arrangements, and tighter integration with supplier planning and scheduling systems.

While the requirements outlined in a buyer's quality system standard can assist a supplier in improving its quality, the fact remains that a supplier bears full responsibility for the quality of its products and services. For example, Hart believes that suppliers have an obligation to study their customer's production processes to see how the supplied material is used and how it relates to the finished product. It is also worth noting that Debruicker and Summe and Roberts stress the fact that suppliers should be more proactive in developing their customer base as a competitive strategy, instead of merely reacting to the quality improvement activities of their customers.

It is clear, then, that changes are occurring in the customer–supplier relationship; the Philips Group coined the phrase "co-makership" to describe this kind of relationship. In spite of the considerable resources being devoted to the subject by most major organizations, there is surprisingly

Reprinted with permission from the publisher, the National Association of Purchasing Management, "The Buyer–Supplier Relationship in Total Quality Management," by D.M. Lascelles and B.G. Dale, *Journal of Purchasing and Materials Management*, Vol. 25, No. 2, Summer 1989.

little literature that deals with the issue of supplier development. This article, based on an empirical research study, deals with current issues in supplier development and the obstacles likely to impair the buyer–supplier relationship.

METHODOLOGY

As part of a research program that focused on the process of quality improvement, the authors formulated a quality improvement change agent hypothesis. The preliminary work carried out indicated that a demanding customer is the most potent change agent in getting a supplier to initiate a process of quality improvement. To investigate further the effect a major customer might have on supplier behavior and on attitudes toward quality improvement, a questionnaire survey of the supplier communities of three automotive suppliers was conducted. Completed questionnaires were obtained from 300 UK suppliers—53 suppliers to customer 1, 136 suppliers to customer 2, and 111 suppliers to customer 3.

The questionnaire responses were subjected to a comparative analysis to determine if any statistically significant differences existed between the responses for the different customers. This was done by carrying out significance tests on the differences between the three sets of questionnaire responses, treating each as a separate statistical sample (see Table I). From the results of these tests it was concluded that there were no significant differences between the responses received from the suppliers to customers 1, 2, and 3.

It is also worth mentioning that 30 responses to the questionnaire survey were received from foreign-based suppliers. This sample was compared with the sample of 300 UK-based suppliers. No statistically significant data could be found from this comparative analysis to indicate that the awareness, techniques, and methods used to manage product and service quality by foreign suppliers are different from those used by UK-based suppliers. In addition, the fieldwork produced no hard empirical data to suggest that the overall performance of foreign suppliers was better than that of their British counterparts.

To gain further insight into the customer–supplier relationship, two of the three customers were studied in depth to see how they interacted with their suppliers. This was done by spending time on-site observing how purchasing and supplier quality assurance personnel went about their work (data was also obtained from semi-structured interviews held with these staff people), analyzing relevant company reports, and by attending a quality improvement seminar held by one of the organizations for its key suppliers. A number of suppliers were also visited in order to gauge their impressions of their respective customers.

Table I Quality Management Techniques Used by Suppliers

Techniques	Suppliers to Customer 1		Suppliers to Customer 2		Suppliers to Customer 3	
	N = 53[a]	%[b]	N = 136	%	N = 111	%
Records of quality related activities	49	92.4	117	86.0	99	89.2
Inspection—of supplies on receipt	46	86.8	124	91.2	104	93.7
Inspection—prior to dispatch	45	84.9	123	90.4	107	96.4
Inspection—during manufacture	44	83.0	117	86.0	99	89.2
Joint quality planning with customers	41	77.3	99	72.8	86	77.5
Documented quality management policy	40	75.5	110	80.9	90	81.1
Statistical process control	40	75.5	96	70.5	72	64.9
Product planning	36	67.9	80	58.8	61	55.0
Quality performance reporting (at board meetings)	36	67.9	63	46.3	65	58.6
Quality performance reporting (at management meetings)	35	66.0	92	67.6	80	72.1
Joint quality planning with suppliers	35	66.0	85	62.5	70	63.1
Project planning and control (for new products or methods)	31	58.5	80	58.8	58	52.3
Review of contracts to identify special or unusual requirements	31	58.5	78	57.3	67	60.4
Vendor rating	31	58.5	85	62.5	68	61.3
Evaluation of customers' packaging and storage requirements	27	50.9	80	58.8	54	48.6
Quality costing	27	50.9	54	39.7	51	45.9
Product testing	26	49.3	85	62.5	68	61.3
Evaluation of competitors' products	24	45.2	74	54.4	59	53.2
Failure mode and effects analysis	20	37.7	67	49.2	50	45.0
Inspection at suppliers' premises	19	35.8	56	41.1	38	34.2
Design brief from marketing/sales	17	32.1	52	38.2	39	35.1

Table I Quality Management Techniques Used by Suppliers (continued)

Techniques	Suppliers to Customer 1		Suppliers to Customer 2		Suppliers to Customer 3	
	N = 53[a]	%[b]	N = 136	%	N = 111	%
Value analysis	17	32.1	36	26.5	34	30.6
Market research	16	30.1	40	29.4	30	27.0
Field trials/product clinics	15	28.3	47	34.6	36	32.4
Interdisciplinary quality groups	14	26.4	44	32.3	30	27.0
Design review meetings	13	24.5	42	30.8	32	28.8
Reliability improvement programs	12	22.6	49	36.0	31	27.9
Product life cycle costing	10	18.9	15	11.0	11	9.9
Quality circles (shop floor)	9	17.0	25	18.4	17	15.3
Quality circles (staff)	8	15.1	15	11.0	12	10.8
Quality circles (multi-disciplinary)	6	11.3	22	16.1	11	9.9

[a] N = number of respondents.
[b] % = percent of respondents.

POOR COMMUNICATION AND FEEDBACK

Communication and feedback in the supply chain is not good. Moreover, suppliers and buyers often do not realize how poor they are at communicating with each other. The vital communication links between the two parties are often taken for granted; communication is a two-way process and must be treated as such. This fundamental weakness in the buyer–supplier interface is a serious roadblock to quality improvement, and is probably an outcome of the traditional quasi-adversarial relationship.

A recent supplier conference, held by one of the customers studied, provided several illustrations of how the buying firm had failed to communicate effectively with its suppliers over the years, resulting in the formation of negative attitudes on both sides. Mistrust, fear, disappointment, frustration, and dishonest acts on both sides were the results. The conference gave both groups an opportunity to air grievances and discuss problems in an honest and open manner, which hitherto had not been a feature of the customer's relationship with its suppliers. The most noteworthy outcome was that for the first time both parties realized they could actually talk to each other. Communication between buyer and supplier, and even the need for improving supplier performance, has been taken for granted in much of British manufacturing industry. This situation probably is summed up best in the following comment by Egan:

> When in 1980, Jaguar started to knobble component suppliers for poor performance of their product, they (component suppliers) were often surprised, because until that time no one had bothered to give them feedback of this kind and they, therefore, could be partly forgiven for believing that everything in the garden was rosy. I say partly because component suppliers did very little to find out how their products performed in service.

The findings of the questionnaire survey indicate that the situation was not much different in 1987. While almost all the 300 survey respondents claimed to know what factors sell their products (usually price, quality, and delivery), further analysis of the data revealed their ranking to be largely subjective. Most suppliers have no quantitative or proactive measure of customer satisfaction. Very few even bother to find out what their customers think; an attitude of "no news is good news" still appears to be the norm.

COMMUNICATION OF REQUIREMENTS

It is up to the buyer to ensure the existence of a clear specification that defines the exact requirements. This in itself, however, is not sufficient to assure conformance. The supplier must be given the opportunity to understand the function of the part it is to supply and to discuss design details before they are finalized, particularly with regard to the manufacturability of parts.

For example, one automotive supplier studied had experienced frequent problems with the performance of *its* castings suppliers. A detailed investigation of the causes of dimensional and metallurgical nonconformances revealed that many of the problems were of the automotive supplier's own making, due to its failure to specify requirements in a clear enough manner, and in not recognizing the unique operating problems that exist in the foundry industry. The firm buying the castings discovered that the quality performance of its suppliers improved when (1) suppliers with the appropriate expertise were selected, and (2) the design and functional requirements of the finished casting were discussed with foundry representatives before the contract was consummated.

The head quality engineer of another firm had no doubt that communicating quality requirements clearly and accurately to suppliers was the biggest single breakthrough his organization could make in improving supplier quality performance. In his firm, technical engineering standards were not always sent to suppliers with the purchase order. When the purchasing manager was interviewed, not surprisingly he disagreed, saying that most suppliers had been serving the firm for some time and should be well aware of the firm's quality requirements. He contended that the engineer's observation was in fact just an excuse used by some suppliers to ship nonconforming items. It should be noted, however, that technical engineering standards are not well communicated *in-plant* in this firm; the organization tends to function on a "need-to-know" basis.

Some purchasing managers and quality engineers seem to think that the quality performance of their suppliers can be achieved almost by remote control—and often are surprised and disappointed when they receive nonconforming items. During the course of this investigation, the authors encountered several people who genuinely believed that they engaged in joint quality planning with suppliers, whereas in fact the communication process was all one-way (from buyer to supplier). Feedback from suppliers was discouraged; in some cases it was ad hoc and ignored, and in others it was never sought in the first place. In such cases, quality planning rarely is joint in nature because suppliers have no voice in the product specification or design. After the initial vendor assessment, some purchasing organizations do not even bother to follow up to ensure that their supplier's manufacturing processes continue to be capable of achieving the required level of quality conformance. Indeed, a number of such companies tend to confuse an assessment of the supplier's quality system with advanced quality planning.

The following three examples of nonconforming materials occurred in customer 1's organization. (The firm's annual purchasing expenditure is approximately £60 million, and 200 different components and parts are purchased.)

- The company experienced a high rate of in-process rejections on certain purchased forgings. The cause eventually was traced to the inability of the supplier's heat treatment process to adequately treat the bottom of the grooves cut into the component. Due to a design flaw, this was a customer requirement that eventually turned out to be impossible to fulfill by this or any other vendor. However, the supplier did not inform the buyer that its process could not meet the specification in full.
- A code was required to be stamped on the outside rim of certain screw heads. The supplier continued to ship screws with the code stamped on top of the head. When questioned by the quality engineer about this nonconformance, the supplier replied, "Why are you complaining now? We have supplied screws coded in this manner for years and you never complained before. Besides, we don't have a machine capable of stamping the outside rim."

- A component was ordered to be manufactured from a specified type of European steel. On receipt from the supplier, the component material was found to be too soft. Subsequent investigation uncovered an interesting situation. The specified steel could be obtained only from a source in West Germany in 50 ton lots, a quantity that far exceeded the buyer's annual requirements. Therefore, the supplier decided to manufacture the components from the "next best" material which was more easily obtainable.

These examples of nonconforming items occurred in a company that prides itself on having an efficient purchasing function, a "lean and mean" attitude toward business, a relatively small supplier base, practicing just-in-time purchasing, and encouraging its suppliers to adopt SPC. This firm is a prime example of managing supplier performance by remote control. Despite its belief to the contrary, this firm does not engage in joint quality planning with its suppliers. There appear to be a number of reasons for this:

- Strategically, the company is cost-driven. The management team is keenly aware of the fact that it is part of a foreign-owned multinational group operating in price sensitive markets. Moreover, the entire output of the plant studied goes to the United States. Consequently, a key company objective is to keep material prices at not less than 30 percent below comparable materials used in its North American operations. One outcome of this sensitivity to cost is that the company seems to manage its supplier base as though it were involved in a commodity trading market. It also actively pursues an international sourcing policy.

Long-term supplier involvement is not a noticeable feature of the firm's purchasing operation, and there are frequent switches from one supplier to another. For example, during 1985, 37 vendors were removed from the company's approved list (almost all for cost rather than quality reasons) and 59 new suppliers added. The quality department's involvement in supplier selection tends to be ad hoc, and cost rather than quality criteria appear to be the basis for selection.

- The company's management is constantly involved in "fire-fighting" activities, perhaps because of an overblown self-image.
- Its communications and feedback systems, both internally and with suppliers, are ineffective.
- The firm's management has an apparent inability to learn from past events, and the same nonconformances tend to recur repeatedly.

Table II Supplier Perceptions of
Their Customers' Quality Performance Expectations

	Suppliers to Customer 1		Suppliers to Customer 2		Suppliers to Customer 3	
	N = 53[a]	%[b]	N = 136	%	N = 111	%
Quality parameter—perceived as being realistic						
Conforming batches	46	86.8	121	89.0	97	87.4
Delivery tolerances	43	81.1	116	85.3	96	86.5
Technical specifications	46	86.8	117	86.0	101	91.0
Improvement to product quality	48	90.6	120	88.2	97	87.4
Quality parameter—perceived as being unrealistic						
Conforming batches	2	3.7	3	2.2	4	3.6
Delivery tolerances	4	7.5	7	5.1	4	3.6
Technical specifications	3	5.6	10	7.3	3	2.7
Improvement to product quality	2	3.7	5	3.7	4	3.6

[a] N = number of respondents.
[b] % = percent of respondents.

SUPPLIERS' PERCEPTIONS OF CUSTOMER EXPECTATIONS

Table II indicates that the large majority of suppliers perceived the quality performance expectations of the three customers as realistic; very few regarded them as unrealistic. In the case of customers 2 and 3, suppliers who regarded quality performance as unrealistic were asked to indicate to whom they had communicated their views. Of the 31 suppliers complaining about customer 2, 18 discussed their problems with the buying firm—12 with Purchasing, 4 with Quality Assurance, and 2 with Engineering. Of the 15 suppliers that felt customer 3's expectations were unrealistic, 9 talked with the buying firm—7 with Purchasing, 1 with Quality Assurance, and 1 with Engineering. Unfortunately, this shows clearly that not all suppliers with reservations regarding customer quality expectations actually communicate their views to the buying organization. The majority of those that do, however, do so via the purchasing department.

Most of the dissatisfaction appears to relate to technical specifications, particularly the lack of consultation over design and product engineering. A number of respondents also criticized the frequency of delivery schedule changes.

Table III Areas of Customers' Approach to Quality
that Suppliers Think Should Be Improved

Area	Suppliers to Customer 1		Suppliers to Customer 2		Suppliers to Customer 3	
	N = 53[a]	%[b]	N = 136	%	N = 111	%
Feedback to suppliers	15	28.3	39	35.1	44	32.3
Communications with suppliers	10	18.9	26	23.4	32	23.5
Product specification data	11	20.8	17	15.3	28	20.5
Delivery requirements data	7	13.2	30	27.0	26	19.1
Advice to suppliers	8	15.1	17	15.3	16	11.8
Expectations of supplier performance	7	13.2	15	13.5	13	9.6
Other	2	3.7	7	6.3	6	4.4

[a] N = number of respondents.
[b] % = percent of respondents.

Table III identifies the areas in which respondents think that a customer's approach to quality should be improved. The three areas of major concern are:

1. Performance feedback to suppliers
2. Ongoing communications with suppliers
3. Precise materials specification data

PURCHASING'S ROLE

The basic responsibility of the purchasing department and the need for a focal point in handling supplier communications are two important factors in developing the buyer–supplier interface. The points of contact between buyer and supplier are often unclear, resulting in an uncoordinated flow of data. Inevitably, not everyone is kept in the picture and misunderstandings arise. More often than not, the allocation of responsibilities among the purchasing, quality assurance, engineering, and related departments regarding the activities of suppliers is poorly defined. For example, in initiating a supplier development program one major firm examined its supply operation and discovered that while procurement, design, production, and quality assurance engineers were all talking with suppliers, no single function accepted the overall responsibility for supplier performance with respect to price, delivery, and quality. This was a crucial discovery, since the company had traditionally defined the role of the purchasing function as "obtaining the right parts, at the right time, at the right price." Clearly, the purchasing function was not achieving this objective, and the company's organizational structure was not adequate for coping with the requirements of effective supply management. To improve supplier performance, the company had to get back to the basics.

CUSTOMER'S CREDIBILITY

A purchasing organization's lack of credibility in the eyes of its suppliers is another barrier to attitude change; suppliers need to be convinced that a customer is serious about quality. Poor purchasing and supply management practices, such as price buying, frequent switches from one supplier to another, unpredictable and inflated schedules, poor engineering design/production/supplier liaison, over stringent specifications, abuse of power by quality engineers, and the use of "loss of business" as a bargaining ploy by the buyer all help to widen the credibility gap. It is not uncommon for a customer to talk quality to its suppliers, and then act quite differently later by focusing on price or delivery performance. Moreover, there is little use in holding quality improvement conferences for suppliers if the purchasing organization continues to adopt an adversarial approach in dealing with suppliers, or is seen to accord a low priority to quality until there is a serious nonconformance. In the words of the quality engineer of one supplier visited, "No one cares about supplier performance until the production line stops."

Customer 2 is a prime example of a major purchasing organization which, over the years, has lost considerable credibility with its suppliers as a serious "quality-minded" company. (The firm now has a real problem with the quality of supplied parts; for example, 30 percent of all initial lots are rejected.) The authors observed that on several occasions the mention of customer 2's name to its suppliers or ex-suppliers would produce a wry smile or a shake of the head. Several claimed that customer 2 bought solely on the basis of price. This attitude was also borne out in some of the responses to the supplier survey. One company visited, which had been rated by customer 2 as a category A supplier, was particularly critical of the way supplier contracts were negotiated, after having lost much of its business on price to a category B rated vendor. Frequent schedule changes also give rise to a lot of ill-feeling among suppliers. In one case, for example, customer 2 changed its delivery schedule with one supplier seven times in two weeks.

Another cause of credibility loss is when a customer has continued to accept nonconforming items over a long period of time, even if unwittingly, and then criticizes the supplier for supplying nonconforming materials. The newly imposed standards of conformance may seem arbitrary and, even worse, the customer's quality system is made to appear inadequate in the eyes of the supplier.

Failure to respond to supplier requests for information or feedback on specification requirements, component functionality, and so on is another way in which a purchaser's credibility can seriously be undermined. For example, a soft trim supplier complained about receiving no feedback after communicating SPC-related queries through the customer's local quality engineer. This supplier now perceives that particular customer to be a bureaucratic purchasing organization rather than a business partner.

MISGUIDED SUPPLIER IMPROVEMENT OBJECTIVES

Buyers often are not sure what they want from their supplier improvement programs. Comments made by questionnaire respondents indicate that some of their customers do not understand the fundamentals of total quality management. Many have formal vendor assessment procedures, but no clear supplier development objectives.

There appears to be a dilution of the quality message as requirements are passed down the supply chain. For example, when faced with demands from customers for quality improvement changes, suppliers frequently react by implementing specific quality management tools and techniques in their operations, and in turn insist that their own suppliers use the same techniques. In reality, very few customers are actively involved with their suppliers in helping solve quality problems; there appears to be an almost blind faith in the power of statistical process control to do the trick. Clearly, many firms believe that if they are using SPC they have a total approach to quality management. Similarly, some of these firms are under the equally mistaken impression that the imposition of a particular quality management technique on their suppliers (as a condition of purchase) is the same as supplier development. Rather than resulting in a positive change of behavior, the outcome tends to result in what Schon calls *dynamic conservatism*, since the imposition is seen as a disruptive threat to the organization. If the organization cannot neutralize the threat, it will comply to the least possible extent with the requirements for change (i.e., dynamic conservatism). Therefore, the implementation of techniques without behavior or attitude change simply means that any benefits gained will likely be short-lived. Quality management techniques must be used as tools to aid the total quality management process; therefore, all personnel should know why specific techniques are being used.

The distinction between the use of techniques and total quality management needs to be clearly articulated and communicated by the senior management team to all employees.

PURCHASING POWER

Purchasing power is a major issue in the buyer–supplier relationship. Lack of purchasing clout was a commonly cited reason by buyers for lack of success in improving supplier quality performance. Moreover, analysis of the responses to the survey revealed that the buying impact of all three customers is generally low, so that the loss of their business would probably have little effect on the sales of most of the suppliers surveyed. The percentage of suppliers' annual sales resulting from business with each of the three customers is shown in Table IV. Clearly, for the majority of the suppliers, business with each of the customers accounted for less than 5 percent of annual sales. Further, while orders from the parent groups of each of the three customers accounted for a larger percentage of supplier sales, they still totaled less than 5 percent of sales in a majority of the cases.

The general view is that a purchaser's influence on its suppliers varies with its purchasing power—the greater a buyer's purchasing power, the more effective are its suppliers' quality assurance activities. During the course of the research, the following examples that support this position were found.

- It is clear that major automotive companies and large public sector purchasing organizations have used their purchasing "muscle" to *force* their suppliers to adopt certain quality management techniques and practices, as a contractual condition of business. On the other hand, one firm (a British Quality Award winner) had little success in changing managerial attitudes toward quality in one of its large raw materials suppliers, due to its relative lack of purchasing power, even though it offered direct assistance to solve nonconformance problems.
- Another British Quality Award winner, therefore a company with demonstrably high quality standards and an established reputation for quality management, still appeared to lack influence over its suppliers even after having reduced its supplier base by almost 40 percent. Of the 20 places on a Department of Trade and Industry sponsored quality activity program offered to suppliers at the company's annual quality convention, only 7 were taken, whereas all 40 places on offer to automotive component suppliers at the Society of Motor Manufacturers & Traders' Drive for Total Quality Conference were

Table IV Percentage of Suppliers' Annual Sales
Resulting from Business with Each of the Three Customers

	Suppliers to Customer 1		Suppliers to Customer 2		Suppliers to Customer 3	
	N = 53[a]	%[b]	N = 136	%	N = 111	%
Percentage of sales to the division in question						
Under 1%	17	32.1	72	53.0	65	58.6
1%–5%	22	41.6	43	31.6	33	29.7
5%–10%	6	11.3	12	8.8	4	3.6
10%–15%	3	5.7	1	0.7	1	0.9
15%–20%	1	1.9	2	1.5	—	—
20%–25%	—	—	2	1.5	—	—
Over 25%	1	1.9	1	0.7	—	—
Unknown	3	5.7	3	2.2	8	7.2
Percentage of sales to the group or corporation to which the division belongs						
Under 1%	17	32.1	54	39.7	33	29.7
1%–5%	21	39.6	51	37.5	40	36.0
5%–10%	7	13.2	15	11.0	13	11.7
10%–15%	3	5.7	3	2.2	11	9.9
15%–20%	1	1.9	3	2.2	6	5.4
20%–25%	—	—	2	1.5	—	—
Over 25%	1	1.9	6	4.4	3	2.7
Unknown	3	5.7	2	1.5	5	4.5

[a] N = number of respondents.
[b] % = percent of respondents.

filled. The purchasing power of the major automotive companies was a significant factor.

Purchasing power alone is not a surefire guarantee of supplier improvement. Companies with considerable purchasing power may well improve the quality of purchased items, but will not necessarily achieve lasting benefits or motivate their suppliers to internalize the benefits of cost-effective quality management to satisfy all customers. There is a tendency for some suppliers to treat powerful customers as sacred cows, leading in effect to "stratified quality control." The survey findings revealed that a number of firms appeared to grade the quality of their products at different levels, according to anticipated individual customer expectations, based on past experience.

CONCLUDING REMARKS

The majority of suppliers studied see the quality performance requirements of the three customers as realistic. However, a substantial number
of them feel that bilateral communications and feedback from their customers could be improved significantly. Not all dissatisfied suppliers
actually communicate their dissatisfaction to their customers. However,
several suppliers indicated a willingness to collaborate more closely with
their customers on component design and product engineering. Such
collaboration would form a solid basis for long-term improvement and
provide a logical starting point for a supplier development activity.

There are no significant differences in quality management techniques
between the supplier bases of the three companies. This suggests not only
that the suppliers comprising the aggregated survey sample can be considered typical of the UK automotive components industry, but also that
the supplier base management activities of the three customers have little
direct impact on the quality management activities of their suppliers. Lack
of purchasing clout appears to be one obvious cause, but purchasing
strategies also have an important bearing on the situation.

Cost reduction is a major element in the purchasing strategies of all
three customers. When they are under pressure, quality appears to assume
a lower priority than price and other commercial considerations. This has
a negative effect on a company's image and its credibility with suppliers.
While customer 1's quality system is not noticeably better than those of the
other two customers, the firm has two obvious advantages—a much higher
share of its user market (so it is perceived as a successful business) and a
smaller supplier base.

There is a good deal of cynicism among a large number of suppliers
that major purchasers in the UK automotive industry are price driven
when negotiating contracts. This causes a negative reaction among some
suppliers. However, these suppliers are missing the point; price is just one
element of the overall product sales package. And while price is nego-
tiable, product and service quality are not. Many suppliers do not appear
to realize that total quality management can provide them with the essential organizational capacity to satisfy all their customer requirements. It is
not unusual for suppliers to indulge in "stratified quality control" by
grading their products according to customer purchasing power.

Suppliers have become an essential part of a quality improvement
strategy aimed at improving the competitiveness of a buying firm. It
appears that there are two major reasons for this—namely, greater global
specialization and changes in the nature of competition itself. Effective
supplier development requires purchasing organizations to treat suppli-

ers as long-term business partners. This necessitates a fundamental shift from the traditional adversarial buyer–supplier relationship to one of co-makership, together with careful selection of suppliers and a rationalization of the supplier base. Some of the developments taking place in the buyer–supplier relationship in the automotive industry typify the co-makership approach. These include:

- The use of long-term purchasing contracts.
- The development of common goals, trust, and dependence.
- Joint problem-solving activities.
- The use of single and dual sourcing.
- Reduction of the supplier base.
- Reduction of the inspection of purchased parts.
- Both parties learning more about each other's business.
- Buyers actively assisting suppliers with quality and operating problems.

Properly implemented, these activities help reduce costs, to the benefit of both parties.

Demanding customers are the prime motivation for long-term quality improvement. However, the degree to which a supplier can be influenced is affected by purchasing power and the extent to which the buyer is perceived by the supplier to be serious about quality. Looking at industry as a whole, many major customers have formal supplier improvement programs, but no clear idea of what they require from their suppliers. Unfortunately, relatively few are actively involved in joint problem-solving activities with suppliers. Before embarking on a formal supplier development program, the purchasing organization must review critically those aspects of its own operation that can adversely affect supplier performance—things such as purchase specifications, communications, training, and organizational roles.

The key steps involved in a supplier development program are: (1) establish and articulate program objectives; (2) set priorities for action; (3) identify key suppliers as potential long-term partners, and make plans to reduce the supplier base; (4) communicate the program objectives and methodology to key suppliers; (5) assess the capability of suppliers to meet purchase requirements; (6) engage in advanced quality planning *with suppliers*; (7) formally recognize suppliers that achieve *preferred* status; and (8) develop an ongoing quality improvement relationship with suppliers, based on a free exchange of information.

CHAPTER 5

LINKING SUPPLIERS through POLICY DEPLOYMENT

OBJECTIVES OF LINKING

What is the purpose of connecting or *linking* suppliers to an organization? Each organization has different objectives. Some may think that quality is more important than price, while others may believe that price is the only factor in a buying decision. Others may have even more diverse beliefs. Like individuals tend to attract other individuals with similar interests and characteristics. The overachiever will attract other overachievers, losers will attract other losers, and so on. Similarly, organizations, which are composed of individuals, tend to attract other organizations with similar beliefs and objectives.

When organizations with similar interests create a long-term partnership, they can implement a cadre of mutually beneficial changes such as the following.

Eliminate non-value-added steps: Both organizations can examine their procurement processes and their internal processes to determine how they can best be re-engineered for the benefit of the partnership. For example, too many approval steps in the requisition process can delay an order from being placed. This hurts the customer who now has to keep excess inventory to cover usage during the time that the requisition is being approved, but it also hurts the supplier who is now given less time to respond to the customer's requirements, which may increase the total cost to provide the material or service being requested.

Eliminate waste: If the parties to a supply partnership can reduce waste in either organization, then the total costs can be reduced and both parties in the partnership can share this benefit.

Reduce setup times: This is a key area that is necessary for the establishment of a just-in-time (JIT) environment. Both parties benefit. If setup times are reduced by the supplier, the customer receives greater flexibility in terms of minimum lot sizes, lower lead times, and more frequent deliveries. The customer could then reduce inventory levels required to cover ordering lead time. On the other hand, if the customer is able to reduce setup time due to some feature of the supplier's product, then again both parties benefit. This improvement could also be shared by both parties when negotiating a new contract.

Electronic data interchange (EDI):   The current explosion in information technology is opening many avenues to shared benefits. EDI is a very recent innovation in business communication methodology. It allows companies to pass standardized business transactions between their computer systems with little human intervention. This can significantly reduce the amount of time required to fill an order and pay for an order. Many companies that have implemented EDI technology use it as a catalyst to re-engineer their procurement processes. This re-engineered process developed with EDI technology has allowed all parties to benefit from fewer errors, faster response to customer needs, and an overall reduction in value-added steps in the process. See the case study at the end of this book for further detail.

Continuous process improvement: Whenever a supplier partnership is established, both parties can benefit from improvements to each other's processes, especially when the supplier tries to provide a product or service that is better *linked* to the customer's needs. The two parties can be assured that the net result of the joint effort expended to improve each other's processes will be to the benefit of both organizations. This is further discussed in Chapter 8.

Feedback of results: In order to manage a process, it is necessary to identify the critical success factors of that process, measure the process, analyze the results, and then act according to the findings of the analysis. Without this feedback component, little can be determined about the direction of changes in the process. Alternatively, if the results are provided to the process owner, then appropriate action and improvement can take place.

Some major technological developments are currently in pilot studies, while others are still in the design phases; these will be discussed in the final chapter, where the future direction of purchasing and supplier quality management is considered.

For additional information, see Abstract 5.1 at the end of this chapter.

THE SUPPLIER WITHIN POLICY DEPLOYMENT

What Is Policy Deployment or Hoshin Planning?

Some people refer to policy deployment as Hoshin planning or management by policy in order to differentiate it from management by objectives. Others refer to policy deployment as strategic quality planning, which is somewhat of a misnomer. In the end, all are very similar regardless of the name. Various authors have written at length on this subject, including King,[1] Akao,[2] and Sheridan.[3] The main objective of policy deployment is to align the organizational forces of the extended enterprise in the same direction so that everyone within the enterprise understands the overall direction of the organizations involved and how each can best support that direction. When properly executed, policy deployment gives each individual in the organization and each organization within the extended organization a sense of commitment and direction and allows them to see how their job fits within the larger scheme.

The Components of Policy Deployment

Policy deployment is composed of a number of levels (Figure 5.1), as described in the following paragraphs.

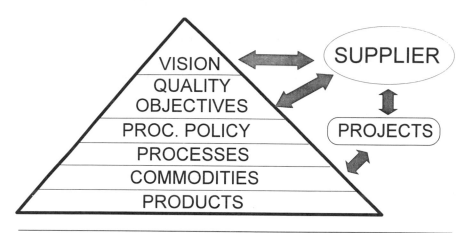

Figure 5.1 The Supplier within Policy Deployment.

Vision: The vision is a description of a desired future state of the organization. It is analogous to a place or a location to which the organization wants to move. There are many roads that the organization can take, but knowing the vision allows the organization to determine the best quality objectives in order to accomplish its mission.

Quality objectives: These are the goals and targets that must be met, as well as the means to get there. These goals or targets, together with the associated means, are referred to as policies. These policies are deployed throughout the organization and hence the name policy deployment. It is important that these objectives be measurable.

Procurement policy: A procurement policy should be developed by the Supplier Quality Management Council. The composition of this council and its responsibilities are discussed in Chapter 10 on implementation. This policy must be approved by the chief executive or president of the organization and then communicated to all suppliers. This communication and deployment process will be further explained at the end of this chapter.

Processes: Once these policies have been developed at the top of the organization, with input from lower levels, and then agreed to, they must be deployed to all the processes and levels within the organization. This includes major business processes, major manufacturing processes, service delivery processes, and administrative processes.

Commodities: These are groups of common or similar items that are mainly utilized in one or a group of processes. A specific product group or service group usually uses some common items or types of items. Similarly, suppliers often specialize in certain types of products or services. For example, chemicals, plastics, steel, office equipment and supplies, fasteners, and computers all may be considered to be different commodities.

Products: The processes within an organization usually require certain products or services that flow through the process or are a part of the steps in the process.

Supplier: A supplier ultimately provides the products and services which are part of the processes mentioned above.

Projects: Projects are selected with each supplier in order to improve the products and services provided by the supplier to the organization.

It is the quality of the products and services coming from the suppliers that must be managed. In order to do this efficiently and effectively, the policy of the organization must be deployed through the different levels mentioned earlier so that the organization can ultimately determine which suppliers to work with more closely. Once key suppliers have been determined, projects are designed to improve the products and services they provide.

Cycle Time Example

It is important for an organization to select suppliers that share its vision of the organization. For example, an organization may have a corporate objective to reduce cycle time. That organization then would benefit from working with a supplier with a similar objective of reducing cycle time. The supplier would try to reduce the time to develop its products, which in turn would benefit the buying organization because their supplier could more quickly respond to their changing needs. Similarly, the supplier would ask its suppliers to reduce their delivery and cycle times so that it would be better able to deliver to the buying organization on time. The supplier would also try to reduce shipping quantities and to deliver more frequently so that the buying organization could reduce its cycle times and award the supplier additional business.

For additional information, see Abstract 5.2 at the end of this chapter.

STEPS IN SUPPLIER POLICY DEPLOYMENT

The Concept of Prioritization ("Don't Chase Too Many Rabbits")

The implementation of a total quality management (TQM) system at Florida Power & Light (FPL) involved working very closely with some of the quality counselors from the Japanese Union of Scientists and Engineers (JUSE). Dr. Kondo and Dr. Kano most frequently consulted. Dr. Kondo advised, "You chase too many rabbits." Personnel at FPL were eager to fix and improve everything at once. At first, many corporate objectives were established, which were then deployed to a large number of departmental goals. Dr. Kondo referred to each of these goals as a rabbit. Trying to accomplish too many goals was equivalent to chasing too many rabbits. This would result in much confusion and the possibility that none of the rabbits would be caught, i.e., none of the goals would be accomplished. What was suggested instead is that an organization needs to prioritize its customers' needs, its quality elements (key characteristics), and its processes in order to determine which areas to address first. Energy must be focused on those areas that ensure that worthwhile goals will be accomplished. This prioritization process is key to the success of supplier policy deployment.

The concept of prioritization is relatively simple. Basically, two main factors must be considered when determining the priority level of any item. The first is the level of importance of an item relative to the other items. The second factor is the need for improvement. If an objective is very important and has a very high need for improvement, then it is a high-priority item. If, on the other hand, it is not very important and it has a low priority for improvement, then it can be considered a low-priority item, which means that time and effort would probably be better spent on something else.

Importance

Most people find it difficult to differentiate between importance and priority, yet importance is only one factor that contributes to priority. Importance addresses the following issues.

Tie to the vision: This is the level of consequence and relevance of an item in terms of the overall vision of the organization. Any effort that is in line with this vision or the corporate objectives designed to meet this vision is highly important.

Tie to a major business process: A high-priority item is necessary for the successful accomplishment of a major business process, such as procurement, customer service, production, etc.

Measured by a customer group: This can also be a relative factor because one process or outcome may be compared to another by the same customer segment. A customer group may judge the importance of an item relative to the need for the process itself or the quality characteristics of the process.

Critical success factors: A high-priority item is closely related to one of the critical success factors of the organization. This would be a factor that is one of the top indicators in the corporate measurement system (which will be discussed later).

Benchmark position: An item that is related to one of the key benchmarking indicators, whether "best-in-class" or a "competitive" benchmark, is highly important regardless of its position or trend.

Need to Improve

The second factor to consider when prioritizing is the need to improve a process, product, service, etc. This factor is also relative. In determining the weight to be given to this factor, the following should be considered.

Satisfaction of the customer group: This is the level of satisfaction with a process as determined by the customer segment being addressed. If the customers are highly satisfied with a particular item, then the need to improve is low and vice versa.

In or out of statistical control: Is the process in statistical control? A process that is not in control should be brought into control so that the concepts of statistical process control can be used to manage the process. This is generally true unless the process does not meet customer requirements in the first place, in which case major changes are needed to force the process to shift into a range that meets customer requirements.

Process capability: Is the process capable of meeting the customer requirements? A process that is in control may not be capable of meeting these requirements. A process that is not capable has a high need to improve.

Trends: Do trends indicate movement in the wrong direction? For example, if an upward trend on a run chart represents good progress, then a downward trend would indicate a high need to improve.

Business environment: Finally, the direction of the business environment should be considered. Are there any developments in the foreseeable future that would significantly alter the direction of the quality characteristics necessary for the satisfaction of the customer?

Prioritization Matrix

One tool used to analyze the combined effects of importance and need to improve in determining priorities is a prioritization matrix (Figure 5.2). This matrix is composed of four columns. The first column is the item (objective, process, or other) to be prioritized. The second and third columns, respectively, represent the weights assigned to the two main factors just discussed: importance and need to improve. Other columns could potentially be included to represent other factors, but for our generic purposes here only these two factors will be considered. Other factors could include feasibility, cost, timing, or any other factor that would significantly influence the prioritizing decision.

PROCESS	(I) IMPORTANCE SUM=100	(N) NEED TO IMPROVE N=1 TO 100	(C) COMBINED WEIGHT C=(I*N)/100
A	20	60	12
B	50	80	40
C	30	70	21

Figure 5.2 Process Prioritization Matrix.

PROCESS	(I) IMPORTANCE SUM=100	(N) NEED TO IMPROVE N=1 TO 100	(C) COMBINED WEIGHT C=(I*N)/100
A	20	90	18
B	50	20	10
C	30	50	15

Figure 5.3 Process Prioritization Matrix.

Importance can usually be given a relative weight. A total number of points (i.e., 100 or 1000) is distributed among the items or elements being compared. These points are distributed based on level of importance. A higher number of points represents a higher level of importance. Similarly, need to improve could be assigned a number from 1 to 10 or a number from 1 to 100, based on the degree of differentiation the organization finds appropriate.

A combined weight is then calculated in the fourth column as the standardized product of columns 2 and 3. The resulting index can be used as a guideline to determine the priorities. It is important to note, however, that these values or numbers should not be used as a substitute for the decision-making process or common sense. They should only serve as a guideline for discussion. Once these values have been calculated, the decision makers need to determine whether they are in fact reasonable and whether cross comparisons make sense.

Figure 5.2 provides an example of a process that was considered to be most important, had the highest need to improve, and ended up with the highest combined weight and therefore the highest priority. Alternately, in Figure 5.3 the process with the least importance and the highest need to improve received the highest combined weight and therefore the highest priority.

Expanded Prioritization Matrix

The tool represented in Figure 5.4 is very similar to the prioritization matrix in Figures 5.2 and 5.3, except that multiple criteria are used to compare multiple alternatives. This expanded matrix can be compared to the concept of the House of Quality in quality functional deployment, except that it does not use the Expanded House of Quality. Instead, it is the house without the roof.

As shown in Figure 5.4, the key corporate quality objectives or elements are listed on the left. The objectives listed in the figure are only examples. Each organization through its policy deployment process must determine its own key quality objectives. Each objective is then allocated a weight representing a portion of a given total, say 100, to indicate its relative priority, i.e., combined importance and need to improve. The different levels of deployment are utilized in the columns to the right to determine which commodity, product/service, and suppliers will be selected as the "rabbits" to be chased. For example, in Figure 5.4, the deployment level being considered is the commodity level. Each of the commodities being compared is assigned a weight from 1 to 5 (or any other range) to differentiate the level of relationship to each quality objective in the first column. The weighted sum of the column is then calculated, and the commodity with the

QUALITY OBJECTIVE	WEIGHT	RELATIONSHIP TO QUALITY OBJECTIVE		
		COMMODITY A	COMMODITY B	COMMODITY C
QUALITY	30	1	3	2
QUANTITY	5	4	5	4
CYCLE TIME	20	2	3	4
RELIABILITY	15	1	2	2
PRICE	20	5	2	2
SERVICE	5	1	5	4
CORP ELEMENTS	5	2	5	4
SCORE	100	220	295	270
RANK		3	1	2

Figure 5.4 Selecting Priority Commodities.

largest sum is considered to have the strongest relationship with the overall quality objectives. Improving the products or services within this commodity will help achieve the corporate quality objectives more readily.

Prioritizing Processes and Commodities

Each of the major processes within an organization needs to be prioritized in order to determine the "rabbits" that will be chased. This is done using a combination of the simple prioritization matrix and the expanded prioritization matrix. Both of these tools can assist in the selection process.

Again, these tools are only guidelines. They are just that—tools. The tools are not the decision makers. The decision makers are the managers of the organization, who should perform their roles with input from all levels. In addition to these tools, decision makers should consider such factors as resource requirements, the validity and relevance of the process measures, the targets and means that will be established for each process improvement, and the internal and external changes that might force a contingent change in strategies. A simple tool such as a prioritization matrix can only be used to guide the thought process; the ultimate decision rests with management.

Once the highest priority processes have been selected, the commodities with the strongest ties to these processes must then be considered for selection. Another matrix similar to the expanded prioritization matrix can be utilized to determine the relationships among the processes and the related commodities. Once the commodities with the strongest ties to the priority processes have been selected, they must be compared to the corporate quality objectives by using another expanded prioritization matrix. This would to help narrow the list and identify those commodities that need the special attention of a commodity team. This process is depicted in Figure 5.5.

Establishing Commodity Teams

The commodity team addresses all the issues related to a selected commodity. The team should be composed of representatives from all the departments affected, such as end users, procurement, engineer-

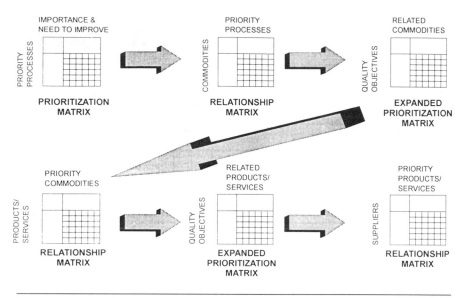

Figure 5.5 Deployment to Suppliers.

ing, marketing, materials management, and finance/accounting. The role of the team encompasses the following.

Communication: Team members need to be aware of all the events, projects, industry developments, technological breakthroughs, and customer needs associated with the commodity for which they are responsible. The team would also be responsible for communicating these issues to all the parties affected. This can be done through formal communications (such as user focus meetings, newsletters or bulletins, surveys, and project status presentations) as well as informal means (such as daily interactions with the groups which the team members represent).

Customer needs: Through communication, team members are responsible for determining the customer needs for the products in their commodity, including development and final approval of specifications as well as operational definitions of the requirements.

Provide assistance: The team is responsible for providing assistance to the suppliers that have been selected for different improvement projects.

Audits: The team is responsible for conducting periodic audits of the key suppliers in this commodity group so as to keep abreast of the suppliers' process capability, production capacity, quality problems and resolutions, etc. More on the auditing and certification process will be provided later in this chapter.

Certification: The team provides a recommendation to the supplier quality council to determine the certification level of each supplier within the commodity.

Feedback: In addition to formally communicating the supplier performance information to the suppliers within a particular commodity, the team is also responsible for developing specific performance criteria by which to measure the suppliers periodically.

Selection: The team is responsible for selecting key suppliers to work with, as well as determining the distribution of business awarded to different suppliers within the commodity.

Negotiation: The commodity team or a subset of the team is responsible for negotiating contractual terms with the suppliers that have been selected to provide certain products within the commodity. Members of the team should be familiar with the suppliers' processes and industry standards, so that they can make informed decisions.

It is important to recognize that this team process initially may be more time consuming for both the suppliers and the team members. However, once long-term relationships have been established, time can be spent on efforts more productive than simply processing daily paperwork for small orders. This could ultimately result in improved overall quality.

It is important not to assign too many commodity teams to each supplier. According to Bill Scherkenbach, at one time Ford Motor Company had as many as seven different teams visiting some suppliers. This resulted in confusion, misdirection, and wasted effort for both Ford and the suppliers. Ford eventually limited the number of teams contacting a particular supplier to a maximum or three. Organizations should be careful not to create a bureaucratic nightmare by assigning too many teams to one supplier.

The decisions of the commodity team must be deployed throughout the organization. As mentioned earlier, the responsibility of the team to communicate is extremely important. All individuals in the organization who are affected by the decisions of the team should have ready access to the information and decisions of the team so that they can align themselves with these decision. This will present a united front to the supplier community and reduce the variability which could otherwise be created.

Selecting Priority Products/Services, Suppliers, and Projects

The methodology utilized here is similar to that used to select the key commodity areas. The matrix tools can be used to further the deployment of the corporate objectives.

Relationship matrix: This tool is used to determine which products and services are most closely associated with the commodities that have been selected (relationship matrix of commodities vs. products/services).

Expanded prioritization matrix: From among those products/services that are most closely associated with the commodity in question, an expanded prioritization matrix is used to determine which most strongly support the corporate objectives (expanded prioritization matrix of corporate objectives vs. products/services).

In addition to selecting the priority products/services, it is important that the organization determine the improvement targets and means for those products/services. These targets and means should support the overall corporate quality objectives. This can be done by benchmarking the products/services being considered with other companies or competitors and by analyzing the major improvement areas required. The feasibility and resource requirements of these targets and means should be discussed among members of the commodity team in order to obtain the commitment of all parties involved. Eventually, this needs to be discussed and agreed upon with the suppliers selected. At this point, it may be necessary to assign a subteam of the commodity team or a specific project team to deal with a subgroup of products/services within the products/services selected.

Once the products/services have been determined, a similar deployment process is used to select the suppliers that can best provide those products/services. Again, two matrices can be utilized: one to determine which suppliers provide the products/services selected (matrix of products/services vs. suppliers) and the other to determine which of these suppliers is most closely tied to the corporate quality objectives (matrix of corporate objectives vs. suppliers). This is similar to the last part of Figure 5.5. This process would allow the organization to focus on those suppliers that can provide the products/services in question and that can do so in line with or linked to the corporate quality goals. The organization should consider suppliers that currently are heavily involved in providing the products/services in question. Good tools to use in this determination are an ABC analysis and a Pareto chart by dollar volume, item quantity, or number of transactions. The organization should also try to focus on those suppliers that are willing to continue or establish a long-term "partnership" with the organization: a supplier that through the years can build a relationship based on mutual trust. The supplier should have the production capacity to meet a large majority of the needs of the buying organization.

Targets and means must also be established for the particular suppliers selected to provide the specific products/services. As with the targets and means for the product/service, these supplier targets and means should support the overall corporate quality objectives, be feasible, meet resource requirements, and have the commitment of all parties involved, including the suppliers selected. Once these commitments have been obtained, project teams should be established, with appropriate representation from the commodity team and the supplier. These supplier quality improvement teams should be given the authority to make improvements in the product/services selected as long as they are in support of the targets and means committed.

For additional information, see Abstract 5.3 at the end of this chapter.

Reducing the Number of Suppliers

Over the years, organizations generally create a large supplier base or list of "approved" suppliers for any given commodity. This is because over time, many suppliers that want to do business with an organization are asked to complete a set of forms and provide certain documentation. Based on this information, these suppliers are then added to the approved list of bidders. Whenever a purchase is being considered, a Request for Quote (RFQ) is sent to most of the suppliers that have previously bid on or have asked to bid on this item. As time goes on, even though the list is updated, it continues to grow—sometimes into thousands of suppliers—and becomes unmanageable.

This is only one reason why world-class companies have decided that the best approach is to reduce the number of suppliers used. This must be done with great care. Some companies have reduced the number from thousands to a few hundred. Significant benefits can be derived from such a reduction in the supplier base, but caution must be exercised in certain areas.

Manageability: As noted in Chapter 1, reducing the number of suppliers can shift the role of procurement personnel from paper-pushing to managing supplier quality. Working with fewer suppliers facilitates the job of managing them.

Variability: Reducing the number of suppliers can reduce the variability of incoming materials or services. This is extremely important in reducing variability of the internal processes that utilize these materials. For example, a part required by a buying organization for an ongoing process has a very clear specification. However, every time the part is purchased from one supplier, the machines in the process must be adjusted before using the part. As more suppliers are selected to manufacture this part, the machines must be adjusted even more frequently. This creates additional work for the buying organization. Also, even after adjusting the machines, the results of the process vary. Bill Scherkenbach[4] addresses these concerns and explains the effect of using various suppliers on the process. As illustrated in Figure 5.6, three suppliers produce the same part within specifications, but each also has its own distribution of the key quality characteristic for the part. If the three distributions are combined, the resulting distribution has much greater variability. In addition, using fewer suppliers and subsuppliers reduces the number of possible outcomes of supplier variability. This is depicted in Figure 5.7. Therefore, it is important that one consider buying not only the product, but also investigating the

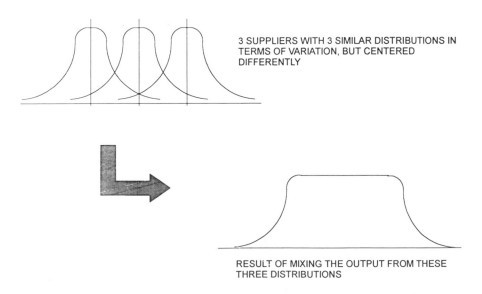

3 SUPPLIERS WITH 3 SIMILAR DISTRIBUTIONS IN TERMS OF VARIATION, BUT CENTERED DIFFERENTLY

RESULT OF MIXING THE OUTPUT FROM THESE THREE DISTRIBUTIONS

Figure 5.6 Supplier Variation. (Source: Adapted from Scherkenbach.[4])

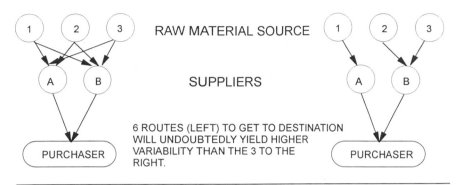

Figure 5.7 Limiting the Number of Suppliers.

suppliers. The point is to not only improve the process that manufactures the product but to further reduce variation by also improving any supplier process preceding it as well.

Price: When reducing the number of suppliers, price becomes a double-edged sword. The original reason to increase the number of suppliers may have been to increase competition, thereby lowering the price. This is not the only way to decrease price, however. By reducing the number of suppliers that provide a particular item, the customer, with the help of the supplier, can better concentrate on improving the supplier's process or possibly modifying the design of the part to add more value to the customer's process. Ultimately, the total life cycle cost of the item can be reduced. Price targets can also be set and achieved in conjunction with the supplier. This has proven very successful for some auto manufacturers. Finally, a larger volume of business will undoubtedly yield a lower price per unit from the supplier. A caution is that a supplier could create a situation similar to a monopoly and try to increase the price unduly. Price should be tied to some industry standard or commodity index and to some type of standardized costing method. These terms would reduce the possibility of price disputes and promote trust in the relationship.

Volume of business: If a single supplier is selected as the sole source for a particular product or service, that supplier's level of business with the customer organization will obviously increase. This should have a positive effect on the price, as mentioned earlier, but both the customer and the supplier should avoid a situation where the business from the customer is the only or overwhelmingly the largest volume of business for the supplier. This could result in the supplier having little extra capacity in case a problem arises. Also, the customer could put the supplier out of business by opting for another supplier. This situation would put an undue burden on the partner relationship.

Supplier partnership: Reducing the number of suppliers helps to strengthen the development of a partnership with the supplier(s). By awarding all its business to one supplier, the customer can streamline the transaction process and thus have more time to understand and manage the supplier relationship. The viewpoints of the customer and supplier should be similar. Both should view the reduced supplier base as a win–win situation. This environment would nurture a sense of trust between the two parties and allow the relationship to be strengthened.

Contingencies and contracts: Even though many benefits may be gained by reducing the supplier base, great caution must be exercised. Some of these benefits as well as potential dangers have been described, but the point is that all long-term sole-source contracts must address these and other pertinent issues so that both parties are properly protected. Some of the other issues may include contingency supply plans, alternative or substitute parts or services, alternative suppliers, alternative transportation, and any other factor that is important in a particular industry.

For additional information, see Abstract 5.4 at the end of this chapter.

Deployment of TQM to Suppliers

Before the supplier policy deployment process reaches the point of selecting priority suppliers, it is important that the supplier community begin to understand the new purchasing/supplier quality management (PSQM) philosophy and the associated corporate procurement policy. Suppliers must understand their new role in this new way of doing business. Once the priority suppliers have been selected, it is time to motivate, convince, cajole, inform, and educate them in this new procurement process. This can be accomplished in various ways.

Symposia: Priority suppliers and eventually all suppliers should be invited to participate in a series of symposia to explain the need for change, the PSQM philosophy, the supplier's new roles and responsibilities, the certification process including ISO 9000, the implementation of TQM including statistical process control, the supplier policy deployment process, the supplier selection criteria, the corporate quality objectives, and the need to link into the PSQM process. The customer organization should be prepared for resistance from its suppliers. Many will consider this to be additional work required by one customer. Some will expect to be paid more for higher quality. By helping suppliers to understand what is in it for them—the potential for more business, long-term contracts, increased market share, improved profits, among other benefits—the customer organization can convince its suppliers to buy into the process. Successful improvement projects can be communicated at future symposia so that suppliers can come to understand how their involvement can improve their overall business success.

Assistance to suppliers on implementation of TQM and statistical process control: Some suppliers will immediately agree to take part in the PSQM process. Others may already have implemented a TQM system or may be in the process of doing so. These suppliers will probably need very little assistance. Others may be totally lost as to what to do next. Some companies have assigned the assistance role to the commodity team that works with a particular supplier. The commodity team can help the supplier with its first and maybe its second improvement projects. Other companies have opted to hire or recommend consultants that can assist the supplier in implementing TQM and in successfully completing the improvement project. Many options are available, and each organization must determine the level of assistance it can provide to the supplier based on available resources and the priority of that commodity. The American Supplier Institute (ASI), created by the Ford Motor Company, is a good example of this "helping hand" practice.

Increased communication and joint development of specifications: Continuous and frequent communication with the supplier is a recommended way to build this buy-in and commitment. In a case where this situation is new to a supplier, many questions would arise at first. Someone must be available to provide ready answers or possibly be willing to visit the supplier's plant to discuss improvement ideas. Another way to achieve participation is for the supplier to work closely with the commodity team to determine the specifications for the product/service to be improved. This should go to the level of operational definitions, i.e., unambiguous descriptions and examples of expectations for function, color, size, purpose, price, reliability, and other key quality characteristics.

Life Cycle Costs

The difference between price and total life cycle cost is significant. Even though price is no longer the most important factor in purchase decisions, it still ranks as one of the highest criteria. Purchase price sometimes includes transportation costs, installation, and training costs, but often that is not the case. The problem is that the original purchase price may not consider such factors as maintenance costs, operating costs, salvage value, throughput or productivity of one machine vs. another, space requirements, availability of parts, warranty costs, obsolescence, disposition costs, reliability of technology, and all the other costs that may be included in the decision to purchase a particular product or service. When comparing price, all of these costs must be considered because the decision will determine which costs will be accrued. This type of analysis is particularly important when deciding on a specific piece of major equipment or on a long-term contract for a critical assembly part or service. When all these costs are taken into consideration, a more realistic comparison can be made among suppliers and among parts.

For additional information, see Abstract 5.5 at the end of this chapter.

ENDNOTES

1. King, Robert (1989). *Hoshin Planning: The Developmental Approach.* Methuen, Mass.: GOAL/QPC.
2. Akao, Yoji (1991). *Hoshin Kanri—Policy Deployment for Successful TQM.* Cambridge, Mass.: Productivity Press.
3. Sheridan, Bruce (1993). *Policy Deployment: The TQM Approach to Long-Range Planning.* Milwaukee: ASQC Quality Press.
4. Scherkenbach, William W. (1991). *The Deming Route to Quality and Productivity—Road Maps and Road Blocks.* Rockville, Md.: Mercury Press.
5. Figures 5.1 to 5.5 ©Advent Group, Inc.
6. Exercises 5.1 to 5.6 ©Strategy Associates, Inc.

EXERCISES

EXERCISE 5.1
DETERMINING THE MISSION OF THE ENTERPRISE

This exercise provides an example of the types of questions that should be answered in any attempt to develop a mission statement for your enterprise. These questions are generally used in the strategic planning process and are designed to identify explicit and implicit assumptions about the organization.

This questionnaire should be answered by key members of the enterprise and by critical external constituents. It is recommended that the questionnaire be distributed to individuals and a written summary of the responses developed. It is probably best if the synthesis of the results is done by a single individual and a written document provided to the entire group. The use of a written report is suggested because it allows individuals an opportunity to review all of the responses and to develop a holistic interpretation of the results before becoming involved in the discussion of details. It is also recommended that the results be discussed in a formal retreat in which members of the group have the opportunity to discuss issues and to develop a mission statement for the enterprise.

Mission Statement Form: This form provides an example of the type of document to be given to participants when they are asked to initiate the development of a mission statement for the enterprise.

Answer these questions concerning _____. Where you have data (or access to individuals with data), use it. Otherwise, provide the most realistic answers you can.

1. _____ exists to do _____?

2. What is distinctive (or even unique) about _____?

3. What are the primary products and services provided by _____?

4. Who are the primary customers (consumers) of the products and services provided by _____? Why have you identified these as the primary customers?

5. What other types of individuals or groups (stakeholders) have a vested interest in _____ (its performance and success)? What is the nature of their interest?

6. What core values (principles) are important to the operation and future of _____ ?

7. What is different (if anything) about _____ and/or its environment now from what it was five (5) years ago? Why is it different?

8. What is likely to be different about _____ and/or its environment five (5) years from now. Why will it be different?

9. What new (different) products and services could _____ provide in the future?

10. What must be done by _____ in order to provide these new products and services in the future?

EXERCISE 5.2
MISSION STATEMENT GUIDELINE FORM

1. Describe your beliefs concerning the mission (purpose) of _____. (Why does it exist and/or why should it exist in your opinion?)

2. Record points from other people's beliefs concerning the institutional mission of _____ that you want to include in your draft of a mission statement.

3. Develop your personal mission statement for _____.

EXERCISE 5.3
ASSESSING VISION STATEMENTS

Questions to be asked about the vision of your organization include:

1. Does the organization have a clearly stated vision?

2. Do the key people (stakeholders—internal and external) know and agree with the vision?

3. What are the boundaries to your vision? Are there time, geographical, or social constraints to the implementation of your vision?

Please rate your existing organizational vision statement on the following criteria. (1 = high, 2 = somewhat high, 3 = neutral, 4 = somewhat low, 5 = low.) To what extent does/is your existing organizational vision statement:

1. Future oriented?   1 2 3 4 5

2. Express creativity and is not merely derived from   1 2 3 4 5
   current conditions and trends?

3. Based on value principles that reflect respect for   1 2 3 4 5
   people?

4. Recognize the history, culture, and values of the   1 2 3 4 5
   organization—even if change is envisioned?

5. Set high standards of excellence, ideals, and   1 2 3 4 5
   expectations for members of the organization?

6. Clarify organizational purpose and set direction?   1 2 3 4 5

7. Likely to inspire enthusiasm and encourage   1 2 3 4 5
   organizational commitment?

8. Reflect the uniqueness of the organization in its   1 2 3 4 5
   competency and image?

9. Ambitious, challenging organizational members?   1 2 3 4 5

It should be noted that this series of questions and criteria can be used to compare the vitality of alternative organizational visions.

EXERCISE 5.4
DEVELOPING VISION STATEMENTS

1. Describe your maximum vision for _____ ten years in the future. (What will _____ be like in ten years if it achieves your ideal vision for it? Be specific!) _____ will:

2. Describe your vision for _____ in five years if it is to achieve your maximum vision for the future. (What would _____ be like in five years if it is in the process of achieving your ideal vision? Again, be specific!) _____ will:

EXERCISE 5.5
GOAL AND OBJECTIVE
ASSESSMENT QUESTIONNAIRE

General questions to be asked about your enterprise and its overarching goals include:

1. Does the enterprise have a clear statement of overarching goals?

2. Do the key people (stakeholders—internal and external) know and agree with the goals?

3. What are the boundaries to your goals? Are there time, geographical, or social constraints to the implementation of your goals?

Please rate the goal and objective statements of your enterprise using the following criteria (1 = definitely meets the criteria, 2 = somewhat meets the criteria, 3 = neutral, 4 = does not meet the criteria, 5 = definitely does not meet the criteria.)

Our enterprise goal and objective statement:

1. Identifies specific goals to be achieved   1 2 3 4 5

2. Addresses significant issues in the life of the   1 2 3 4 5
    organization

3. Is consistent with the organizational mission   1 2 3 4 5

4. Is realistic   1 2 3 4 5

5. Is challenging   1 2 3 4 5

6. Is feasible   1 2 3 4 5

7. Encourages a focus on performance   1 2 3 4 5

8. Encourages individuals to ask the question,   1 2 3 4 5
    "What will I be doing?"

9. Provides enough specificity that achievement   1 2 3 4 5
    measures could be developed

10. Progress toward goals is verifiable   1 2 3 4 5

11. Goal achievement is verifiable   1 2 3 4 5

EXERCISE 5.6
OVERARCHING GOAL IDENTIFICATION

Based on your understanding of the vision of the enterprise:

1. Identify the three most important issues facing _____ over the next five to ten years.

    1.

    2.

    3.

2. Please rank these issues based on the following criteria: (1) urgency—does the issue need immediate attention; (2) seriousness—significance of consequences if issue is not addressed; (3) growth potential—potential that situation will worsen if issue is not addressed; (4) overall negative impact on institution.

Urgency	Seriousness	Growth	Impact
1	1	1	1
2	2	2	2
3	3	3	3

3. Identify (in rank order) what you consider to be the three most important goals for the organization to adopt for the next five to ten years.

    1.

    2.

    3.

4. What are the benefits (positive aspects) of selecting your highest ranked goal as an overarching organizational goal?

5. What are the costs (negative aspects) of selecting your highest ranked goal as an overarching organizational goal?

6. What are the costs (negative aspects) of not selecting your highest ranked goal as an overarching organizational goal?

7. Assuming your highest ranked item were adopted as an overarching organizational goal for the next five to ten years, what organizational objectives should we adopt for the next two to five years. Place them in rank order from most to least important.

    1.

    2.

    3.

8. What are the benefits (positive aspects) of selecting your highest ranked objective?

9. What are the costs (negative aspects) of selecting your highest ranked objective?

10. What are the costs (negative aspects) of not selecting your highest ranked objective?

ABSTRACTS

ABSTRACT 5.1
MAKING TOTAL QUALITY WORK:
ALIGNING ORGANIZATIONAL PROCESSES,
PERFORMANCE MEASURES, AND STAKEHOLDERS

Olian, Judy D.; Rynes, Sara L.
Human Resources Management (HRM), Vol. 30, Issue 3, Fall 1991,
pp. 303–333

Throughout this article, four 1991 survey sources are used: the KPMG survey of 62 companies, 2 Conference Board surveys of 149 firms and 158 Fortune 1000 companies, and the AQF/Ernst & Young study of 500 international organizations. The cornerstone of this 30-page article revolves around the authors' statement: "The goals of total quality can be achieved only if organizations entirely reform their cultures. Total quality (TQ) is increasingly used by companies as an organization-wide system to achieve fully satisfied customers through the delivery of the highest quality in products and services. In fact, TQ is the most important single strategic tool available to leaders to effect the transformation of their organizations. Traditional management, operations, finance and accounting systems are reviewed against changes that are needed in organizational processes, measurement systems, and the values and behaviors of key stakeholders to transform the status quo and shift to a total quality culture that permeates every facet of the organization."

Total quality must reflect a system-wide commitment to the goal of serving the strategic needs of the organization's customer bases, through internal and external measurement systems, information and authority sharing, and committed leadership. The article contains the following pertinent data: (1) organizational synergies critical to achieving a pervasive culture; (2) the essentials of TQ; (3) organizational processes that support TQ; (4) establishing quality goals, including a look at "Six Sigma" and "Benchmarking;" (5) training for TQ; (6) recognition and rewards; (7) measuring customer reactions and satisfaction; (8) developing four areas of measurement: operation, financial, breakthrough, and employee contributions; and (9) stakeholder support. Of significant added value are over 60 references on the subjects discussed, which is reason enough to obtain a copy of this extremely worthwhile article, in spite of its formidable length.

ABSTRACT 5.2
INVENTORY: DO YOUR POLICY AND PRACTICE STACK UP?

Kivenko, Ken
Automation (PDE), May 1988, pp. 51–52

A major factor in productivity and financial return rates of an organization in the 1990s is management policies and practices for inventory control. Attention to detail in the key areas of planning, purchasing, and assuring quality can yield high payoffs if management can remember to "walk the talk." The use of a manufacturing resource planning (MRP) system, which demands the commitment of top management, can prove invaluable during the planning stage.

On the other hand, purchasing personnel face a dramatic change in the way they do business. In the past, purchasers who were blamed for previous problems overcompensated by increasing their order quantities and bringing in material early. Managers should now realize that purchasing personnel should work more closely with suppliers as team members. They will help to keep material costs down and inventories in check by ensuring high quality of incoming goods and on-time delivery.

In terms of assuring quality, management can reduce work in process by encouraging the use of quality control tools such as design reviews and prototype testing, employee participation, vertical communication, employee training, statistical quality control methods, automation, and customer feedback charts. If inventory is to be controlled, management must communicate effectively to all levels of an organization and keep in mind that some of the things they are doing can affect the company negatively and raise work in process. No references or graphs are provided.

ABSTRACT 5.3
BUYERS AND DISTRIBUTORS: IT'S TIME FOR TEAMWORK

Forbes, Christine
Industrial Distribution (IND), August 1991, pp. 20–24

The call from purchasing managers and distributors is unanimous. The purchasing and distribution field has changed from one of inventory management and sales to a more holistic, value-added approach, featuring total quality management. The change that has had the most impact on the industry has been the shift toward a smaller supplier base, limiting the number of vendors for each product, and working more closely with suppliers. This new movement is called Total Cost, because it takes into account the total cost to the customer over and above the initial price. Late delivery, poor service, and faulty parts are viewed as part of the price of a product. Thus, industry leaders who have embraced Total Cost are willing to pay a higher initial purchase price when total cost benefits are guaranteed.

Therefore, organizations on the brink of Total Cost breakthrough are selecting the "best and the brightest" distributors. The primary benefits brought on by this change are improved efficiency and cost, more conclusive performance tracking, and stronger supplier relationships (or partnering). Distributors and purchasing professionals agree that many factors led to these changes, but the main catalyst has been an emphasis on value-added services. These services are generally a physical adaptation to a product, such as an optional stereo for a car.

Whereas the most important customer demand is product quality, the quality requirements vary sharply according to the customer's size, needs, and the extent to which the customer's own quality system has developed. For example, Amoco demands quality from its distributors by monitoring distributor nonconformance through such variables as delivery, product quality, and administrative errors. Several priorities must be constantly examined by the purchasing and distribution organizations so that they can successfully embrace the changes around them.

Communication is a priority area where improvement is needed, and new technological channels can help. Purchasers also note that distributors have fallen behind in education and technical ability. More specifically, purchasers want more new product information, better knowledge of the product, and, most importantly, they want distributors to do their own screening to determine the best, most cost-efficient products. Limited graphs and no references are provided.

ABSTRACT 5.4
COMPETITION AND QUALITY RISE
AS BUYERS WEED OUT SUPPLIERS

Anonymous
Total Quality, May 1992, pp. 1–3

"Even though partnering might feel like railroading to suppliers at first," says one quality improvement facilitator, her company's relationships have all ended up being mutually beneficial. This article consists mainly of quality and production managers sharing their stories of how partnering works for them. Many were told by customers to begin TQM initiatives or they would stop doing business with them. While this created a furor, it did help companies to take seriously the needs of the customer. The result has been higher quality products and service from suppliers and a more trusting relationship from customers. One manager reports that his company is tied into its customer's computer. "We now order their supplies for them," he says. "We just see what they have scheduled, and we make their boxes accordingly. They never place an order." The advantages of supplier partnering are in financial benefits, as well as in real limitations, says the author. Companies highlighted in the article include Packaging Corp. of America (Goldsboro, North Carolina), Motorola, Velcro, GM, Pacific Southwest Container (Modesto, California), and Square D.

ABSTRACT 5.5
REDEFINING THE MANUFACTURER–SUPPLIER RELATIONSHIP

Aleo, Joseph P. Jr.
Journal of Business Strategy, September–October 1992, pp. 10–14

Kodak, with half of all components used in manufacture supplied by outside vendors, has focused on realigning the company's supplier base as a central strategy, says the author. Supplier reduction (a) winnowed out vendors unable to meet quality standards, (b) improved vendor responsiveness, and (c) made the smaller supplier base easier and less costly to manage. Kodak's Office Imaging Unit developed three tools for assessing supplier performance:

- **Supplier performance rating system:** Each month, Kodak sends suppliers a quality rating report with a 100-point rating standard to rank lot-acceptance rates. A supplier can earn up to 60 points on quality and 40 points for on-time delivery. Kodak tabulates combined performance ratings and awards citations of excellence to its best suppliers.
- **Quality assurance audit:** Auditing teams conduct an audit of the supplier's quality system and an audit of the product itself.
- **Supplier team improvement process:** A supply team from five Kodak operational departments reviews all historical data and reviews and revises all part and assembly drawings. Then, a duplicate package is sent to the supplier for advance review. At a joint meeting, both Kodak

and supplier teams examine each aspect of the products and outline long- and short-term improvement goals.

The remainder of the article describes Kodak's Early Production Supplier Involvement program, designed to more closely involve suppliers in the design and manufacturing development of a product.

1. **Selection:** Kodak compares suppliers on a decision matrix and selects the top candidate. If the supplier is interested, nondisclosure and supplier–customer agreements are executed.
2. **Involvement:** Working together, Kodak engineers and the supplier produce drawings, outline critical-to-function characteristics, and evaluate prototypes. If the supplier meets agreed-upon program goals, the supplier continues to the next phase.
3. **Certification:** The certification stage defines product characteristics and how they will be checked and gives direction on how quality objectives should be met.
4. **Continual improvement and feedback.**

(©*Quality Abstracts*)

CHAPTER 6

SUPPLIER CERTIFICATION

We have just traveled the path of supplier policy deployment in Chapter 5. One of the major expected outcomes of following this path is a set of priority suppliers that seem to be strongly linked to the objectives of the buying organization and that have the capability of providing the products or services of most importance to the organization. At this point, however, these suppliers have not undergone a thorough evaluation of their capabilities and objectives by the buying organization. The buying organization must continue to be wary of the products and services provided by its suppliers unless some verification of the capabilities of their internal and external processes has been completed. This approach is referred to as supplier certification.

OBJECTIVES OF SUPPLIER CERTIFICATION

Some of the objectives of supplier certification include:

- **Verify** that the suppliers being selected for long-term relationships with the organization are capable of meeting the needs of their customers in all areas. This does not just mean the needs of the incoming quality inspectors, but also includes any of the other processes within the organization that may utilize the particular product or service directly or indirectly.

- **Motivate** suppliers to continue to improve their processes and the resulting products and services through incentives given for attaining higher levels of certification.
- **Improve** key supplier processes. This would benefit both the supplier and the customer organization and would strengthen the win–win relationship that is being developed with the supplier.
- **Assess** continuously the supplier capabilities to determine whether a supplier that has attained a certain level of certification maintains that level, needs to be upgraded, or needs to be downgraded.

CERTIFICATION PARADIGMS

The history of certification programs has brought about many changes in the concepts and ideas being utilized by industry leaders. Some of the changes that have taken place are shown in Table 6.1. Some leading organizations have shifted completely to the new paradigms, while others have done so partially. Each buying organization must consider all the benefits and risks of shifting to the new paradigms before making a blind move.

For additional information, see Abstract 6.1 at the end of this chapter.

THE SUPPLIER AUDIT

Verification is one of the first objectives that needs to be met when trying to certify a supplier. It is extremely important to determine if the supplier is worthy of being considered for a long-term relationship with the buyer. One of the ways to do this is through a supplier audit.

In a supplier audit, the buying organization establishes the criteria it wants to verify that the supplier meets. Some of the criteria should be standard for all suppliers of the firm, while others are more com-

Table 6.1 Certification Paradigms

Old paradigm	New paradigm
No procurement strategy	Purchasing/supplier quality management council provides policy and direction, with supplier quality management as a key policy
One-time procurement	Long-term partnerships
Lowest price	Lowest long-term ownership cost reduced through joint cost targeting
Specifications arbitrary or to meet worst case	Established through design of experiments
Poor assessment of process capability	Goal of minimum process capability (Cpk) of 2.0 to 8.0 through use of design of experiments
Measurement through AQLs or parts per million	Cpk, cycle time, yields, statistical process control charts on key characteristics
Few incentives	Incentives built into selection process and performance criteria
Reliability testing included accelerated life tests	FMEA, Taguchi, Weibull
Individual departments talking to suppliers for their needs	Commodity teams coordinating corporate objectives and assisting supplier with quality improvement
Cycle time not considered	Important part of overall TQM effort

modity or industry specific. For example, a standard criterion might be the need for the supplier's management to be fully committed to a quality philosophy of meeting or exceeding its customer requirements. Industry-specific criteria might be the conductance of copper cable, the rigidity and porosity of the jacketed insulation, or other quality characteristics that affect the functionality and reliability of electrical cable. The following are a few of many potential areas of concentration for supplier audit teams.

Management: Commitment to quality, style, empowerment, educational background, previous experience, etc.

Design process: What is the design process? Is it systematic? Does it involve appropriate affected areas or only R&D?

Procurement: Is the procurement process fast? Are levels of authority clearly defined? Are customer requirements considered in the bidding process? Is price considered before quality? Are all affected parties involved in major procurement decisions? Does the supplier have up-to-date procurement systems? Does the supplier use or plan to use electronic data interchange?

Quality assurance: How does the supplier assure the quality of the process output? Is it inspection driven or does the supplier methodology include prevention-based methods?

Receipt inspection: Does the organization simply accept all products as supplied? Does it have different policies for different levels of supplier certification? Is the supplier's goal to reduce the amount of incoming inspection by certifying its own suppliers? Are there clearly documented specifications that can be used to inspect at receipt? Is there a clear way of separating rejected materials from acceptable materials? What are the return policies?

Materials management: Does the supplier have up-to-date material management systems? Are there policies for the optimization of stocking levels? Is just-in-time manufacturing practice followed?

Materials storage, handling, and shipping: Are there controls for shelf life of time-dependent raw materials? Are volatile or toxic materials properly secured, labeled, handled, and protected to safeguard against environmental accidents? Are modern, up-to-date material handling equipment used and proper maintenance procedures followed? Are products properly protected during shipping through adequate packaging?

Process management: Are process controls in place? Are employees trained to recognize out of control conditions and know what actions to follow to bring the process back into control? Are analysis techniques used to prevent special causes and to manage or reduce common causes and the variability of the processes? Is there a good tie from the process management area to improvement processes?

Inspection, testing, and examination: Are first item samples sent for testing and inspection before approval of initial shipments from a new supplier? Are follow-up inspections made until the supplier attains the appropriate certification level according to the acceptable risk of a defect?

Specification and change control: Is there a set methodology to keep track of and assure that specification and process changes are recorded and approved by all involved before implementation of the change, that all employees affected are properly trained in the new procedures, and that lots are properly tracked to reflect the process in effect when the lot was manufactured?

Calibration and lab controls: Does the supplier have a periodic maintenance and testing schedule to calibrate all measurement devices? Is the schedule in place in the lab area as well as on the manufacturing floor or anywhere else that measurements are made?

Quality information: Has a quality information system been put in place, whereby information can be tracked by lot, supplier, timing, process status, customer, rejects, costs, or any other data field that the supplier or the buying organization may feel is an important quality characteristic?

Nonconforming material control: Is there a method in place to identify and tag nonconforming materials, whether incoming or work in process? This material must be excluded from the regular flow of work in order to avoid the possibility of it being combined with acceptable material.

Corrective action process: Does a method exist to follow-up on corrective actions identified by all levels of employees? This could range from a suggestion system to a more sophisticated team improvement project tracking system.

The preceding list of areas of concentration is not meant to be exhaustive. Buying organizations need to determine the areas that are most important to them for the particular supplier or industry being audited. The supplier's input can also be heard in this area. Caution should be exercised in determining the audit areas because the amount of time spent in the audit is intrusive to the supplier. On the other hand, the buying organization needs to address all the areas that it deems important, and the supplier should cooperate if the demands are reasonable.

The buyer organization can set up a scoring mechanism for its suppliers which would somehow measure the degree to which the supplier meets the requirements in each of the different areas. These measurements could include some minimum requirements that the supplier must meet before being considered for certification, as well as minimum levels of compliance.

For additional information, see Abstract 6.2 at the end of this chapter.

TYPES OF CERTIFICATION

Some of the different types of certification processes in use throughout manufacturing and service industries today are described here.

Some Specific Certification Programs

Each buying organization could determine the criteria it deems important and the process it will use for supplier certification. The main reason an organization would use these criteria is that it is in a very unique industry and has very specific needs that would not be covered by one of the standard industry criteria. The following are some examples of organization-specific certification programs.

Florida Power & Light

This Deming Prize winner created a comprehensive certification program, which was first called the Vendor Quality Improvement Program and then was modified and renamed the Supplier Excellence Program. When it was first started, the program included three levels of certification and motivation for the suppliers that had been selected to participate during the supplier policy deployment process.

Quality Vendor: This was the first level of certification. To attain this level, a supplier had to demonstrate its commitment to the concepts of quality improvement (QI). This included the supplier's understanding and application of the concepts of QI. The supplier first needed to provide a description of its quality process. This document was reviewed and then either approved according to minimum expectations established by FPL or feedback was provided to the supplier concerning the weak areas, along with suggestions for improvement. Once this document was found to be satisfactory, an improvement project that was of importance to both FPL and the supplier was selected. A review team from FPL worked with the supplier to provide guidance to the supplier and to eventually verify that the project exemplified the application of QI concepts. At the conclusion, the supplier provided a self-assessment of the improvement project. This assessment was reviewed by the FPL review team, and if the supplier provided sufficient evidence of application of QI concepts, it was awarded the Quality Vendor designation. As part of this designation, the supplier was given a bid advantage on procurement evaluations for all products/services it provided. This advantage provided great motivation for suppliers to gain the FPL Quality Vendor designation.

Certified Vendor: This was the second level of certification, and it required a much more specific approach. The supplier had to demonstrate the use of statistical process control (SPC) on the critical quality characteristics of a specific product/service utilized by FPL, a minimum process capability (Cpk) of 1.00 for the same characteristics, and the deployment and integration of the QI process into the overall management of the supplier. An additional bid advantage was given to the supplier on an item-by-item or specific service basis.

Excellent Vendor: This was the highest level of certification for FPL suppliers. To reach this level, a supplier had to first attain the Certified Vendor status and demonstrate process capability Cpk greater than or equal to 1.33 for all key characteristics of all the products and services provided to FPL, as well as the use of reliability techniques in the design and improvement of those products and services. An additional bid advantage was given to suppliers that reached this level.

Motorola

This Malcolm Baldrige Award winner has a very extensive supplier certification program. Motorola works with its suppliers for their continuous improvement. Any supplier that wants to continue to do business with Motorola is asked to apply for the Malcolm Baldrige Award. This provides a great self-assessment tool for the supplier and for Motorola to review progress.

General Motors

GM's certification program is referred to as PICOS, which stands for the Purchased Input Concept Optimization System. GM has been very forceful with its suppliers in reducing costs and improving quality. Quality audits are performed to determine if the supplier's process is capable of providing a quality product to GM.

Chrysler

This organization has partnered with its suppliers to provide concurrent engineering on the key assemblies and parts for its new car models. The program is voluntary. From 1989 to 1992, the program saved Chrysler a total of $160 million in the cost of incoming parts.

Ford

Ford's program is called Q1 Certification. It is a very comprehensive program of quality audits, assistance, and teaming with its suppliers. It is regarded as one of the benchmarks of the industry and is similar in many respects to the Michigan Consolidated Gas program, which is described in the case study at the end of this book.

Standard Industry Certification Processes

Rather than developing their own certification processes, some companies use standard industry certifications. This is a much easier approach because these processes are readily available and they represent the most important generic requirements to verify that the supplier is following good quality management practices. These programs do not specifically certify any particular product or service of the supplier, but instead examine the processes and methods that the supplier organization follows. It is then left to the buying organization to assure that the quality specifications for the specific item or service are met. Some of the standard industry certification processes are as follows:

- **ISO 9000:** This is an international specification that has been accepted by over 100 countries. A more detailed discussion of this very important certification process is provided in Chapter 7.
- **Malcolm Baldrige National Quality Award:** When an organization applies for this award, it must perform an in-depth self-appraisal. The appraisal includes seven major areas of review. This assessment is provided to the National Institute of Standards for review by a Board of Examiners and Judges composed of quality experts. An award winner must demonstrate excellent

preventive-based quality processes, thorough deployment of these processes, and significant improvement results at world-class levels. Therefore, a Malcolm Baldrige Award winner can probably be considered to have good quality processes and to provide quality products or services. Again, specific products must be certified individually by the buying organization against its specific requirements.

- **Governor's Sterling Award for Quality and Productivity**:   This is the State of Florida's quality award. It is patterned after the Malcolm Baldrige Award, but has been expanded to include some sectors not included in the Baldrige. For example, this program includes awards for healthcare organizations and government organizations.
- **The Deming Prize:**   This is one of the most prestigious quality awards. It is given in Japan. One of the categories is the international award. Florida Power & Light is the only company outside of Japan that has ever won that award. The criteria are very systematic and follow the teachings of Deming, Juran, Ishikawa, and many of the Japanese quality gurus. The award program is administered by the Japanese Union of Scientists and Engineers (JUSE).

It is important to reiterate that even though a supplier may have received one of these awards or certifications, it is still up to the buying organization to determine if the criteria are sufficient for their own quality needs. Most importantly, the buying organization must be sure that its own quality specifications are being met adequately for specific products and services.

Influence of Certification on Supplier Selection

We have discussed some of the different ways that suppliers can be certified. Some of these certifications are unique to the buying organization, while others are more standard. One thing seems to be common among those suppliers that are certified: the "certified" label seems to influence buying decisions. This influence is not limited to the organization that provides this certification.

As shown in Figure 6.1, 71.5 percent of the respondents to a survey conducted by *Electronic Buyers News* concurred that they were influenced by knowing that a supplier under consideration had received some form of certification, either standard or specific, as defined ear-

% OF BUYERS INFLUENCED TO BUY FROM A SUPPLIER
THAT HAD WON A QUALITY AWARD
OR RECEIVED SOME SUPPLIER CERTIFICATION

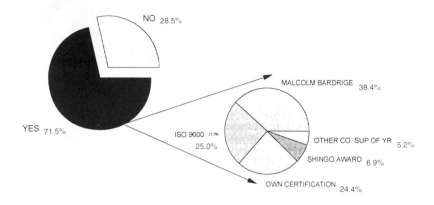

Figure 6.1 Certification Influence. (*Source: Electronic Buyers News,* November 12, 1992.)

lier in this chapter. Of these certifications, the respondents most frequently selected the Malcolm Baldrige Award as the certification that most influenced them. ISO 9000 certification and individual company certification were the next most frequently identified. It is important to note that other awards and other company certifications were also influential.

ABSTRACTS

ABSTRACT 6.1
NO GAIN WITHOUT PAIN

Black, Sam P.
The TQM Magazine, March–April 1992, pp. 47–49

In 1979, Caterpillar Tractor Co. decided to launch a program of supplier certification similar to Ford's Q1 system. Twelve years later, 84 percent of the company's business goes to certified suppliers. The author explains the five basic conditions or rules for suppliers:

- Understand and agree to all quality requirements identified in specifications.
- Resolve all major and/or chronic quality problems to the satisfaction of all Caterpillar user plants.
- Develop and document a quality plan outlining the process and product controls used to assure conforming products.
- Prepare to provide to a visiting certification team evidence that your quality system is working.
- Define and institute a system to achieve annual quality improvement.

Like other companies, Caterpillar has adopted a strategy for reducing the number of suppliers by moving more business to certified suppliers. More recently, explains the author, the company has demanded that its suppliers have an ongoing annual quality improvement program coupled with an education process for their people. Caterpillar opened places in its class in internal statistical quality control to suppliers who wanted to participate, charging only a very nominal fee. It also has developed a small liaison team with suppliers who require technical assistance, which could result in mutual quality improvement. Some of the pain experienced in the development of an efficient supplier quality system comes from resistance to change, says the author. He gives examples of resistance that the company's own buyers may put up in response to what they see as "interference" in their jobs. He emphasizes the importance of nurturing trust and a "win–win" concept. He also describes Q-NET, Caterpillar's database with information on quality indicators that is available to the whole supplier community. "Invariably, when an error did occur," says the author, "it came about when the supplier broke a cardinal rule, which is to change the process or base materials without first advising Caterpillar." (©*Quality Abstracts*)

ABSTRACT 6.2
EVALUATING SUPPLIERS

Wind, James F.
The TQM Magazine, January–February 1992, pp. 333–336

Since purchased parts often reach to 65 percent of all manufacturing costs, an ongoing supplier rating system is vital to a manufacturing operation. The author describes a large *Fortune 500* multidivision corporation which embarked on a supplier certification program. After investigating 17 suppliers suggested for consideration, only 3 had a good record of consistent shipment. All 17 had been selected for reasons other than their quality performance. The author explains how critical conformance is: a table shows that product received from a supplier capable of producing 1 percent nonconforming parts (10,000 ppm) can disrupt an assembly operation 25 minutes for every part used at a given workstation. Another table lists state-of-the-art rating elements, such as "rejected lots severity comparison," "part count accuracy," "technology rating," etc. He suggests a computerized rating system that rates only significant elements and that maintains credibility within the company and with the supplier. (©*Quality Abstracts*)

CHAPTER 7

ISO 9000 and PURCHASING/ SUPPLIER QUALITY MANAGEMENT: A VIEW to the FUTURE

Frank Voehl

PROLOGUE: THE COMING OF THE GLOBAL MARKETPLACE

Globalization has become a reality in the time since ISO 9000 was published in 1987. For today's suppliers, all but the smallest or only local commercial and industrial enterprises are finding that their principal marketplace competitors include enterprises that are headquartered in other countries. Thus, marketing strategy and product development must be done on a global basis to effectively compete.

Additionally, the term *global quality* continues to grow in importance as a factor in supplier quality marketplace success. The rapid implementation of the European Community (EC) single-market arrangement has become a driving force in the pursuit of global quality by placing new pressures on all worldwide producers who want to trace or even compete with European organizations. The EC approach rests on the use of ISO 9000 standards as the documentation of requirements for its third-party certification scheme for quality systems registration, as well as for auditing compliance with the requirements.

OVERVIEW

ISO 9000 Defined

What is ISO 9000? Let's start by first defining ISO as a term. According to Sprow, it is short for *isos*, the Greek term for equal, homogeneous, or uniform, which is a transformation of the acronym for the International Organization for Standardization. This was done deliberately because IOS sounds too much like chaos, and the word order changes inevitably with different languages. One observer has quipped that ISO 9000 stands for International Strategic Opportunity for the '90s, which it certainly might be. (It sounds a bit like the transliteration of the Union of Japanese Scientists and Engineers into the acronym known as JUSE.)[1]

Quality by Consensus

ISO 9000 began with the launch of Technical Committee 176 in 1979 to deal with generic quality principles to satisfy the need for an international minimum standard for how manufacturing companies establish quality control methods. This included not only control of product quality, but maintaining uniformity and predictability as well. Consumers wanted assurance that in the new world market—whether buying telephones, bread, wheat, or widgets—they would be getting reliable quality for their money today, tomorrow, or next year.

To accomplish this, 20 actively participating countries and half again as many additional observer countries met and created, by consensus, a series of quality-system management standards called ISO 9000, which was finally issued in 1987. The standards were based in large part on the 1979 British quality standard BS 5750, as well as on the Canadian standard CSA Z299, the American ASQC Z1.15 standard, MIL Q 9858A, and to a limited degree the JUSE-based Deming Prize guidelines.[1]

ISO 9000 was a great success from the start. It was the first ISO standard to go beyond nuts and bolts and attempt to address management practices. It quickly became the most widely known, widely adopted ISO standard and has sold more copies than any standard ISO has ever published. Although it is voluntary so far, over 50 countries have adopted it as a national standard. According to a recent survey, 82 percent of European blue-chip companies are familiar with its content and 64 percent have initiated action to become registered to ISO. Although the numbers on this side of the Atlantic may not be as high, it is of interest here.[1]

The Interrelationships between Quality Assurance and ISO 9000

To understand the impact that ISO 9000 can have on the supplier organization, it is first necessary to focus on the interrelationship that exists between quality assurance (QA) and ISO 9000. The approach that manufacturing organizations have taken to achieve the quality edge has traditionally been QA, and over the past ten years QA in the United States has evolved into total quality. Increasingly, training and education organizations are looking to use the same route to capture markets. Total quality involves a systematic approach to identifying market needs and honing work methods to meet those needs. Organizations can develop and run their own QA and total quality management programs, but many prefer to adopt a recognized standard and to seek external approval for their system. In the United Kingdom, BS 5750 is the standard for QA and total quality systems. Internationally, BS 5750 is known as ISO 9000. The two standards are identical in all but name.

Many supplier organizations in Europe have begun to explore how they can adopt this standard; a few have attained the coveted BSI kitemark (certification symbol).[2] Part of the reason why so few American organizations have achieved certification is the fact that BS 5750/ ISO 9000 was initially designed for manufacturing industries. Its language and approach are alien to service organizations, which predominate the growth segments of the American scene. However, its underlying principles, which concentrate on meeting customer needs, are fully applicable in the new marketplace of the global village. Somehow, then, we need to find a way of applying ISO 9000 to U.S. suppliers across the board if we are to recapture competitive advantage.

The ISO 9000 standards are a single system originally designed to cover all manufacturing, later extended to the service industries, and now being experimentally used across the world. ISO 9000 certification could become a requirement for any supplier that wants to do business in the international marketplace, even though at this time that notion seems to be a bit of a stretch. While the strains of this stretching of BS 5750/ISO 9000 show all too clearly, it remains a very general set of principles about good management. Of the 20 standards (modules) contained in ISO 9004, most have direct application, as shown in Figure 7.1.[3]

Getting a Feel for ISO 9000 Integration

The 20 separate standards (or modules) in the ISO 9000 series are fairly easy to relate to supplier organizations. While some are less applicable than others to supplier organizations, most are directly related to the details of purchasing/supplier quality management (PSQM). In Figure 7.2, the standards that seem to be highly relevant to the PSQM supplier education process are related to a simple model of purchasing and conducting a supplier training course.

Fundamentals of the Quality Assurance Management System

The words quality assurance in the context of total quality have a certain mystique about them, giving the impression of a complex set of skills which few will ever acquire. The early developers of QA no doubt kept themselves in the consulting business through continuing

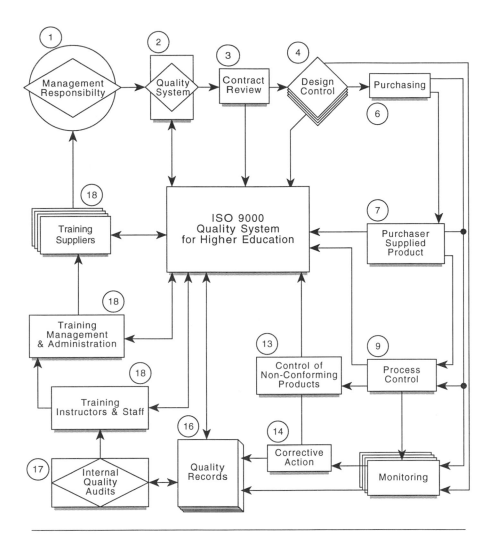

Figure 7.1 Flowchart of ISO 9000 Standards for Purchasing/Supplier Quality Management.

to foster that image. However, the reality is that QA is a fancy term for any well-run management system. This means that QA is not esoteric, or complex, or beyond the reach of nonspecialists. If it were, what would be the point of it? Any QA system that is going to work has to be simple, fitting comfortably alongside—or even inside— everyday working practices.[3] It has to be economical, in that it saves more than

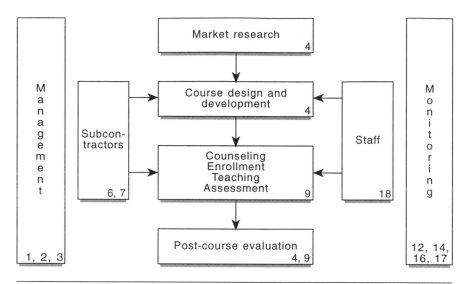

Figure 7.2 Relationship of ISO Standards to Purchasing a Supplier Quality Management Training Course. (Source: Freeman, Richard (1992). *Quality Assurance in Training and Education.* London: Kogan Page Limited.)

it costs. And it has to be long lasting, not just a here today, gone tomorrow type of program.

In essence, total quality involves an approach to organizing work which ensures that:

- The mission and objectives of the organization are clear and known to all.
- The systems through which work will be done are well thought out, foolproofed as well as possible, and communicated to everyone.
- It is always clear who is responsible for what.
- What the organization considers to be quality is well-defined and documented.
- Measurement systems are in place to check that everything is working according to plan.
- When things go wrong—and they will—there are proven ways of making them right.

These management systems can be divided into undocumented, documented, and ISO 9000 (QA) systems.

Undocumented System

In the undocumented system approach, the only way to find out how something is done is to ask someone. "Ask Harry, he always knows." "Try Mary, I think she's done that before." In very small organizations, this can often (although not always) work well, but as an organization grows, this "system" falls apart. Different people do things differently. Essentially, the undocumented system is not a system at all. It is a *laissez-faire* approach in which the organization never decides how anything is to be done in a formal way. For many organizations, this type of approach has been a way of life.

Documented System

Most undocumented systems are intensely frustrating and unproductive. Soon, task by task, methods are developed for how things should be done. A purchasing system here, a marketing plan there...but do people adhere to these methods? Perhaps—and perhaps not. How would anyone ever know? That is one of the problems with the evolution of documented systems. It is one thing to set down on paper how tasks should be carried out, but quite another to ensure that those intentions become practice.

Additionally, even if a documented system is fairly well observed in practice, it still lacks any means of reviewing and improving itself. ISO 9000 overcomes that problem.

ISO 9000 QA Approach

The ISO 9000 QA approach to management is very similar to the documented method, but adds three essential extras:[4]

- A method to monitor how well the system is being adhered to
- A method for correcting mistakes
- A method for changing the system if it has become obsolete

This error-correcting aspect of ISO 9000 is very important. Mistakes and failures will occur, and the ISO 9000 based quality system recognizes that possibility and prepares for it.

Three causes of failure are recognized:

- Human error
- Failure of input materials
- Obsolescence of the existing method

The quality system carefully distinguishes among these causes. In the first case, the error or omission is corrected; in the latter two, the material or method is amended. ISO 9000 is, therefore, both a self-correcting and a learning system. It changes to reflect changing needs. It is known as a QA rather than a traditional quality control type system.[5]

GETTING STARTED WITH ISO 9000

The Documentation Process

This section provides an overview of the heart of the documentation process for establishing a QA-based ISO 9000 system for the organization. It looks at the basic building blocks that need to be created (see Figure 7.3):

- Mission
- Methods
- Interface points
- Standards

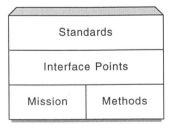

Figure 7.3   Documentation Building Blocks.

Mission

ISO 9000 starts with a clear sense of what the organization is to achieve: its mission. Dr. Deming calls this Constancy of Purpose. It is a timeless, qualitative statement, such as:

- To be the best provider in our area
- To maintain the highest possible level of repeat business in our area
- To have a reputation for excellence among customers in our area

In a well-established supplier organization, it may seem unnecessary to document the mission. "We all know what we do here." "It's obvious what this place is for." Often, however, different people have different ideas of where the organization is and where it is heading. It is pointless installing a QA-type ISO 9000 system in an organization that has no shared view of what constitutes success.

In summary, a mission statement is:

- A statement of what the organization is to achieve—its core purpose
- The vision of where the organization is going to be in 10 to 20 years
- The guiding principles and shared values that need to be internalized by all employees
- *Not* a set of objectives or targets

Methods

Once the mission has been agreed upon, QA systems compel the organization to document the methods by which things are to be done. It is usually fairly clear what tasks need to be done, although in new organizations even the list of tasks may be unclear. In more mature organizations, despite superficial order, there may be strongly conflicting views about how each task should be done and, in particular, who should do it. "No one told me I had to use a tracking system. I've always done it my own way."

Essentially the problems come down to a lack of agreement on:

- What needs to be done—*what*
- The method of doing it—*how*
- Who should do it—*who*

Interface Points

An additional concept in total quality is the interface point. According to quality theory, the critical point at which quality can effectively be assured is the interface between two functions: when person A hands a job over to person B. An interface involves a preparer, a receiver, and a task. The receiver expects to carry out a particular stage of a process. One of the fundamentals of total quality is that clean handoffs at the interface points between departments or functions are necessary to ensure maximum quality and productivity.

This looks a bit abstract before considering what is expected to happen at an interface. The receiver expects that the preparer has done his or her job completely and in the agreed upon manner, because the receiver cannot do his or her job unless the preparer has done the same. Given that this handoff of work from preparer to receiver is so critical to doing a good job, the interface is often called a *critical interface*. By finding all the critical interfaces in an organization, fixing them, monitoring them, and continually improving them, a virtual total quality system is created. (In modern total quality management jargon, the receiver is often called an *internal customer* and the preparer an *internal supplier*.)

In practice, everyone is both a preparer and a receiver. Few tasks are initiated in isolation. Most involve carrying out the next stage in a sequence of processes.

Standards

As previously stated, the receiver expects that the task will be handed over in a completed state and in the agreed upon form. Total quality systems assume that there are agreed upon standards and/or formats that define how tasks are handed over. Meshing these standards is a critical part of setting up a total quality system. The process can often prove controversial, because opinions differ on how well tasks need to be done. One person might insist that all policy manuals be typeset, while another might think that typewritten (or even handwritten) will suffice. These problems are easily resolved if there is general agreement to use the most common definition of quality: fitness for purpose. This means ensuring that all debates on quality are tested against customer expectations. For example, the professional view of the administrator bows to the reality of what purchasing is willing to pay for.

The Building Blocks of an ISO 9000 System for Suppliers

As shown previously in Figure 7.1, most of the 20 ISO 9000 modules are considered to be directly applicable to the field of PSQM. The following is a brief synopsis of the seven most misunderstood items/modules, from the viewpoint of supplier organizations. These seven modules are the building blocks of the ISO 9000 system around which the other 13 modules take shape. The details on each of the 20 modules contained in the ISO 9000 standards can be obtained from the ISO 9000 Forum. ISO 9004 is a good starting place for most supplier organizations, according to members of the ISO 9000 Forum queried on the subject.

Module #1: Management Responsibility

Management responsibility involves the four areas of quality policy, procedures, organization, and performing management visits. It is central to ISO 9000. If there is any suspicion that management—at all levels, including the highest—is not taking the total quality system seriously, then the ISO 9000 assessors will conclude that the system is not effective. This is summarized forcefully in the introduction to ISO 9000:

> The management of a company should develop and state its corporate quality policy. This policy should be consistent with other company policies. Management should take all necessary measures to ensure that its corporate quality policy is understood, implemented and maintained.

There is a very practical reason for this insistence on management involvement. Because total quality is itself a management system, and because an organization cannot run with two management systems, an ISO 9000 system can only work with total commitment from senior management.

A key management responsibility in setting up a quality system is defining a quality policy in a form that all employees, shareholders, and stakeholders can use and understand. The policy documentation can be organized into four levels: the basic policy statements, the governing procedures, the work instructions to be followed, and the quality review. To be effective, they must be clear and specific.

Policy Statement

A quality policy statement might cover:

- Who is responsible for setting up and running the system
- How the system is to be monitored and reviewed by management
- For which functions/tasks defined procedures will be written
- How the implementation of those procedures will be monitored
- How failures to adhere to the procedures will be corrected

The quality policy guidelines set forth in the ISO 9000 International Standards for Quality Management are simple and direct, easy to understand, relevant, ambitious, and achievable.[6]

Procedures

Not everything that an organization does can be subject to the full rigor of a quality system. To attempt to do so would be overwhelmingly time consuming. More practically, an organization identifies the functions or tasks where performance *critically affects* the service *as perceived by the users.* (In practice, ISO 9000 compels that certain tasks be covered, as will be explained later.) Meanwhile, an organization must first decide what its critical functions are, such as:

- Business and operations planning
- Assessment
- Research and development
- Learning resources
- Work experience
- Selection and appointment of staff
- Staff development

Procedures would then be written for each of these. A procedure is a clear and systematic method that sets out how a function is to be carried out and who is responsible for each part of it. It should be honest and realistic—the way things generally are as opposed to a hoped for result. Overcommitment and embellishment are traps that often get many companies into trouble on the road to certification/registration. Companies wind up hanging themselves on too much rhetoric that is impossible to audit against. Thus, when the assessors evaluate what is really happening, the organization fails the certification because it cannot live up to its documentation.

Work Instructions

In order for procedures to be easily understood and followed, they must be short and must avoid unnecessary detail. Sometimes, however, more detail is needed to ensure that a job is done in a precise manner. Where this is the case, the extra detail is put into a work instruction. For example, a procedure might contain the paragraph:

> Mini-vans for trips shall be ordered by the trip organizer at least seven days prior to any trip, using Form ABC99.

Form ABC99 then becomes the work instruction that tells the organizer exactly what details are needed and by whom.

The distinction between procedures and work instructions is defined as follows:

Procedures
- Refer to a process that includes many subtasks
- Outline what needs to be done

Work instructions
- Refer to just one task
- Provide detailed guidance on how to complete the task

The management representative is often a key position and role in making ISO 9000 come alive. Choosing the best available vs. the most readily available person is a key decision to be made early in the journey.

Quality Review

The essential management role is the quality review, which is further emphasized by the self-adjusting nature of total quality systems. The management review is the engine for that process. At its simplest, the review needs to decide:

- Organization structure, including adequacy of staffing and resources
- Structure and design of the quality system
- Achieved quality of end-product or service
- What information is needed to be sufficiently certain that the quality policy is being implemented, as well as other information based on purchaser feedback, internal feedback, and process/product performance
- What information is needed to decide whether the policy needs amendment
- How frequently these data need to be collected

As ever, it is important to decide what is critical and genuinely indicative of the health of the organization. The more data management asks for, the less it will be able to make sense of. Also, the cost of data collection must be considered. The more that management asks for data that is not automatically collected as part of day-to-day work, the more the costs of the quality system will rise. The efficient and economic way to resolve this is to scan the procedures once they have been written in order to identify data that exist in the system that will be of value in assessing the overall health of the system. There will, however, be two types of data collection : random and systematic.

Both operational data and total quality system data should be used to ascertain problem areas. The management review should contain a sensible balance between the two. Enough data should be provided to convince management that nothing *critical* could be going wrong, but no more. (See the article entitled "PSQM Feedback within the Corporate Measurement System," at the end of Chapter 9.)

The Quality System Loop

A final way to check on the role of management is to examine the quality loop and determine whether everything has been included.

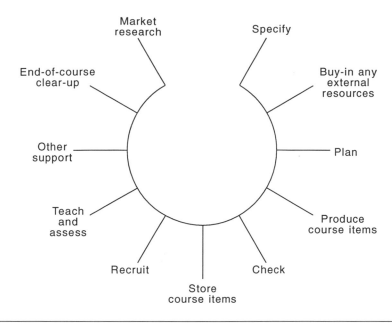

Market research

Specify

End-of-course clear-up

Buy-in any external resources

Other support

Plan

Teach and assess

Produce course items

Recruit

Check

Store course items

Figure 7.4 Quality System Loop for Purchasing a Supplier Quality Management Training Course. (Source: Freeman, Richard (1992). *Quality Assurance in Training and Education.* London: Kogan Page Limited.)

Figure 7.4 is a preliminary model for purchasing a supplier quality management training course and is provided as a springboard for discussion.[7]

Module #2: The Quality System

It is one thing to have a policy, but quite another to turn it into a system that can deliver that policy. It is the responsibility of management to devise, promulgate, and monitor such a system. In one sense, everything that is done as part of the ISO 9000 system is part of the quality system, but here we are looking at the specification of that system and the documentation that goes with it.

Where does management start? It starts with the age-old question, "What kind of a business are we really in?" and then with the new total quality question, "What is really critical?"

These two questions must to be asked and carefully answered in order to (a) avoid a blind and inappropriate application of ISO 9000 (designed for a specialty manufacturing organization) to the supplier organization and (b) prevent the system from tackling irrelevant detail. *For a total quality system to work well, it is essential that it concentrate on the things that make a difference.* What might these be? Each supplier is different, but the following areas might prove critical in most supplier organizations:

- How market needs are identified
- How needs are turned into product specifications
- How employees are recruited and counseled
- How progress is monitored
- How customer satisfaction is assessed
- How staff are selected
- How staff are developed
- How processes (rather than individual products) are evaluated

Once such a list has been compiled (almost certainly by a bottom-up process involving staff and line employees at all levels), it is management's job to decide which items are critical and, therefore, for which there will be a quality policy. Most organizations make this initial list too long.

Once a list of critical functions has been prepared, a policy is needed. This will set out in broad terms management's quality approach to each function, e.g. the policy for recruitment and training might be:

> All employees shall receive written details of the courses in which they have expressed interest. These details shall include: the prior knowledge and skills assumed for the course, the course aims and objectives, the learning time, the methods of assessment, the qualification awarded and career/ training routes available at the end of the course. Before enrolling, each employee shall be interviewed by a Human Resources counselor.[7]

This is a policy statement and is, therefore, short on operational detail. For each function that has been identified as critical, the policy statement will be followed by a detailed, written operational procedure. Although the quality policy should be regularly review, it should not be full of transient detail that requires frequent updating. The goal should be a balance between a policy that is too vague to be meaning-ful and one that is too detailed.

Module #3: Marketing

The marketing section is responsible for establishing quality re-quirements for the product, including determining need, defining market demand and sectors, and determining customer requirements and communicating them accurately within the company. Marketing should also prepare a product brief, which contains performance data, installation, fit, standards, packaging, and quality assurance informa-tion. This area is also charged with documenting the customer feed-back information system.

Module #4: Design Control

For the purposes of this example, design control is not needed and therefore is not included.

Module #5: Purchasing

The procurement section is responsible for the quality of pur-chased materials, components, and assemblies. Quality of services such as calibration and special processes should also be considered. This should all be planned and controlled, so that a program of con-tinuous improvement can be maintained and quality disputes quickly settled.

At a minimum, the procurement system should include require-ments for specs, drawings, and purchase orders; selection of qualified suppliers; agreement on quality assurance and verification methods; settlement of quality disputes; and receiving inspection plans, con-trols, and records.

Module #6: Internal Quality Audits

Even if the quality policy and the procedures are well prepared, there is no guarantee that they will be followed. Auditing is the means by which the organization verifies that the procedures have been implemented. Regular checks (audits) are made in a specific and systematic manner to identify whether or not adherence to the procedures exists. This inevitably involves the potentially threatening process of interviewing the people doing the work, who can easily assume that they are being inspected. However, this is not the case at all. This impression has to be regularly dispelled by reminding everyone involved that it is the procedure that is being audited, not the person.

The entire management review system and the self-improvement nature of total quality systems demand that the system be continually checked to determine whether it is performing according to plan. This checking process is called *auditing*, because the methods used are very similar to those in financial auditing.

Auditing works by regularly checking each procedure to determine whether the work is being done as set out in the statement. Any deviations are recorded as *noncompliances*, which have to be corrected. The process of putting right a non-compliance is called *corrective action*.

Through the quality management system, a timetable is drawn up which ensures that all procedures are audited on a regular basis. For example, the most important procedures might be audited once a year, while the less important ones are audited once in two or three years.

One or more auditors are appointed for each procedure. When it is time to audit that procedure, the auditor visits the section that uses the procedure and, in an auditing meeting, works step by step through each statement in the procedure to check for evidence that the step has been applied.

It is at this point that the difference between good and bad procedures can often become apparent. In a bad procedure, precisely what evidence constitutes compliance may be very unclear. In a good procedure, the nature of evidence of compliance should be obvious. For example, "The company shall agree to a list of performance outcomes with the suppliers" is vague because it does not say what constitutes evidence of agreement. If the procedure is reworded, this vagueness can be eliminated: "The company shall prepare a list of performance outcomes agreed to with and signed by the supplier's management committee." It is now clear that the auditor will be looking for items on the signed list. These clear-cut pieces of evidence are called *quality records*.

Module #7: Quality Records

It is clear that successful auditing depends on evidence being available to demonstrate that the procedure has—or has not—been followed. Anything used to record compliance is called a *quality record.*

It is possible to introduce a total quality system that specifies numerous new and complex records that will have to be kept as quality records. However, this is not the way to introduce total quality. It results in deep resentment from all the staff who have to run the system and fortifies the belief that ISO 9000 is just additional paperwork.

An efficient and successful quality system will seek every opportunity to use everyday working documents as quality records. Almost certainly, the existing document formats will need some revision in order to become quality records, but the important thing is that the number of documents is not increased.

Module #1 Revisited: Management Reviews

The ISO 9000 system begins and ends with the commitment of management, and the final part is the management review. A quality council composed of senior management holds regular review meetings to assess how well the system is meeting the needs of the organization and the customer and how well the system is being run. Such a review would receive summary reports on the system, which might document areas such as:

- Adherence to the audit schedule—Are audits being done on time?
- Implementation of corrective action—Are problems revealed by audits being corrected in the agreed upon manner and promptly?
- Procedure review—Are procedures being regularly reviewed by their users and amended if needed?
- Mission—Is the mission statement still appropriate?

The overall approach is self-regulatory and self-improving, with heavy emphasis on documentation and audit, as previously discussed.

IMPLEMENTING ISO 9000

Issues to Consider

Having identified and summarized the major components that constitute ISO 9000 for suppliers, it is time to turn to the implementation issues. The following is a sample of the types of issues that ISO 9000 will require management to consider:

- What management must do in order to effectively run the quality system
- What a total quality system is
- How auditing should be done
- Checking customers' requirements
- Controlling product/materials design
- Ensuring that precisely what is needed is purchased
- Keeping track of the learning process
- Using appropriate assessment methods
- Ensuring that out-of-date products, information, and materials are not used
- Keeping appropriate records
- Maintaining safe working practices

Management Reviews for Implementation

Day in and day out, employees will be carrying out tasks and functions according to the agreed upon procedures and work instructions. At regular intervals (perhaps once a month), some part or other of the procedures will be under audit. The entire process becomes an integral part of how work is done and how it is managed. However, just as any process or system needs to be evaluated from time to time, so does any quality system. This evaluation process is called management review, as previously discussed.

As with any evaluation system, if steps are not taken early to collect the data as work proceeds, it may be difficult, expensive, or even impossible to collect the data later. This is particularly important because if compliance cannot be proven, noncompliance is assumed. No news is bad news in ISO 9000. This means that management must be explicit about the data to be evaluated in its reviews. Data will tend to be of two types: routine statistical data and ad hoc surveys. The types of routine statistical data that management might seek include:

- Percentage of audits carried out within one week of target date
- Number of noncompliances detected per audit
- Percentage of corrective actions carried out within the time period agreed upon between auditor and auditee
- Percentage of total noncompliances that belong to each procedure
- Average length of time since each procedure was last reviewed
- Number of procedures not reviewed in the last twelve months

All these types of data are easily plotted on time graphs so that management can see the trend in performance.

The other category of data that a management review group might seek is ad hoc reports. For example, the group might want to review:

- Employee views on how well the quality system supports them in their day-to-day work
- Suppliers' views of the quality system
- A sample of quality systems in similar establishments

Obtaining ISO 9000 Certification

Whether or not to seek external recognition of the total quality system is a matter of choice. If the decision is made in favor of external recognition, then the system must be assessed against either the ISO 9000 standards or another quality standard such as the Malcolm Baldrige Award.

The role of a certification body is to assess the quality system in depth in order to determine whether it meets the standards set out in BS 5750. The certification body requires a fee, which is negotiated in terms of the size of the organization and the complexity of its quality system. A quality manual and procedures must be submitted, but otherwise documentation is kept very simple. The certifying body then:

- Reviews the documentation
- Visits the premises to interview quality staff and other employees and to generally see the total quality system in practice

- Produces a report which either confirms that the standard has been met or indicates the changes needed in the system to meet the standard

Including the certification process alongside the other steps in this chapter, the full sequence for obtaining ISO 9000 is as follows:

1. Obtain the necessary parts of ISO 9000
2. Design the system as set out in the *ISO 9000 Compendium*[6] published by the ISO 9000 Forum. (In practice, the assistance of an external consultant will probably be required for this step.)
3. Choose a certification body
4. Schedule a certification body visit
5. Receive certification or amend the system

Choosing a Certification Body

A list of certification bodies can be obtained from BSI or from the National Accreditation Council for Certification Bodies (NACCB). In choosing a certification body, it is best to identify one with plenty of experience in working with the type of business in which the organization is involved. The better this type of business is understood by the certification body, the better they will be able to understand the subtleties of adapting ISO 9000. It is also a good idea to check with other similar organizations to determine which certifying body they used (if any) and what their experience was. If a certifying body with a poor track record is chosen, difficulties can be expected as they adapt to the specific needs of the organization.

EPILOGUE: THE DRIVING FORCE BEHIND TQM

Total quality began in those markets where Japan and the United States were in direct competition. It has continued to expand wherever markets are characterized by an ever-increasing demand for quality and reliability combined with a reduction in price in real terms. Thus, TQM is particularly common in automobile manufacturing, process industries, and electronics, areas where today's products are far more reliable than those of a decade or two ago.[8]

As the worldwide trend toward privatization continues, it is likely that PSQM will become more competitive. Particularly with the aid of high-tech media, customers will less and less frequently automatically turn to their nearest local provider. It is, therefore, reasonable to expect that providers will increasingly find themselves competing in terms of quality, satisfaction, and price. Mandatory total quality and ISO 9000 could well be on the way.[9] Today's choice may be tomorrow's mandate.

Overall, the goals of an integrated ISO 9000 based total quality system can be summarized as:[10]

- Listen to the voice of the customer
- Focus on the needs of the market
- Achieve top quality performance in all areas, not just in the product or service
- Establish simple procedures for quality performance[11]
- Continually review processes to eliminate waste[12]
- Develop measures of performance
- Understand the competition and develop a competitive strategy
- Ensure effective communication
- Seek continuous improvement

When comparing QA-based ISO 9000 programs to total quality, the most significant difference is that total quality adds customer focus and cost to the quality debate. QA essentially ignores cost (or money in any form), whereas total quality uses cost as a critical performance measure.

It is not the intent here to draw any firm conclusions as to the merits of ISO 9000 versus TQM. Indeed, there is too little evidence of the application of either method in PSQM to validate conclusions. What can be said, however, is that suppliers cannot expect to escape the current drive toward higher quality and customer focus. Therefore, a more sensitive measure of performance will be required, as well as a means of improving past performance. However, in phrasing such a need, it points toward some form of quality assurance. Perhaps ISO 9000 will fit that need. Perhaps TQM will, or some combination of the two. If neither does, some other approach will soon be required. The time is right. The stakes are high. The message is clear.

ENDNOTES

1. Sprow, Eugene (1992). "Insights into ISO 9000." *Manufacturing Engineering,* p. 73, Sept. 1992.
2. Freeman, Richard (1992). *Quality Assurance in Training and Education.* London: Kogan Page Limited, p. 10.
3. Sink, Scott (1991). "The Role of Measurement in World Class Quality." *Industrial Engineering,* June 1991.
4. Spizizen, Gary (1992). "The ISO 9000 Standards: Creating a Level Playing Field for International Quality." *National Productivity Review,* pp. 331–346, Summer 1992.
5. Note on traditional quality control: Quality control is a much more widely known term than QA, but the distinction between the two is not always well drawn. Quality control is essentially a method of inspecting for, and rejecting, defective work (although some of its statistical methods can be used to prevent defective work from occurring). As such, there is no concept of preventing the problem in the first place. QA is essentially *preventive,* as the word assurance implies. It means preventing errors, not correcting them repeatedly.
6. Source: *ISO 9000 Compendium,* 3rd edition. Geneva: ISO, 1993.
7. Freeman, Richard (1992). *Quality Assurance in Training and Education.* London: Kogan Page Limited, p. 22.
8. Total quality is based on the assumption that suppliers will only prosper in their markets if they are able to both improve quality and reduce costs. While this notion is not novel in manufacturing, it is perhaps revolutionary in services. Administrators frequently request additional resources so that they can improve quality. Total quality says that you must improve quality with fewer resources, because if you do not, your competitor will.
9. Total quality assumes that there is a hidden source of fat in any organization (Freeman, 1992). That source is the cost of quality, also known as the price of nonconformance (PONC) or the cost of not doing things right the first time.
10. Jackson, Susan (1992). "What You Should Know about ISO 9000." *Training,* pp. 48–52, May 1992.
11. Ozeki, Kazuo and Asaka, Tetsuichi (1990). *Handbook of Quality Tools: The Japanese Approach.* Cambridge, Mass. and Norwalk, Conn.: Productivity Press.
12. According to Dr. Asaka of JUSE, most problems can be classified as follows: (a) problems related to worker skills or attitudes: pure mistake, not following the operating procedure, skills not yet adequate, concern for quality not strong enough; (b) problems related to the workplace QA system: the quality characteristic to be assured is not well defined, operating standards are incomplete, manage-

ment points are unclear, casual attitude about QA methods, quality control process chart not yet complete; (c) lack of motivation to solve the purchasing administrator's or agent's problem: no desire to delve deeply into the problem and solve it, purchasing administrator's or agent's leadership in setting improvement goals and in making improvements is inadequate; (d) problems in the workplace culture: never delving deeply into problems, blaming the workplace custom; (e) problems originating in another department: design error, error in determining customer specifications. Asaka believes that if problems are solved in a haphazard manner, a problem might mistakenly be identified as a recurring worker error when the true cause is the daily training and quality control education being provided to workers. Try to create an atmosphere in which everyone is motivated to build quality into their work processes, he taught.

An administrator should look for the root cause of any problem that occurs, consider if he or she (not others) is causing the problem, and implement the basic policies needed to correct it.

13. Figures 7.1 and 7.3 ©Strategy Associates, Inc.

CHAPTER 8

SUPPLIER CONTINUOUS IMPROVEMENT

As mentioned in the first few chapters, one of the key components of a purchasing/supplier quality management (PSQM) system is the improvement of the supplier's processes, products, and services as they most affect the buying organization's processes, products, and services. This is one of the most important components of PSQM, because the improvements that are gained are mutually beneficial to both parties and serve to create a stronger tie between the supplier and the buying organization.

In order to make this tie as strong as possible, the two parties should select an improvement project that is of mutual benefit. The supplier should then, with the possible assistance of the buying organization, demonstrate its understanding of an improvement method by applying it to the improvement project jointly selected. This will provide evidence to the buying organization that the supplier knows how to improve and is committed to improvement of all key supplier processes and not just the project selected.

The supplier and the buying organization should consider working together on the design of certain products and services. Often the buying organization does not do so and does not utilize the industry knowledge of the supplier. Yet a good supplier will usually understand its industry and sometimes some of the customer's needs even better than the buying organization. By working together on the design aspects, a strong potential exists for the development of a higher quality product or service at a lower life cycle cost.

Some of the common objectives of the improvement project might be to reduce overall life cycle cost, reduce variability and improve the process capability of key quality characteristics, improve reliability, and improve maintainability. Each organization should understand its key quality characteristics, as explained in previous chapters, and the objectives of the improvement project should be linked to the same. This will help to align the supplier's efforts with those of the buying organization.

Both the supplier and the buying organization could utilize basic research, market research, customer feedback, process analysis, benchmarking, value analysis, quality function deployment, concurrent engineering, business reengineering, and the Systematic Improvement Method[1] in the design and improvement of processes, products, and services. Some of these approaches will be described in this chapter. Some are more applicable to design, while others are more applicable to improvement of processes, products, and services. Other methods may also be applicable, and the supplier and buying organization should determine which is most applicable to the specific improvement project.

IMPROVEMENT STRATEGIES

Various strategies have been utilized to achieve improvement over time. Some of these strategies are depicted in Figure 8.1, which is adapted and expanded from Bob King's book entitled *Hoshin Planning, The Developmental Approach*.[2]

Incremental improvement and wandering: In the past, this was the strategy most frequently exercised by companies that had the desire to improve. The organization would identify a need to improve and assign some project effort to effect the improvement. Once the improvement was realized, the project was considered completed and

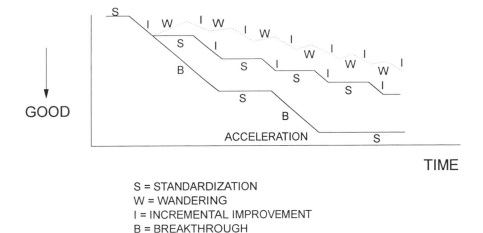

Figure 8.1   Improvement Strategies.

no further emphasis was put on the improvement area because it was considered to be solved. This invariably led to deterioration of the improvement gains over time.

Incremental improvement with standardization: Another approach, which has come into much wider use especially in companies utilizing a total quality management system, is to institute an incremental improvement effort constantly to the areas with the highest priority. Once improvements are made, the processes are standardized and deployed throughout the organization so that the gains are preserved over time. This method is what most Japanese companies refer to as *kaizen.*

Breakthrough improvement with standardization: This strategy is used mostly in companies that utilize policy deployment, benchmarking, and business reengineering approaches. The goal is to leapfrog the competition through major gains in processes, products, and services. These companies are careful to standardize the changes once the improvements are gained, thereby assuring that they are not lost over time.

As can be seen from Figure 8.1, the approach that could probably yield the most significant improvements is breakthrough with standardization. However, this strategy is riskier than the others. A breakthrough improvement is much more difficult to achieve than an incremental improvement. If the breakthrough improvement is made, then the gain would be significant, but because of its difficulty, the chances of success may be less. The organization should consider which strategy it should implement for each area of improvement. Sometimes the organization must incur the associated risks in view of the anticipated returns, while other times a more conservative approach is best. The different approaches that will discussed in this chapter are more applicable to one strategy than the other. For example, the Systematic Improvement Method[1] is most applicable to the incremental improvement and standardization strategy, although it can also be used successfully in breakthrough improvement with standardization. The potential for applicability is summarized in Table 8.1. The higher the number in the square, the higher the applicability of the approach to the strategy.

Some of the approaches mentioned in Table 8.1 will be described in the remainder of this chapter, including benchmarking, value analysis, quality function deployment, concurrent engineering, and business process reengineering. Then, a methodology that was developed by Advent Group, Inc., called the Systematic Improvement Method,[1] will be presented.

Benchmarking

This approach was popularized by the well-known author Robert C. Camp through his work at Xerox. In his book entitled *Benchmarking*,[3] he provides the following definition:

> Benchmarking is the search for industry best practices that lead to superior performance.

In his book, Camp proposes a ten-step process that could lead an organization to significant improvement of its processes. These steps then could lead a supplier and the buying organization to work together toward major common gains. There are different types of benchmarking, and all of them could result in significant improvements for both parties. The different types of benchmarking include internal, competitive, functional, and generic. Camp[3] expands upon these in his book. This approach has been used successfully by many firms to improve their processes. It is one of the most widely used approaches to improvement.

Table 8.1 Applicability of Quality Approach
to Improvement Strategy

Approach	Strategy 1: Incremental improvement and wandering	Strategy 2: Incremental improvement with standardization	Strategy 3: Breakthrough improvement with standardization
Basic research	1	2	3
Market research	2	3	3
Customer feedback	3	2	1
Process analysis	1	3	2
Benchmarking	1	2	3
Value analysis	1	2	3
Quality function deployment	1	1	3
Concurrent engineering	1	1	3
Business reengineering		1	3
Systematic Improvement Method		3	2

Value Analysis

This methodology began in the late 1940s in the purchasing department of General Electric. The key to value analysis is the functional approach. Although value analysis started in private industry, today it is more prevalent in the public sector. It has some similarities to the quality function deployment approach, which will be discussed next, and is used extensively in the private sector. In a recent issue of *NAPM Insights* (December 1993), the history, methodology, applications, and benefits to be derived from this approach were addressed in various articles. The approach is systematic and addresses the needs of the buying organization in creative ways. It provides for prioritization of the needs of the buying organization and considers all possible alternatives to providing the required functionality. These alternatives are then compared in terms of value (i.e., importance vs. costs), and the best mix is selected. Both service providers and manufacturers are using this improvement method.

Quality Function Deployment

Quality function deployment (QFD) focuses on use of the House of Quality to determine customer needs. It couples the quality characteristics that the organization can provide with the deployment of these needs, from the design of products and services through each of the components down to the process that will deliver the ultimate product or service. QFD was developed in Japan by quality experts such as Yoji Akao,[4] Macabe, and Fukahara, among others. Bob King[5] has written one of the most thorough books on this subject, entitled *Better Designs in Half the Time, Implementing QFD, Quality Functional Deployment in America.* Mr. King proposes a four-phase approach to QFD: organization, descriptive, breakthrough, and implementation. This method has been highly successful in reducing design time considerably. It is also the same method described earlier in Chapter 5, as applied to supplier policy deployment.

Business Reengineering

This methodology has become more popular in recent times. Its premise is to do away with the old way of doing things. Start from scratch and determine the fundamental needs of the business, and design the most effective and efficient process to address those needs. In their book entitled *Reengineering the Corporation,* Hammer and Champy[6] put forth most of the current ideas regarding this methodology. They define it as follows:

> Reengineering is the fundamental rethinking and radical redesign of business processes to achieve dramatic improvements in critical, contemporary measures of performance, such as cost, quality, service, and speed.

Hammer and Champy[6] discuss examples from various companies such as IBM Credit, Ford, Kodak, Hallmark, Taco Bell, Capital Holding, Bell Atlantic, and others. All to some degree realized significant benefits from redesigning their processes. Another example is Florida Power & Light, which because of entering a changing competitive market has looked at reengineering some of its key business processes, such as procurement. It has even considered some major changes such as payment upon receipt, which could potentially save

Florida Power & Light and its suppliers some significant overall processing costs.

Concurrent Engineering

This method has become very popular and has had great success in American industry. For example, automotive designers who worked on the likes of the Saturn from General Motors, the LH series from Chrysler, and the Taurus from Ford all utilized this methodology. Electronics, computer, service, healthcare, and many other industries have also used this technique successfully. The concept is relatively simple. All parties are involved from the beginning of the design project. The needs of all parties are considered. This may take a little longer, but in the end all concerns are addressed and redesign is significantly reduced. The problems associated with designs that later cannot be manufactured or maintained are reduced.

SYSTEMATIC IMPROVEMENT METHOD

This process was left for last because it has one of the most far-reaching application potentials. It was developed by Advent Group, Inc.[1] and has been successfully implemented at various locations. The method has as its predecessor some of the same concepts as the quality improvement story used widely in Japanese firms for continuous improvement and made popular by Dr. Hitoshi Kume[7] in his book entitled *Statistical Methods for Quality Improvement*. Both of these methods are the result of applying the scientific methods and the Shewhart/ Deming cycle to the continuous improvement of processes, products, and services.

The Deming cycle is more commonly defined as Plan-Do-Check-Act or PDCA. Very basically, this applies a simple concept. The first phase is to *plan* what is to be done, including expected results or goals. Once a good plan has been developed, it is time to *do* what was planned, i.e., follow through or implement the plan. After the *do* phase, it is necessary to *check* to determine if things went according to the plan, i.e., determine if expectations were met. Depending on the results of the *check* phase, in the *act* phase a determination is made as to whether there is more to be done or changes need to be made because

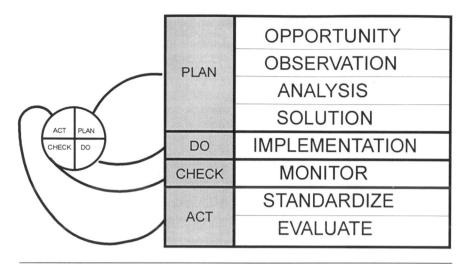

Figure 8.2 Systematic Improvement Method.

expectations were not met. Once the cycle has been completed and if all expectations were met, then the process is moved to another area with a higher priority or the cycle is restarted at the *plan* phase to continue the improvement. Each time the cycle is completed is referred to as a "turn of the PDCA wheel." Each turn of the PDCA wheel implies that some incremental improvement has occurred.

The PDCA cycle can be expanded into eight different steps which provide for the continuous improvement of any process, product, or service. These eight steps are referred to as the Systematic Improvement Method, as shown in Figure 8.2

Opportunity

In this phase it is important to understand the overall scope of the improvement effort and the reason why effort is being devoted to improve it. The priority of the improvement area selected vs. other areas must be considered. This priority should consider customer requirements, importance of the improvement area or process, the degree to which customer needs are being met, and therefore the need to improve the process. The processes with the greatest importance and the greatest need for improvement should be addressed first. This step is similar to some of the prioritizing methods that were mentioned in the earlier sections of Chapter 5. Some form of measurable indicator should be used to determine if progress has been made after improvements are implemented. A specific target for improvement should be agreed upon, as well as a schedule for the improvement activity. Most importantly, a team of individuals from the different areas affected should be selected. If this improvement effort is taking place at the supplier, then a representative from the buying organization should be included if possible. Similarly, if the effort is taking place at the buying organization, a representative from the supplier should be part of the team if possible.

Observation

This step is intended to dig deeper into the existing conditions. It is important to thoroughly understand the process. What are the steps and logical flow of the process? What departments are involved? How long do different steps take? What is the value added by each step in the process? The situation needs to be stratified. The concept here is to reduce the area of emphasis from the broad scope of the project to a specific problem or opportunity that can be addressed. The specific time, place, symptoms, departments, conditions, positions, etc. when the problem or opportunity exists should be identified. In addition, process information should be gathered, including quality and process indicators, specification limits, process capability analyses, and historical trends. Site visits may be required to gather nonnumerical observations, i.e., morale, feelings, conjectures, complaints, concerns, suggestions, and any other information that may pertain to or be useful in the upcoming analysis. The difference between the current level of the quality characteristics or process indicators and the level they *should be* at can be considered as either a problem or as an opportunity. This *should be* level can be thought of as an objective or target of the team. A definitive statement of this existing condition can be referred to as the problem or opportunity statement.

Analysis

Once the opportunity area has been narrowed to a workable, analyzable piece, the analysis step can begin. The objective in this step is to break down the opportunity by looking for the causes and effects leading to the problem or opportunity. This process would typically start with the use of the original seven quality control tools (see Figure 8.3) and other tools. Using these tools, the team would try to identify the most likely root causes of the problem or opportunity and develop tests or experiments to verify their findings with data and observation. If possible, the problem with the alleged causes could even be reproduced, as long as the risk of recurrence of the problem is not high.

Solution

Once the root cause has been verified, the team can determine the best solution to eliminate or reduce this root cause. The team must utilize much creativity in this endeavor. They should consider breaking away from their current paradigms to try new and innovative solutions, although sometimes the most obvious and simplest solution is best. A team should usually select one solution to implement at a time or the effect of various solutions may be combined. If the team can determine the individual effects of each solution, then it is acceptable to implement multiple solutions. Multiple solutions are generated and are linked back to the root causes. A multi-criteria selection method is utilized, which should at least consider the degree to which a solution eliminates or addresses the cause, the feasibility and risks of the solution, and the cost/benefits associated with the different solutions. Other considerations may include the effect of the selected solution on other areas. Will it cause other problems? The objective is to select the most effective solution considering all the preceding factors and any others the team deems appropriate. One of the key determinations that the team should complete at this step is the selection of an indicator that will be affected by the selected solution, which in turn will affect the original overall indicator of the project. This indicator will be used in the following steps to check if the solution is effective.

Implement

This is the *do* portion of the PDCA wheel. Now that a solution has been selected, the next step is to implement that solution. The key, however, is not to make a full-scale implementation at this time; instead, a limited implementation is usually in order so that in the following step a determination can be made as to whether the solution that was selected was truly as effective as expected before spending the time and energy required for a full version. Therefore, one of the first parts of this step is to determine the scope of the pilot test. It should be broad enough that the effectiveness of the solution can be measured, but narrow enough to be feasible. The team should discuss the boundaries that would suffice. Note that for a small solution with minimal impact, a pilot test may not be necessary. Again, the team should discuss the pros and cons of this option and decide if a pilot would be beneficial. The team should get the buy-in of all the departments or suppliers involved in or affected by the solution. A force-field or pro and con analysis could be performed to identify the issues and concerns that should be addressed in order to ensure the successful implementation of the solution. An action plan, including answers to the what, who, and when of each of the implementation steps, needs to be developed. Training the personnel affected by the pilot test should take place. Finally, the solution should be implemented, making sure that the appropriate means for monitoring the selected solution indicators have been well established.

Monitor

This step corresponds to the *check* phase of the PDCA cycle. Because the solution has by now been implemented, the purpose of this step is to verify whether or not the solution has been effective. Has the implementation created the expected results? Has the indicator that was set up to track the effectiveness of the solution changed in the proper direction and amount? The team should convert the effects to monetary terms as much as possible. They should compare the actual value of the indicators to the target value. All effects—good or bad—should be listed. This information can be helpful in future implementations. Some of the negative effects may need to be addressed prior to proceeding with a full-scale implementation in the *standardize* step. The length of time devoted to the *monitor* step should include at least a few repetitions of the process. This would allow the solution to be "tested" sufficiently before a full implementation is attempted.

Standardize

The next two steps are part of the *act* phase of the PDCA cycle. In the *standardize* step, the team assesses whether or not the results of the *implementation* step were successful and to what degree. Depending on the outcome, at this point the team needs to decide whether to proceed with the full implementation or to "go back to the drawing board," i.e., go back to the *analysis* step to either identify and verify a new root cause, to the *solution* phase if it is determined that the solution did not address the root cause, or the *implementation* phase if the solution was not properly implemented. The decision to proceed with the full implementation should consider all the data gathered in the *monitor* step. Based on comparisons to the original objectives, the pilot results can also assist in the decision process. The concerns that may have been identified during the pilot should now be addressed before considering the full implementation. This may require one additional cycle of implementation in a revised pilot mode before proceeding to the full implementation. Once the decision is made to proceed with the full implementation, procedures should be modified, new responsibilities should be explained to the people affected, and full training should take place. Careful monitoring of the indicators should continue during this phase to ensure that expected results are being achieved. Otherwise, the need for corrective action can be identified and instituted as soon as possible. Once the full implementation has been successful, monitoring responsibility should be assigned to the departments or suppliers (or both) that have the most control over each indicator. Finally, the solution should be considered for replication in other areas of the buying organization or to other suppliers (except for proprietary improvements). Replication is one of the best ways of multiplying the effects of improvement efforts to all applicable areas.

For additional information, see Abstract 8.1 at the end of this chapter.

Evaluate

The last step in the Systematic Improvement Method is also part of the *act* phase of PDCA. In this step, the team assesses what it learned from the process itself. The team can determine if there are better ways to have addressed certain steps in the process, if the process itself can be improved, or if certain team selection criteria can be improved for the next effort that the team will undertake. The team should review the original full scope of the project and determine if there are still other opportunities or problems that should be addressed; if so, the team should restart at the *opportunity* or *observation* step again. If the overall scope of the project has been successfully attained, then the team can either suggest another high-priority improvement area to address or be disbanded. The monitoring responsibilities still continue, not as part of the responsibilities of the team, but instead as responsibilities of the departments or suppliers assigned in the *standardization* step.

The Systematic Improvement Method is applicable to many improvement situations. It should be used only as a guideline. Such a series of steps should not be used exclusively in a dogmatic way. The improvement team should be given the flexibility to deviate somewhat from the exact methodology if they deem it necessary or expedient for the overall success of the improvement process. The team should, however, go back and verify the steps later if possible. The methodology should assist the team, rather than the team having to work for the methodology.

USE OF QUALITY TOOLS

Often there are different understandings of the term *quality tools.* For example, in the Japanese school there are the original quality control tools and the new quality control tools. The original quality control tools (Figure 8.3) are comprised of seven tools that are mostly used for quality improvement efforts associated with a systematic improvement method such as the one described in the previous section. The new quality control tools are mostly associated with strategic planning, organization, and project management.

By using the original quality control tools, a team working on an improvement should be able to analyze a large majority of the opportunities or problems that it faces. These tools have application in various parts of the Systematic Improvement Method. This does not mean that only one tool is applicable to one step, but rather the tools can be useful in various steps. The application of these tools is treated more thoroughly in other books; therefore, the focus here will be on the

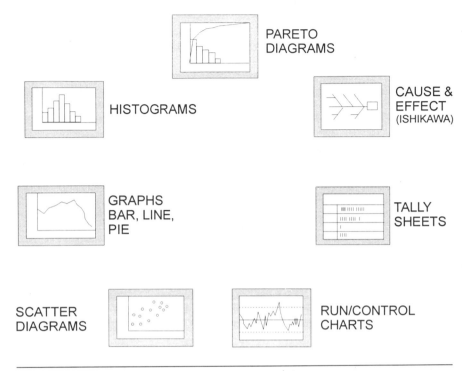

Figure 8.3 Original Seven Quality Control Tools.

use of some of these tools in the Systematic Improvement Method for a supplier-related improvement project.

IMPROVEMENT CASE STUDY

A case study will now be presented in the supplier area using the Systematic Improvement Method and some of the original quality control tools mentioned in the previous section. This case was adapted from a case presented at the Thirteenth Quality Control Seminar for Procurement and Materials Departments, sponsored by the Japanese Union of Scientists and Engineers (JUSE). The case has been modified to follow a storyboard approach using the steps of the Systematic Improvement Method. The logical flow of the case is presented in Figure 8.4 to 8.8.

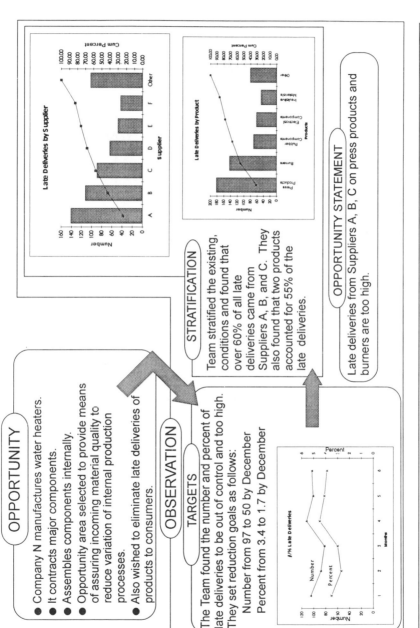

Figure 8.4 Case Study Using the Systematic Improvement Method. (Adapted from JUSE seminar case.)

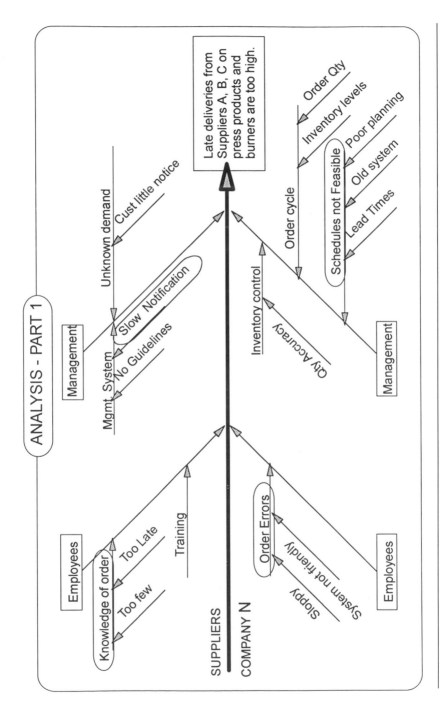

Figure 8.5 Case Study Using the Systematic Improvement Method. (Adapted from JUSE seminar case.)

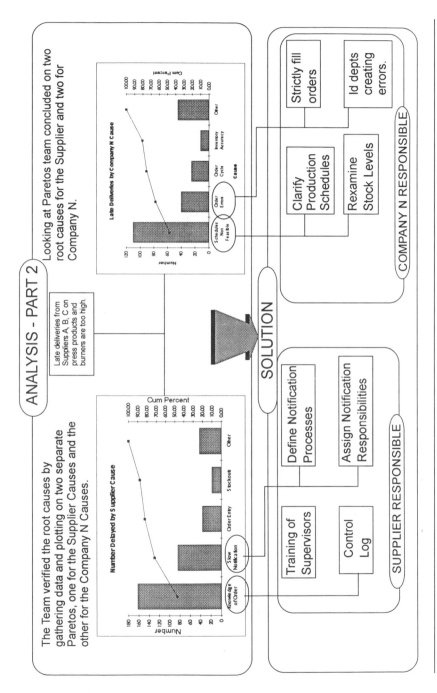

Figure 8.6   Case Study Using the Systematic Improvement Method. (Adapted from JUSE seminar case.)

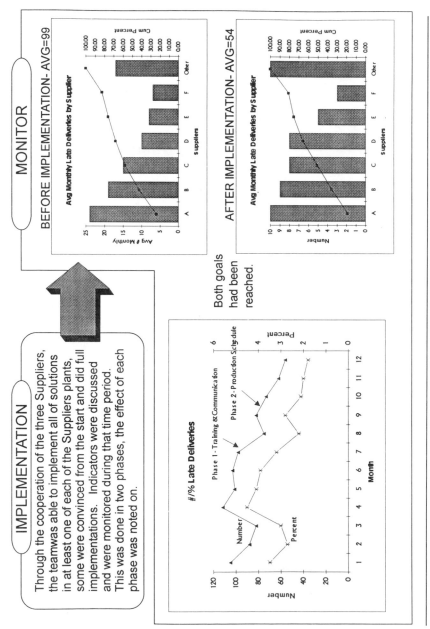

Figure 8.7 Case Study Using the Systematic Improvement Method. (Adapted from JUSE seminar case.)

EVALUATION

The team was very happy with the results of this effort. They recognized that there were still other areas that needed to be addressed within the opportunity area of Late Deliveries. During their meetings they had found out that other companies were making some significant re-engineering changes to their ordering processes. Now that they had reached their goals they felt that the next effort should concentrate on the process itself. They had started some Benchmarking with some of the Suppliers and with other companies that they felt would warrant the effort.

STANDARDIZATION

Once the team recognized that it had achieved its goals of reducing both the number of Late Deliveries and the Percent Deliveries that are Late, it wanted to institutionalize the changes to be sure that these improvements were not lost. The following changes were made at either the Supplier or the Company:

- Procedures for ordering were modified and all employees were trained.

- New communication systems were documented and issued as standards.

- The new Production Schedule was accepted and approved for implementation at all sites.

- Replication to other Suppliers was started based on the results of this improvement.

Figure 8.8 Case Study Using the Systematic Improvement Method. (Adapted from JUSE seminar case.)

VARIABILITY REDUCTION

Most of the methods that have been discussed can be used not only to make absolute improvements in the indicators of quality characteristics, but also to reduce the variability of these indicators. This is one of the areas of greatest importance because it is often the variability of the process that creates conditions that are unacceptable. The concepts of statistical process control and process capability are discussed in Chapter 9. World-class quality corporations today include these concepts in their specifications from their suppliers. Not only are they interested in a process or product that is focused near the center of the specification limits, but they also want to ensure that the process will always produce products or services within these limits, which is why process variability reduction methods have had a recent resurgence. Many teams that have used the methods described in this chapter often describe their goals as the reduction of process variability. This is usually done to gain control of a process; then, after control of the process is achieved, movement of the mean is addressed.

ENDNOTES

1. Fernandez, Ricardo R. (1993). *Process Management and Improvement.* Miami: Advent Group, Inc.
2. King, Robert (1989). *Hoshin Planning: The Developmental Approach.* Methuen, Mass.: GOAL/QPC.
3. Camp, Robert C. (1989). *Benchmarking—The Search for Industry Best Practices that Lead to Superior Performance.* Milwaukee: ASQC Quality Press.
4. Akao, Yoji (1991). *Hoshin Kanri—Policy Deployment for Successful TQM.* Cambridge, Mass.: Productivity Press.
5. King, Robert (1989). *Better Designs in Half the Time—Implementing Quality Function Deployment in America.* Methuen, Mass.: GOAL/QPC.
6. Hammer, Michael and James Champy (1993). *Reengineering the Corporation.* New York: Harper Business.
7. Kume, Hitoshi (1985). *Statistical Methods for Quality Improvement.* Tokyo: The Association for Overseas Technical Scholarship.
8. Figures 8.1 to 8.8 and Table 8.1 ©Advent Group, Inc.

ABSTRACTS

ABSTRACT 8.1
START AT THE VERY BEGINNING

Brown, Philip and Cousins, Paul
The TQM Magazine, May–June 1992, pp. 116–120

Three key drivers for TQM impact the purchasing function, say the authors: (a) quality in all we do, (b) greater flexibility in the manufacturing capability, and (c) lower costs. The primary focus of purchasing's relationship with suppliers used to be reducing costs in a way that resulted in confrontation. But with the new concern for zero defect quality so that purchased products can be accepted directly into the production line, real trust is important, and trust is not built on aggression. The authors discuss ten factors that are most significant in building successful relationships with suppliers:

- Price
- Quality
- Delivery
- Reputation
- Commercial viability
- Level of technology and skills
- Innovative potential
- Flexibility
- Communication
- Culture

Communication between purchasing and suppliers emphasizes both (1) the human interaction between companies and (2) electronic data exchange so as to cut paperwork and staff time on frequent small orders. While this level of supplier partnership may be developed with no more than, say, 20 percent of suppliers, the significance of these partnerships, the authors say, is far greater. They also mention a computerized "Vendor Management Model" which helps evaluate potential suppliers against critical factors. (©*Quality Abstracts*)

CHAPTER 9

SUPPLIER MEASUREMENT AND FEEDBACK

CLOSING THE LOOP

Returning to the original description of the purchasing/supplier quality management (PSQM) model as described in Chapter 3, it is comprised of four major components:

- Customer–supplier relationships
- Linking
- Improvement
- Feedback

The first three of these were addressed in previous chapters. The feedback component is the focus of this chapter.

It is this feedback component that helps "close the loop" of information and progress between the buying organization and the suppliers in the process. If a good customer–supplier relationship is to the established and maintained, it is imperative that a common communication of expectations be established. Both parties need to speak the same language. When one party believes that there has been a break-down in the system, the other party should be able to agree. To facilitate this, the criteria for determining that a breakdown has taken place must be perfectly clear, agreed upon, and understood operation-ally by both parties, but a solid monitoring and communication system needs to be established so that both parties are aware of the situation as soon as it occurs and can take appropriate action. This communica-tion should flow in both directions—from the customer to the supplier as well as from the supplier to the customer. As was discussed earlier, the two hats are interchangeable depending on the situation, and therefore the communication needs to flow in the direction of the corresponding requirement (see Figure 9.1).

Without this feedback component, the "loop" is broken. When conditions exist that do not meet the expectations of both parties, only one party may be aware of the situation and may expect the other to act upon it. How can the other party act if they do not know about the situation? This creates tension and dissatisfaction between both par-ties, which serves to destroy the strong customer–supplier relationship that both parties have been striving to develop.

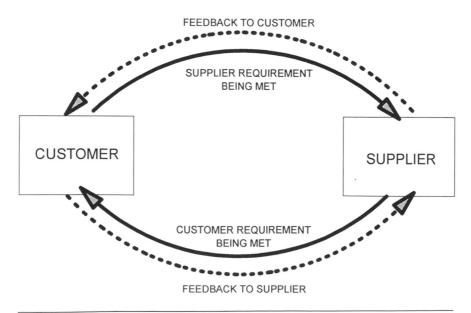

Figure 9.1 Feedback Directions.

This is why the feedback component is so important. It is analogous to preventive maintenance of capital equipment. It is the periodic oil change in a car. Every time that the feedback takes place and is done with a positive win–win attitude, trust is increased and the relationship is further strengthened.

FACTORS TO CONSIDER

In order to maintain this customer–supplier relationship, all the factors that are important to both parties should be measured and feedback on them should be provided periodically. (For additional information, see Abstract 9.1 at the end of this chapter.) As mentioned earlier, these factors could include the quality characteristics or objectives that are most important to the customer (quality, delivery, service, cost, safety, reliability, cycle time, quantity, and others), the amount of business provided by the particular supplier, the extent of their link to the quality objectives, their frequency of deliveries, invoice errors and resolutions, payment cycle times, or whatever factors are important to maintaining the customer–supplier relationship and the achievement of common goals.

These factors can be selected from the efforts that were done in the linking component of PSQM (see Chapter 5). Some high-level indicators are needed, but some more specific product- and shipment-related indicators should also be maintained for use in problem analysis and continuous improvement. The high-level indicators will track overall progress, but the more specific process-driven indicators will allow both parties to determine root causes and to develop improvement solutions.

For additional information, see the article entitled "PSQM Feedback within the Corporate Measurement System" at the end of this chapter.

FEEDBACK METHODS

There are various ways to provide feedback. It can come in the form of individual contacts, formal meetings, written periodic reports or correspondence, electronic data interchange, or some combination thereof.

Personal Feedback

This type of feedback includes individual and group communication. It is usually done in a one-on-one meeting of the two parties or in a team meeting. This is usually one of the most effective feedback sessions because both parties not only submit their views of the existing status or results for the past period, but they also have the opportunity to interrogate the other party. This questioning and interaction leads to a much clearer understanding and a stronger commitment to the objectives.

In a project team meeting, the subject matter will center around the limited objectives of the team. In a commodity team meeting, the discussion will center around broader issues and may even include reports from project teams. Again, however, personal and team interaction is the key characteristic of this type of feedback. One version of this type of feedback is a team presentation. This is probably the most formal and costly form, but it serves as an incentive and as motivation to the team.

Written Periodic Reports

Written is the key word here. This type of feedback is more formal than personal feedback in that a written report is developed. The report may be simple or complex. Some reports may be periodic in nature and thereby simpler and more of a summary. The supplier report card (discussed later in this chapter) is a good example. Other types of written feedback include statistical process control charts, use of the quality control analysis tools, documentation of procedures, and supplier audit reports, as discussed earlier. These may, of course, be used in conjunction with other types of feedback, such as personal feedback, to provide a more humanistic and committed view.

Electronic Data Interchange

This method of communication has recently taken on a life of its own. It started in the automotive and transportation industries, where a lot of written communication of a very frequent and standard nature was being sent by mail or fax to business partners. Electronic data interchange (EDI, see the American National Standards Institute X12 Subcommittee) has become very widely accepted in communication of business transactions because it creates a much more standard approach. Most companies begin their implementation of EDI with procurement transactions, even though there are many types from which to choose. Purchase orders, bills of lading, receipts, invoices, and sometimes even payments are automated using this method.

Other areas are becoming more popular for transmission of business partner data. Companies are increasingly finding that the expediency and standardization of the X12 transactions can adequately handle most of their current needs and many needs they do not even know they have. For example, companies are starting to use EDI for periodic assessments of key quality characteristics, whereby the key specifications are sent via EDI. New standards are being developed so that even graphics and drawings can eventually be sent using this technology. Some companies already require each supplier to send statistical process control data for the lot being shipped along with the shipping notice or even before. This way the customer can verify that the process is in control. Production schedules, inventory levels, and shipment schedules are also being sent through EDI. This methodology is very instrumental in joining companies together and strengthening their customer–supplier relationships.

Many new technologies similar to EDI will probably be developed in the future. The use of data superhighways such as INTERNET or other on-line services will eventually allow the flow of key pieces of information between customers and suppliers to take place in an efficient, standard, and friendly fashion. This is when many of the feedback issues will be best addressed. Conceptually, the customer could eventually get on-line information about a supplier's process and the supplier could get information about the customer's production process and schedule. *Talk about a partnership!*

STATISTICAL PROCESS CONTROL[1]

Tracking a specific measure to determine if trends are headed in the right direction is an elementary means of statistical process control (SPC). Simple trend and run charts can be used to keep track of some of the indicators to start with, but eventually the most important indicators and, in particular, any product specifications should be monitored using SPC techniques. Some of these techniques will be discussed in this chapter as part of the feedback portion of PSQM.

Definitions

There are many definitions of SPC, but let's develop one here:

- A systematic approach to process decision making
- A way to collect, display, and analyze data in order to make decisions
- A way to determine if a process is acting within specifications
- A way to determine if a process is acting within its normal variability or if something else happened that is affecting the process
- A way to identify opportunities for improvement
- A way to move toward prevention rather than detection and correction
- A way to determine when to take action instead of tampering with a process

A few concepts should be understood if one is to utilize SPC successfully.

Process: A process is a set of steps and decisions that are followed to achieve some purpose or outcome. The purpose of SPC is to understand a process as a system. This understanding increases one's ability to manage the process. It leads to a knowledge of the causes and effects that interact within the process to create the ultimate results or outcome.

Variation: Every process has variation. Nothing is exactly what it is made out to be. There is always variability in all process variables. If you were to measure the time it takes you to get to work in the morning, you would find that it was always different. The diameter of a ball bearing from an assembly line changes from bearing to bearing. Process temperatures and pressures in a chemical plant vary from batch to batch. Most of this variability is natural and is caused by the forces inherent in the process itself.

Common cause variation: Naturally caused variation is inherent in a process just by its design and operation. This type of variation is usually referred to as common cause variation. It is predictable because it is a part of the process itself. This type of variation can only be changed by changing the process itself.

Special cause variation: This type of variation is different and distinct from common cause variation in that it is attributed to a special or assignable cause. It is less frequent than common cause variation and is not usually predictable.

Population and sample: This is the data from the entire process. Because obtaining the data from the whole population is usually cost-prohibitive, a sample or a small subset of the population is studied and analyzed.

Distribution: A group of data points usually follow a certain pattern. These patterns can be visualized on a histogram (see Figure 9.2). A histogram contains many tiny bars that eventually create a smooth curve, which is referred to as the theoretical distribution. Because of the central limit theorem, all averages of samples will be close to a normal distribution or bell-shaped curve.

Detection: The original way to assure quality was through the use of detection techniques. It was believed that application of inspection methods to detect a poor quality product would separate the poor product from the good so that only the good product would be sent to the customer. This was a very inefficient way to assure quality because action to fix the problem would only be initiated after the fact.

Prevention: This mode of quality control is more upstream of the process. Measures are taken of the process at it happens. These measures are taken throughout the process rather than just at inspection at the end of the process. Problems with the process are identified early by the workers, who can make adjustments in the process and reduce the potential for poor product at the end of the process. This method improves quality by improving the process itself. In order to do this, the process and its causal relationships must be understood.

Types of Measures

Variable: This type of data comes from some measurement on a continuous scale. It could be process or product characteristics such as temperature, length, weight, pH, time, or strength. An Xbar–R chart is usually used to monitor and control processes whose key measurements are variable in nature.

Attribute: These data are a result of counting or classifying a characteristic or feature of a process or product. This could be the number of entry errors on a purchase order, invoice errors per month, percent of invoices with errors, defects per square foot of electrical insulating blankets, etc. These types of measures are usually controlled using a p chart or a c chart.

Statistics

Over the years, professionals who work with a lot of data have developed measures to describe the sample and population data they are analyzing. These measures are referred to as descriptive statistics. They can be categorized as follows.

Measures of central tendency: These are used to define the center of the distribution being analyzed. Three measures are usually used:

- **Mean:** The arithmetic average that is denoted by Xbar for the sample mean and μ for the population mean
- **Median:** The data point which 50 percent of the sample is above and 50 percent of the sample is below
- **Mode:** The most frequently occurring data point in a sample

Measures of dispersion: These are used to determine how much variability there is in the sample, i.e., how spread out the samples are. The most common of these measures are:

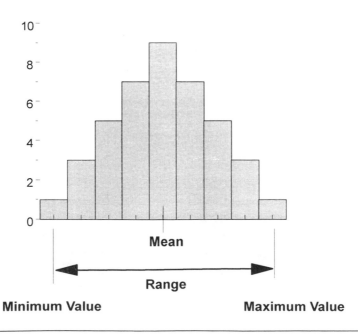

Figure 9.2 Statistics.

- **Range:** The difference between the minimum and the maximum in the sample, denoted by R.
- **Variance:** The sum of the squared differences of each data point from the mean of the sample, denoted by s^2 for a sample variance and by σ^2 for a population variance
- **Standard deviation:** The square root of the variance, denoted by s for the sample standard variation and by σ for the population standard variation

The mean, range, minimum, and maximum are displayed in Figure 9.2

One of the most important concepts in SPC is understanding the portion of the total normal distribution that falls within a certain number of standard deviations from the mean. In Figure 9.3, 68.3 percent of the distribution falls within ±1 standard deviation from the mean, 95.5 percent falls within ±2 standard deviations from the mean, and 99.7 percent or the great majority of the distribution falls within ±3

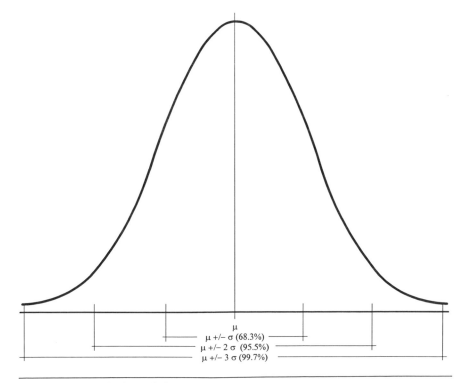

Figure 9.3 Bell-Shaped Curve.

standard deviations from the mean. This means that for any distribution of sample means that are normally distributed, the chances of being outside of 3 standard deviations is very small—less than 0.3 percent. This condition creates the basis for some of the most powerful tools in SPC, one of which is control charts.

Tools

Two sets of tools are used in SPC. The first is usually utilized at receipt or final inspection, while the second is used during the process. Each type of measure also requires a different type of tool (see Tables 9.1 and 9.2).

The different tools, methods, and charts in Tables 9.1 and 9.2 can be used, as mentioned, in different applications. Various books deal with this issue of SPC in its entirety. For example, Hitoshi Kume's[2] book entitled *Statistical Methods for Quality Improvement* is an excellent short manual on the subject. A definitive work on the subject of statistics is Duncan's[3] book on *Quality Control and Industrial Statistics.* In the following section, an application of an Xbar–R chart will be developed, describing how such a tool could be used in a PSQM environment.

Case Using an Xbar–R Chart

For purposes of illustration, a very simple case from the automotive industry is selected. One of the most common parts utilized in automotive manufacturing is the ball bearing. It has a few important characteristics, among which are diameter and hardness. This example will concentrate on the diameter. Note that these bearings are used in

Table 9.1 Receipt and Final Inspection

Type	Attribute measure	Variables measure
Physical	Visual	Visual
Military plan	MIL Standard 105E	MIL Standard 414
ANSI	ANSI Z1.4	ANSI Z1.9
ISO	ISO Std. 3951	ISO Std. 2859
Inspection	100% Sort	100% Sort

Table 9.2   Process

Type of data	Attribute measure	Variables measure
Individual		X–moving range chart
Average		Xbar–R chart
Fraction defective	p chart	
No. of defective units	np chart	
No. of defects	c chart	
No. of defects per unit	u chart	

other subassemblies and on later assemblies of a truck. If the process that produces the bearings can be controlled, then one of the key characteristics of the subassemblies that utilize the bearings and later the functionality of the truck wheel assembly will be controlled as it pertains to the bearings. Examples of Xbar and R charts for these bearings are shown in Figure 9.4 and 9.5. The average of the process is centered exactly at the center of the specification.

The specification is 10 mm ± 0.01 mm. This will become important in calculating the capability of this process. The first thing to do is to determine if the R chart (Figure 9.5) values are in statistical control (see next section). If these values are in control, then the Xbar chart (Figure 9.4) can be analyzed. Otherwise, it is advantageous for the team to first work on reducing the variability of the process; once the variability is in control, then the team can look at the Xbar chart. In this case, the R chart is in control because none of the values fall outside of the upper and lower control limits and no patterns are evident. Therefore, the team can analyze the Xbar chart. Looking at this chart, the process

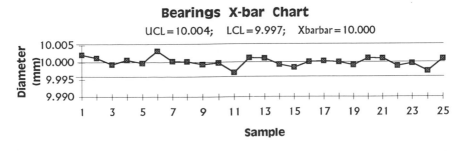

Figure 9.4   Bearings Xbar Chart.

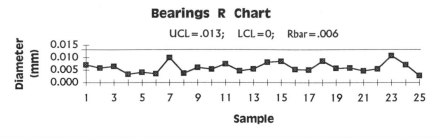

Figure 9.5 Bearings R Chart.

appears to be in control, but three points are very close to the control limits: samples 6, 11, and 24. The team should examine these three cases to see if there were any special causes that created the situation. This may help identify an area that can then be improved using some of the methods described in Chapter 8, especially the Systematic Improvement Method.

This type of SPC data can also be used for certification of the quality of a shipment. Some buying organizations now require their suppliers to provide such data with every shipment or at least periodically. These data can also become part of the supplier certification process (discussed in Chapter 6). One of the key benefits of this type of data is that it creates a common understanding of the actual process behavior between the customer and the supplier. Through joint analysis it can also help establish the causal relationships in the process, which provides a basis for greater trust between the two parties.

For additional information, see Abstract 9.2 at the end of this chapter.

Process Status

Statistical Control

Each process has a set of key quality characteristics that can be used to determine if the process is meeting the needs of its customers. If a quality or product characteristic is being managed using a control chart (as mentioned in the section on tools), then it is considered to be in statistical control (or in control for short) if the sample statistics that are being plotted stay within the statistical control limits that have

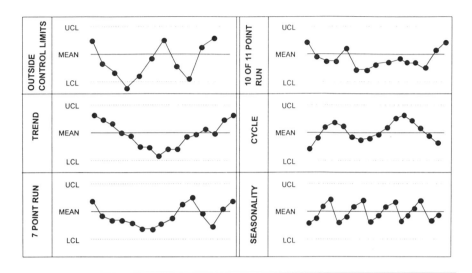

Figure 9.6 Control Chart Patterns.

been calculated for that type of chart. In addition, no particular pattern can be present that would imply the existence of a special cause. Some of the different patterns that would imply the presence of a special cause are shown in Figure 9.6. Any other nonrandom pattern would also imply the existence of a special cause.

Process Capability

A process is considered "capable" if it is producing products that consistently fall within specifications. A statistical index has been developed to quantify the degree to which a process falls within specifications. This index measures how much of the process distribution falls within the specifications. It is calculated as shown in Figure 9.7. There are actually two indices. The first, which is designated Cp, measures the whole distribution without regard for the location of the center of the distribution vs. the specification limits. The second index, called Cpk, is more accurate because it takes the worst situation into consideration (i.e., whether any of the tails of the distribution are outside the specification limits).

A process is considered to be capable if the Cp or better yet the Cpk is greater than 1. Most world-class companies urge their suppliers to provide products and services with a Cpk greater than 1.33 or 2.

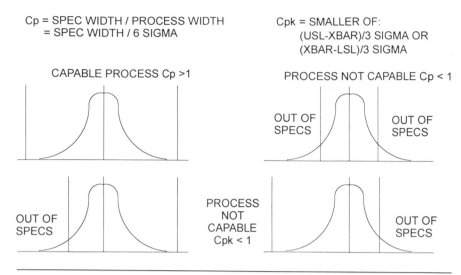

Cp = SPEC WIDTH / PROCESS WIDTH
= SPEC WIDTH / 6 SIGMA

Cpk = SMALLER OF:
(USL-XBAR)/3 SIGMA OR
(XBAR-LSL)/3 SIGMA

CAPABLE PROCESS Cp >1

PROCESS NOT CAPABLE Cp < 1

OUT OF SPECS

OUT OF SPECS

OUT OF SPECS

PROCESS NOT CAPABLE Cpk < 1

OUT OF SPECS

Figure 9.7   Process Capability.

This is more difficult to achieve, but by working together with their customers, suppliers have been very successful in meeting these requirements.

Let's continue the case that was started earlier for control charts. The Xbar–R chart showed that the process was in control but that some points were a little close to the upper and lower control limits. Now the Cp and Cpk of this process can be calculated to determine if the process is capable. This should only be done once the process has been determined to be in statistical control. For this example:

$$\text{Spec Width} = \pm 0.01 \text{ mm}$$

$$= 0.02 \text{ mm}$$

$$\text{Cp} = \frac{\text{Spec Width}}{6\sigma}$$

$$= \frac{0.02}{6\,\overline{R}/d_2}$$

$$= \frac{0.02}{6(0.006 \,/\, 2.326)}$$

$$= 1.29$$

According to this index, the process is capable. This is of course if the major assumption is true (i.e., that the process averages and ranges are normally distributed and are centered at the center of the specifications). All the estimates were made assuming that this assumption is true. This assumption can be tested by plotting the data collected on normal probability graph paper or using some other distribution test such as a chi-square test. If the assumption is true, it can be concluded that the process is capable. If the distribution is not totally symmetrical or the specifications are not symmetrical or equal on both sides, then a stronger test can be run to test the tails of the process distribution. This is called a Cpk index. In our case:

$$Cpk = \text{smaller of } \frac{\text{Upper Spec Limit} - \overline{\overline{X}}}{3\sigma} \text{ or}$$

$$\frac{\text{Xbar bar} - \text{Lower Spec Limit}}{3\sigma}$$

$$= \text{smaller of } \frac{10.01 - 10.000}{3\overline{R}/d_2} \text{ or}$$

$$\frac{10.000 - 9.99}{3\overline{R}/d_2}$$

$$= \text{smaller of } \frac{0.01}{3(0.006/2.326)} \text{ or}$$

$$\frac{0.01}{3(0.006/2.326)}$$

$$= 1.29$$

In this example, both Cp and Cpk are identical. This only occurs in the best-managed processes. Generally, they will not be the same, and the Cpk will be a stronger indicator of process capability. Our example shows a process that is in control (except for some potentially dangerous samples) and is capable!

This capability index is being used very extensively as a key measure of quality. A supplier that can provide products or services with capability indices above 1.00 has processes that are mostly capable. This measurement can be a key indicator in a periodic supplier report card, along with other measurements that the customer finds important. This indicator can also be used to rate suppliers in the supplier selection process (see the case study at the end of this book for more detail). The ratings can be developed periodically and fed back to the supplier for discussion, as mentioned earlier in this chapter.

SUPPLIER REPORT CARD

One of the feedback methods discussed earlier is a written periodic feedback report. Some companies have established a standardized report that they use to rate their suppliers and can send to their suppliers. This gives the suppliers first-hand knowledge of the buying organization's viewpoint of their performance. If the feedback is detailed enough, it can provide an excellent basis for improvement opportunities within the supplier's organization. A sample format for a supplier report card is provided in Figure 9.8.

Summary information: This includes the supplier's name, locations included in the report card, time period, and summaries of some of the indices that are reported elsewhere in the report card.

Quality objectives: The report card may include the current status of key quality characteristics or objectives of the buying organization as affected by the supplier. For example, if the buying organiza-

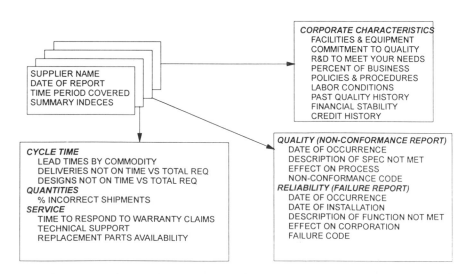

Figure 9.8   Supplier Report Card.

tion has a cycle time quality objective, then it would be appropriate to track order lead time, deliveries not on time, or designs not on time by supplier. This information can be used to rate the supplier and should also be provided to each supplier. Each supplier would be provided with its own information. Strict confidentiality must be maintained. An index of all suppliers, anonymously summarizing the best and worst, could be developed so that each supplier could benchmark its own performance against the aggregate.

Specific detail reports: This section includes individual data points related to the performance criteria that are being tracked. For example, any instances of quality or reliability problems could be reported. Along with this information, the supplier would be informed of the effect of the problem on the buying organization. This would allow the supplier to understand the areas that need the most improvement.

Organization characteristics: Another part of the report card could include the buying organization's viewpoint of the supplier's facilities and equipment, commitment to quality, research and development, labor conditions, policies, finances, credit history, etc. This is not an all-inclusive list. It should include whatever the buying organization finds is important for the viability of the supplier and the potential for a long-term customer–supplier relationship as described earlier.

SUPPLIER SCORING METHODS

There are basically three methods that are in common use to rate and score suppliers, some of which have already been mentioned or applied throughout this book.

Categorical: This is one of the simplest semi-quantitative methods used to rate suppliers. It relies on the judgment of key personnel affected in the buying organization. This might include the purchasing buyer, purchasing manager, engineering, or manufacturing. All rate the supplier on a plus (+), minus (–), or neutral (0) basis on specific characteristics or performance criteria that the buying organization deems important. These ratings are then summarized and are given to the supplier. The ratings could be used in the supplier selection and order award process. More advanced users of this method would have performance data to support the ratings that were provided.

Weighted point: This method is similar to the categorical in that specific characteristics and performance criteria are first selected. There are two big differences, however. The first is that the characteristics and criteria are *weighted* before a rating is given. The second is that once the weight has been established, a numerical rating (from 1 to 5, 1 to 10, etc.) is assigned to each criterion by each of the members on a team from the buying organization. The sum of the products of the weights and the scores is used to compare one supplier to another. The members of the team should be persuaded to utilize data to support the ratings, and the ratings should have specific definitions attached to them. The regular and extended prioritization matrices discussed in Chapter 5 are examples of this type of scoring method, although they go beyond the standard weighted point approach. The House of Quality method (described later) is a further extension of this methodology.

Cost ratio: This method utilizes the concept of life cycle cost to first determine all costs associated with the acquisition, use, and disposal of a particular product or service from a specific supplier. Life cycle costs were explained in Chapter 5. These costs can be classified into different categories or they can simply be taken as a total. A ratio of these costs for each supplier is calculated relative to the total purchase price. If the total costs were classified, then the individual category costs are used to create separate cost ratios for each category. The total cost ratio is used to adjust the bid price. An adjustment in the bid price is then made by multiplying the bid price for each supplier by one plus that supplier's total cost ratio:

Adjusted bid price = Bid price × (1 + supplier total cost ratio)

This adjusted bid price is then compared to bids from other suppliers. This method is not in total alignment with the principles discussed earlier for PSQM because price or cost seems to be most important, but it has been used successfully and should at least be considered.

House of Quality: This method is very similar to the weighted point method discussed above, but it places much greater emphasis on customer needs, quality characteristics, and supplier policy deployment. This method compares best with the method described in Chapter 5. Gopalakrishnan et al.[4] have written a very good article on the use of the House of Quality for internal customer–supplier relationships.

SUPPLIER SELECTION

In previous chapters some of the discussion centered around supplier policy deployment and the selection of suppliers with which to start a long-term customer relationship. Once these suppliers are selected, it is time to begin working with them to implement TQM within their organization. One final question remains, however: how to select which supplier will be awarded a particular order and how much of the order. This concept is difficult to grasp. Initially, the feedback information that is being collected can be used to rate the suppliers. Using either a weighted point or House of Quality approach, the suppliers can be rated in order to decide which supplier to award what percent of the business. At this point, it may be to the buying organization's advantage to keep a few suppliers that are able to provide the product or service. The total purchase volume can simply be proportionately allocated to the best suppliers with the highest ratings. This would create split orders, which is contrary to the concept of reducing the number of suppliers. However, an organization that starts with ten valid suppliers for one part or service and reduces the number to three has already made a significant improvement. Eventually, a highly certified supplier may be capable of supplying the total order for that product or service. The buying organization needs to assess the benefits and risks of such a decision.

The buying organization may want to consider awarding rating points to a supplier based on the level of certification it has achieved. This can create a highly motivated field of suppliers who will join the PSQM program and proceed as fast as possible in order to gain the competitive advantage over other suppliers.

ENDNOTES

1. Fernandez, Ricardo R. (1993). *Statistical Process Control.* Miami: Advent Group, Inc.
2. Kume, Hitoshi (1985). *Statistical Methods for Quality Improvement.* Tokyo: The Association for Overseas Technical Scholarship.
3. Duncan, Acheson J. (1986). *Quality Control and Industrial Statistics.* Homewood, Ill.: Irwin.
4. Gopalakrishnan, K.N., McIntyre, Barry E., and Sprague, James C. (1992). "Implementing Internal Quality Improvement with the House of Quality." *Quality Progress,* September 1992, pp. 57–60.
5. Figures 9.1 to 9.8 ©Advent Group, Inc.

ABSTRACTS

ABSTRACT 9.1
AFTER PRODUCT QUALITY IN JAPAN: MANAGEMENT QUALITY

Yahagi, Seiichiro
National Productivity Review, Autumn 1992, pp. 501–515

This is one of the most important new articles to come out of Japan in 1992. The author proposes the use of expert systems that feature a 12-factor model organized into 41 "elements" for measuring subfactors. Japanese management has moved beyond product quality, says the author, to an emphasis on total integrated management (TIM)—management concerned about each facet of the company and interrelating them into a concerted, comprehensive corporate management policy of innovation. The author has developed an expert system to measure the 12 factors that determine management quality, divided into 41 subfactors. He views six factors as critical to the success of a company: management cycle, business structure, management resources, management design, corporate culture, and management performance. His consulting organization conducts an annual survey of the management practices of Japanese firms, and in this article he presents the results of the most recent survey, which represents input from about 200 firms. Graphs and charts show comparisons between the worst-scoring and best-scoring companies, and creative graphics are used to illustrate the author's analytical technique and to summarize questionnaire responses. From this comparison, he formulates a number of principles: (a) management quality factors must be well-balanced, (b) management cycle is the key to the management quality loop, and (c) the dynamics of TIM must be considered. The author recommends using an annual questionnaire to first analyze management factors within a company and then developing a multiphase action plan to restructure an organization for TIM. This article is must reading for anyone who wants to stay on the leading edge of new application-oriented technology.

ABSTRACT 9.2
QUALITY FORECASTING DRIVES
QUALITY INVENTORY AT GE SILICONES

Duncan, Robert M.
Industrial Engineering, January 1992, pp. 18–21

When GE Silicones sought to apply SPC to inventory control, they turned to the *Finished Goods Series* (FGS) software from E/Step Software, Inc. of Teiton, Washington. This PC-based program is a demand forecasting and inventory management package that has facilities for identifying and reviewing those items that require something other than routine handling. The package includes a simulation model to allow experimentation with various strategies for handling exception items before the changes are actually made. A Pareto analysis was carried out to identify the few critical items to be tracked. Then five years of demand history was loaded into FGS and an optimal model was determined for each scenario. The author describes how FGS detected seasonality, how it handled adaptive smoothing and error tracking, and how to determine where a chosen model is no longer appropriate. "There is not enough time to review every SKU's error," he says. "But using techniques of statistical process control and control charting, it is possible to detect exceptional errors." He discusses how the program was used to filter the previous month's demand, identify trend changes, lower forecast error, tighten outlier sensitivity, and, where appropriate, manually override the program's forecast. The author explains that as the forecast is refined for a product, the program can be made more sensitive to variation by lowering the standard deviation level, which will trigger tracking signals. The article includes examples of charts and analyses produced by the program. "As a general rule," says the author, "GE saves about $10,000 in inventory for each hour spent using the simulation software to review exceptions." (*©Quality Abstracts*)

ARTICLES

BUILDING THE SUPPLIER-FOCUSED ISO 9000 QUALITY MEASUREMENT SYSTEM

Frank Voehl

> *If you can't measure it, you can't manage it.*
> Peter Drucker

INTRODUCTION

While many organizations are embarking on some form of a quality assurance system, which often involves ISO 9000 either today or in the future, few have implemented an accompanying measurement system that can be used to figure out how good a job is being done. Because so few have done this well enough to be examples for industries to follow, it is difficult to do any real benchmarking in this area.

From the studies conducted on the practices of excellent companies, however, some operating models have resulted. One of the most useful is the Corporate Measurement System (CMS), based on the work of Jack Rockart of MIT and others. This model suggests the use of a vital few critical success factors, which are linked to the business objectives and processes, around which to build the ISO 9000 corporate indicator system.

What formerly took three years or more to accomplish can now be done in three to six months using available software packages such as COMSHARE or PILOT. In addition to implementation speed and economy, the CMS approach is extremely flexible in terms of environment, future needs, and changes. Finally, it is user-friendly, with high-level macros and commands that greatly facilitate its use.

Source: This material is adapted from *Building the Corporate Measurement System* by Frank Voehl (©1992 Strategy Associates, Coral Springs, Fla). Used with permission of the author.

OVERVIEW

Organizations embarking on a supplier-focused ISO 9000 system need a measurement system that is simple and flexible in design, easy to use and modify, and is integrated into key functions and processes. The information provided needs to be timely and accurate and must be perceived by employees as truly useful and not just another way that management can monitor them. Instead, what is needed is a measurement system that people can use to better manage their efforts and to link all areas of the company, from the field or office to the corporate vision.

The following are the attributes that are needed in ISO 9000 measurement (the term ISO 9000 measurement system should be understood as a supplier-focused quality assurance system):

- Simple system that is easy to understand
- Employee commitment and motivation
- Specific objectives, procedures, and guidelines for use
- Consistent, continuous monitoring
- Assignment of specific responsibility and accountability
- Top management interest and support
- Timeliness
- Good lines of communication
- Good monitoring staff who provide competent analysis
- Periodic reports
- Useful and relevant information
- Accurate, reliable information linked to the ISO 9000 strategy and business objectives

SUPPLIER-FOCUSED MEASUREMENT SYSTEM PRINCIPLES AND OBJECTIVES

There are two guiding principles to be followed when developing ISO 9000 measurement systems: (1) people on the front lines of the organization respond best to information relevant to their piece of the world and (2) when people have relevant information about things they deem important and can influence, they become very committed to using the information.

The following is a summary of ISO 9000 measurement system objectives:

- Translate the vision to measurable outcomes all employees understand.

- Focus and align the direction of employees based on measurable results.
- Track ISO 9000 breakthrough and continuous improvement results.
- Foster accountability and commitment.
- Integrate strategic plans, business plans, quality, and benchmarking.
- Provide standards for benchmarking.
- Problem-solve business operations.
- Provide a basis for ISO 9000 reward and recognition.
- Create individual and shared views of performance.

MEASUREMENT SYSTEM OVERVIEW

Two types of measures must be considered when implementing an ISO 9000 measurement system: outcome (or macro) measures and process (or micro) measures.

Outcome measures are often called macro due to their broad nature, which generally reflects an after-the-fact type of indicator. Examples are return on investment, or equity, overall customer satisfaction, etc.

Micro, or process, measures represent work-in-process types of situations and are often used for "upstream control" or prevention of problem situations. Most effective measurement systems have a combination of macro and micro indicators.

Micro measures act as tripwires to enable examining processes to determine whether speed of actions can be increased and time, cycle, and steps decreased. Macro measures help to focus on measuring the results of leadership on the ISO 9000 outcomes and help to communicate the vision to find out whether the message is being received. Conversation among people in the field needs to be encouraged to help determine if the processes attributable to a particular corporate function enhance or inhibit the ability to create external customer satisfaction. In other words, do the functions and processes enhance or inhibit the journey along the path of ISO 9000?

CATEGORIES OF MEASURES

There are seven general or broad categories into which most types of ISO 9000 measures can be classified or grouped: accuracy, responsiveness, timeliness, customer satisfaction, cost, safety, and corporate responsibility.

The first three—accuracy, responsiveness, and timeliness—refer to the manner and speed with which the organization conducts its business transactions. The fourth category—customer satisfaction—can also include employee satisfaction when employees are viewed as internal customers. The fifth and sixth categories—cost and safety—can be broken down into a wide variety of subcategories. The final category—corporate responsibility—is often replaced in smaller organizations with a more relevant category that relates to the competition.

Templates, or flowcharts, are used to first link all existing measures to the corporate vision and objectives. Once existing indices are linked, gaps and missing indices are identified and added to the system where appropriate. Decisions are also made to modify or eliminate existing indices as new ones are added. Overall, there are generally between 25 to 50 detailed indicators that are distributed among the seven broad categories.

ROLE OF THE ISO 9000 CONSULTANT

The following services can be provided by the consultant in support of the ISO 9000 measurement system:

- Coach and guide the executive management team in the planning, development, and administration of the ISO 9000 measurement system.
- Assist corporate management in developing a linked chain of business objectives for the overall organization.
- Facilitate the development of critical success factors for key business areas, including elements of measure, related indices, and benchmarks.
- Develop a detailed master plan for implementation, including resources and infrastructure required.
- Pull together current measurement indices, help analyze their validity and usefulness for ISO 9000, and recommend areas for streamlining and improvement.
- Consolidate all measurement efforts into an ISO 9000 measurement system.
- Integrate ISO 9000 measurement into other existing corporate systems (such as strategic planning, business planning, quality, etc.) and ensure that this is done in a simplified manner.
- Work with staff and management to assign accountability and ownership for results at all levels.
- Oversee the design of support systems and controls, including screen format and system prototypes, including the selection of application software, where required.

- Validate the integrity of measures and indices and ensure measurements are working properly and accurately.

SUMMARY

The pursuit of ISO 9000 without an accompanying measurement system can resemble the proverbial shot in the dark: everybody knows where they want to go, but no one is sure of the miles traveled so far or the distance yet to go. Focused measurement can act not only as the integrator but also as the monitor of progress. We would never think of driving a car for long distances without checking the gas gauge. All too often, however, ISO 9000 can run out of gas because the gauges were not put in place at the beginning to track progress along the way.

NOTE

For further information on ISO 9000, see Chapter 7.

CHAPTER 10

STRATEGY FOR IMPLEMENTATION

The major steps for implementing an effective purchasing/supplier quality management (PSQM) system are outlined in this chapter. Keep in mind that the action plan to be unveiled is not a prescription; each organization exists in its own unique set of circumstances. Therefore, unfortunately, no universal blueprint for execution can be provided. However, there are guidelines or principles that point the way to proper PSQM implementation. These guiding principles act as signposts on the road to PSQM. The signposts that tell us which way to turn will be highlighted in this chapter. Hence, in the following pages a sound and principled approach to excellence in PSQM will be delineated, but it is by no means the only approach. Each organization must consider all the alternatives and the associated benefits and risks before deciding which strategy is most suitable.

MANAGEMENT COMMITMENT

The first step in the implementation of PSQM is gaining the support of upper management. Because this approach touches so many areas of the organization, it is important to obtain the support and eventually the approval of the top management of the organization. With this kind of commitment, others who may be less willing to change will become more cooperative and will listen more readily to other ways of doing things.

The PSQM Champion

A champion is needed at first to get the ball rolling. The ideal PSQM champion would be a chief executive officer with a fundamental understanding of total quality management and the role of the supplier. Someone with the ear of the CEO would be advisable. However, the focal point might be a director or vice-president of procurement or even an experienced purchasing agent. The champion should be someone who deals with the buying organization's supplier network on a daily basis and who is well known and respected throughout the organization. Whoever is chosen, gaining top management commitment requires, first and foremost, understanding management's perspective and salient needs.

Selling the Concept

Like with any good lawyer or debater, one must initially try to understand the other side's point of view. In other words, know your target audience's argument better than they themselves do. Demonstrating an understanding of key issues and concerns wins trust. In effect, credibility is being built by diagnosing before prescribing. At this juncture, management is listening because you have taken the time to do the same. Next, present your case, highlighting benefits, just as any good salesman would. Finally, spell out mutually advantageous desired outcomes and suggest some viable courses of action.

Suggested Tactics

Once mutual understanding has been established, the following are some basic tactics for obtaining management buy in:

- **Inform management:** Enlighten the leadership of the organization by providing them with information on the virtues of PSQM. Suggest that they watch relevant videos or listen to audio cassette programs. Prompt key decision makers to attend public seminars or bring in a consultant to deliver a customized PSQM awareness seminar.
- **Learn from the best**: One way to benchmark is to examine the "best practices" of competitors. Show management PSQM in action. A field trip to an organization that is doing the right things can make for an eye-opening experience.
- **Start small**: Choose a small part of the company in which to launch a pilot project with a high payoff potential. Small successes generate curiosity. Everyone likes a winner. Build momentum toward organization-wide deployment of PSQM. These successes will help to solidify the commitment that has been initiated and will build the foundation upon which others in management can join in the PSQM bandwagon.

ESTABLISH A DESIGN AND IMPLEMENTATION TEAM

Each area in an organization usually has its own particular needs, which are associated with the products and services it receives from its suppliers. If each area were allowed to discuss these needs individually with each supplier, mass confusion would result. The suppliers would receive different instructions depending upon with which area of the organization they were communicating. This situation would ultimately be harmful in trying to establish or maintain a customer–supplier relationship. A unified effort should be considered to design a common system that would be used to develop and maintain these customer–supplier relationships throughout the organization. This effort can be unified by establishing a PSQM design and implementation team (DIT).

Team Member Selection

Some key questions to assist in determining team structure and selecting team members are as follows:

- Who could provide the information that would help render a good design of the PSQM system?
- Who could be responsible for implementing this system and a pilot project?
- Who will be affected by the PSQM system?
- Who has the time available to devote himself or herself fully to this effort until the implementation effort is complete?
- Are the potential team members well respected by their internal customers and by the supplier organizations?
- Does the assembled team reflect the different disciplines within the buying organization (i.e., purchasing, engineering, manufacturing, marketing/sales, finance/accounting)?

Roles of the Design and Implementation Team

The DIT is in charge of engineering a PSQM system that will facilitate integrating the voice of the suppliers with the voice of the buying organization. The team will be charged with the design and implementation of a PSQM system that will enable the requirements of the internal customers within the buying organization to be met or exceeded by their suppliers. Once those requirements have been met, the system will in turn allow the internal customers to better meet the needs of their external customer. In order to accomplish this, the following roles are suggested for the DIT:

- Assess the expectations that internal customers from all areas of the organization have of their suppliers. This should include the highest executive levels as well as all departments directly affected by a potential PSQM system.
- Compile a list of corporate quality objectives and express them as the buying organization's expectations of its suppliers.
- Benchmark and research methods used by best-in-class organizations that are well known for the success of their PSQM systems. Certain organizations are mentioned throughout this book, but there are certainly others from which to choose. The literature (especially professional magazines, articles, etc.) is an excellent source.
- Using the information gathered, define the work flow, steps, activities, roles, and responsibilities of the processes within the proposed

PSQM system. This should be done in such a way that the expectations previously determined can be maximized. An organization may decide to follow suggestions from previous chapters in this book in designing the system or can choose to modify them as it sees fit for internal reasons.

- Design the PSQM organization structure and assist upper management in the selection of individuals who will be assigned to a PSQM council (organization and the roles are explained more fully later in this chapter). The subcommittees (described later) do not need to be established this early in the process. They can be established after the pilot phase of this project.
- Along with the PSQM council, the DIT should develop an implementation plan. This plan will describe the steps needed to implement the overall PSQM system through at least one cycle (pilot phase). The outcome of this step would be a plan that has been bought into and approved by the PSQM council.
- Design the initial internal training program and, along with the newly created PSQM council, deliver this program to internal parties who would probably be involved in an initial pilot project.
- The DIT assists the PSQM council through one cycle of the PSQM system. This would include supplier quality deployment, symposia, project selection, support, continuous improvement, monitoring, and possibly certification. These implementation steps will be more thoroughly explained in the following sections of this chapter. Figure 10.1 is also helpful in understanding the process flow.
- Based on the results of the pilot project, the DIT, along with the PSQM council, evaluates the effectiveness of the PSQM system to gain the benefit of lessons that can be learned and applied in enhancing the system prior to undertaking future projects.
- Finally, the DIT and the PSQM council make appropriate adjustments to the PSQM system in preparation for standardization of the system throughout the buying organization.
- Once the PSQM system has been standardized, the PSQM council will continue in existence to carry forward the work, but the DIT will be disbanded, with members of the team joining either the PSQM council or some of the other committees or commodity teams, as described later in this chapter.

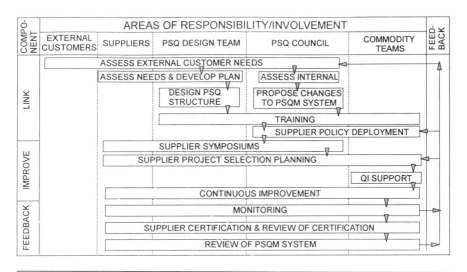

Figure 10.1 PSQM Implementation and Operations.

PSQM IMPLEMENTATION PLANNING

The key to PSQM implementation planning is linking the supplier to the strategic quality plan. A good place to start is by inviting some suppliers to a strategic planning retreat, during which issues such as the following will be addressed: Where are we (the buying organization) going? Who among you (the suppliers of choice) are going our way? Naturally, a broad contingent of ultimate customers are also involved in strategic planning sessions. The customers are heard out so as to glean information about their needs and desires, all of which must be prioritized in order of importance. A series of quality improvement goals and objectives flow from the customers' needs and desires. By now, the DIT has done significant research and benchmarking with other organizations and should be very familiar with the most successful systems that have been implemented. Their input and that of the PSQM council members is also crucial in setting up a plan that can be acceptable to the key parties involved in the implementation effort.

Some of the basic ingredients that go into planning primarily involve asking the what, why, who, how, and when of things. The following questions can be asked to guide the planning process:

- What do we want out of the customer–supplier relationship?
- What are the desired goals?
- What road will take us there?
- What resources are needed to make it happen?
- What criteria or benchmarks will govern accomplishing our task?
- Why do we want the customer–supplier relationships to work this way?
- Who could contribute important information for making a sound decision regarding the customer–supplier relationship?
- Who are the parties responsible for executing the implementation and later the operation and improvement of the PSQM system?
- How can we clarify roles and relationships and coordinate our efforts?
- How will we know we are on track to an effective customer–supplier relationship?
- If not on track, what process will we employ to get back on track?
- How long before we reach proposed benchmarks?

The preceding questions are fundamental to any quality business initiative. Quality is an inside-out approach: it begins with the buying organization and proceeds to the supplier enterprise. Should these questions be answered ambiguously or not answered at all, the partnership will be jeopardized, the result of which will be unacceptable product or service quality. Note that there are no predetermined correct answers to these questions. The answers will differ according to what is right for each organization. Nonetheless, a one-year plan is suggested in which the vision, goals, and objectives for a successful PSQM system are defined. The buying organization might consider starting with a small, manageable pilot project, especially if the partnering arrangement is new to both the supplier and customer organizations. The pilot effort should prove a valuable reference for future applications.

For additional information, see Abstract 10.1 at the end of this chapter.

Project Management Tools

This entire implementation effort can be considered a project until it has been standardized and has become part of the way business is conducted at the buying organization. It is important to ensure that the plan that is developed can actually be implemented. A set of project management tools and methodologies are available to assist in this effort. This subject is covered quite extensively in the literature; therefore, only a few of the tools will be mentioned in this section. Two of the tools that are most commonly used today are the Gantt chart and the critical path method (CPM). The Japanese Union of Scientists and Engineers also refers to the CPM as the arrow diagram. It is one of their "Seven New QC Tools," as designated by Mizuno[1] in his book on the subject.

A useful tool for planning, scheduling, and organizational purposes is the Gantt chart (Figure 10.2). In short, the tool provides information as to where one should be along the path to task completion, who is responsible for task accomplishment, and when the job should be done.

Figure 10.2 is a very simplified version of the implementation plan broken down into three phases. The legend shows the corresponding patterns for the scheduled and actual times for each phase. The long vertical bar represents the current time. By comparing the current time and the actual time, the chart indicates if the phases are on schedule and if schedules have changed. By analyzing a chart such as this, the DIT can determine if their implementation plan is on schedule, and if

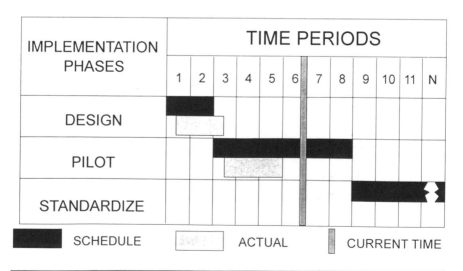

Figure 10.2 Simplified PSQM Implementation Gantt Chart.

not why. Additionally, they can develop countermeasures to get the project back on track. Without a simple tool such as this, expectations are unclear and the project would be difficult to manage.

PSQM STRUCTURE

In order for a system to be properly designed, the activities, decisions, and flow of the system need to be established, but the environment or structure that will assist the system to function with as little resistance as possible and in an organized way also needs to be determined. For this reason, one possible PSQM structure is presented in this section (see Figure 10.3). It is composed of four main entities:

- PSQM council
- PSQM planning, improvement, and performance (feedback) subcommittees
- Commodity teams

Each of these entities will be explained further in this section.

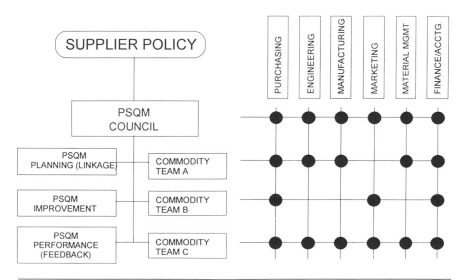

Figure 10.3 PSQM Structure.

Purchasing/Supplier Quality Management Council

The purchasing/supplier quality management council (PSQMC) is an interdepartmental team that is responsible for managing the supplier–customer relationship. It consists of high-level management, each representing a business unit or collection of units from all areas involved in the PSQM system. Questions similar to those asked to determine the membership of the DITs should be asked at this juncture. The answers will determine the makeup of the PSQMC. Unlike the DIT, the mission of the PSQMC is ongoing. The mission of the DIT is shorter in length because the team only exists during the design and implementation pilot phases (see Figure 10.4).

The role of the PSQMC includes the following:

- Develop policy for the PSQM system
- Direct the implementation of the PSQM system throughout the organization
- Monitor the effectiveness of the PSQM system periodically
- Review and evaluate the PSQM system periodically and determine changes that might be needed to improve the overall system
- Allocate resources to support the efforts of the PSQM system
- Approve certification of suppliers to different levels
- Represent the buying organization during award visits to supplier sites

IMPLEMENTATION PHASES	PSQM STRUCTURE			
	DIT	PSQC	SUB-COMMITTEES	COMMODITY TEAMS
DESIGN	●			
PILOT	●	●		
STANDARDIZE		●	●	●

Figure 10.4 PSQM Structure Timing.

PSQM Planning, Improvement, and Performance (Feedback) Subcommittees

Three subcommittees are formed under the PSQMC:

- **PSQM planning subcommittee** is primarily responsible for linking up with potential suppliers and selecting those that fill the buyer organization's expectations.
- **PSQM improvement subcommittee** works on improvement by advocating TQM to supplier organizations, assisting suppliers with quality improvement projects, and helping with certification.
- **PSQM performance (feedback) subcommittee** is responsible for feeding back information to the supplier on specific priority concerns such as quality, quantity, and delivery. Based on the feedback, suppliers can take corrective action to reduce variance in key business processes.

These subcommittees are activated once the standardization phase (see Figure 10.4) is initiated. At this point, sufficient knowledge and experience with the process have been gained. Lessons learned have been applied, and subcommittee membership criteria can easily be derived.

Note that these subcommittees do not have to be comprised of the same personnel who serve on the PSQMC. The subcommittees may consist of people who report to PSQMC members, past members of the DIT, or endless other combinations. The important thing is to ensure that the committees are staffed by people who have access to necessary information for sound decision making, who will implement the decisions, and who will be impacted by them.

Commodity Teams

Various commodity teams are established during the standardization phase (Figure 10.4). Each commodity team is charged with working to improve a set of products or a group of items of highest priority. The teams are composed of representatives from those departments that play a role in the commodities chosen. These teams will contribute to everything from identifying customer needs to the selection of the suppliers.

In Figure 10.3, Commodity Team B includes only purchasing, marketing, and finance/accounting. This commodity might be a customer research service that would require the cooperation of these three departments. Similarly, commodity A requires all departments except marketing. A typical commodity that would require this type of representation might be a manufacturing-related raw material.

Again, it is important to stress that this is only one possible PSQM structure and not the only way to organize a PSQM system. The structure may vary according to industry, personnel, supplier base, and so forth. Each organization should take great care in deciding how it wants to manage the supplier–customer relationship and the organizational structure to support it.

PSQM TRAINING OF INTERNAL STAFF

Once you know what to do and why you are doing it, the next step is addressing how to do it. Learning the "how to" involves skill building. Skills are the product of education and training, which is where we turn our attention next.

Education and training go hand in hand. Education is tantamount to knowledge or theory. Training is the development of skills and abilities. Education without training is empty. Training without education is blind. Education and training must occur at all levels of a company. In fact, education and training must reach suppliers. If suppliers do not develop along with the organization, the stage is set for a complete disconnect and the ensuing failure of the PSQM system.

Although, as mentioned previously, education and training must be disseminated organization-wide, top management should receive more extensive exposure. Managers will become the role models and teachers who will be responsible for creating a life-long learning organization.

If an education and training endeavor is to be effective, it must reach everyone—from the chief executive to procurement personnel. Every employee must at least have a fundamental understanding of the customer–supplier relationship. All education/training programs must cover how the linking subsystem (supplier selection), the improvement subsystem (continuous improvement of products and services), and the feedback subsystem (supplier performance measurement and auditing) are interrelated.

In addition to learning systems thinking, all teams should be provided with specific training in systematic problem-solving methods and group dynamics. Education and training programs should also focus on managing expectations so as to minimize conflicting expectations regarding roles and goals. In short, every organizational actor will have a part to play and objectives for guidance. An example of an education and training plan is provided in Table 10.1.

Table 10.1 Example of Education and Training Plan

Topic	Participants
TQM system and philosophy: Customer focus, policy deployment, measurement systems, systematic improvement, process management, and team concepts.	Organization-wide
PSQM system and philosophy: Show how PSQM is an integral part of TQM. Explain the customer–supplier relationship and the linking, improvement, and feedback subsystems. This would be a high-level management course.	Members of the PSQM structure
Purchasing/supplier quality policy deployment: Linking the supplier system to the overall organization quality systems. Tying the supplier capabilities and improvements to the goals of the organization.	PSQM structure members and commodity team leaders
Customer–supplier relationship: The value of the relationship to both parties, long-term aspects, and partnering.	Members of the PSQM structure, all commodity team leaders and members, and all procurement personnel
TQM tools: The original problem solving-tools and the new management tools.	Members of the PSQM structure and all commodity team leaders and members
Systematic Improvement Methods: A systematic approach to continuously improve existing and new business processes.	Members of the PSQM structure and all commodity team leaders and members

Table 10.1 Example of Education and Training Plan (continued)

Topic	Participants
Feedback and measurement systems: Internal baselines, statistical process controls, process capability studies, quality costs, and variability.	Members of the PSQM structure and all commodity team leaders and members
Benchmarking: External and internal comparisons of indices and processes in order to replicate or apply improvements made by others into your own processes.	PSQM structure members and commodity team leaders
Facilitative leadership: How to increase employee participation, encourage teamwork, simplify work processes, and empower direct reports.	PSQM structure members and commodity team leaders
Meeting management and team building: Keeping meetings focused and running efficiently (i.e., planning the structure of group sessions). Identifying, diagnosing, and removing blockages that hinder team effectiveness.	Commodity team leaders and members

SUPPLIER POLICY DEPLOYMENT

*"What is our business?" is not determined
by the producer but by the consumer.*

Peter F. Drucker

Policy deployment is a process by which business plans are linked with customer requirements. The buying organization and its suppliers of choice must have their respective business plans in alignment if the partnership is to last.

The buying organization should start with its vision and with determining its quality objectives. These initial phases include determining customer quality characteristics and prioritizing them. Two major factors need to be considered when prioritizing quality characteristics. The first is the degree of importance the item holds relative to other contenders, and the second is the need for improvement. A characteristic that is highly important and in great need of improvement qualifies as a top priority.

It is advisable that goals meet the following criteria: Goals should be **S**pecific, **M**easurable, **A**chievable, **R**ealistic, and **T**rackable. Goals that meet the criteria could be referred to as SMART goals, and the acronym is helpful in remembering these important criteria. This model helps one remember the criteria for successful goal setting. Ken Blanchard[2] refers to this model in his book entitled *The One Minute Manager*.

Once the goals have been set, the buying organization should design a procurement policy, which should tie in to the organization's quality objectives. Subsequently, the organization should deploy these objectives and the procurement policy throughout the organization in a cascading manner to determine the processes, commodities, and products with the strongest link to the original direction. This is then narrowed down to the most important suppliers that can provide those products. Finally, improvement projects are selected for the suppliers that are most important to the buying organization and that are willing to participate in the PSQM system and establish a long-term customer–supplier relationship.

Clearly, policy deployment is a customer-driven management system with the explicit goal of linking market and customer requirements to individual and team objectives. It is a process by which a few clear strategic focuses are converted into well-defined tactical goals.

PSQM will work only if the buying organization and its suppliers align their respective goals and objectives. Such alignment requires everyone involved to commit to effective communication, coordination, and cooperation. These ingredients, and these ingredients alone, will engender the requisite trust.

SUPPLIER SYMPOSIA

Acting on the belief that the supplier (the party or entity responsible for input to the process) plays a significant role in the ultimate success of any business endeavor, it follows that the buying organization should set up a group meeting with its suppliers. Now it is up to the buying organization to sell the benefits of the PSQM system to its supplier base. During these symposia, the buying organization should stress how partnering can enhance the economic stability and long-term viability of both the supplier and the buyer. In effect, what is being advocated is a more principled approach to supplier–customer relations that requires separate and distinct organizations to work together for their long-term mutual success. (See Chapter 4 for a detailed explanation of the customer–supplier relationship.) This new relationship replaces the old procurement approach in which the buying organization relentlessly negotiates price with the supplier, even to the extent of endangering the subcontractor's existence.

Suppliers that buy into the idea of partnering are considered potential suppliers of choice. Ultimately, the symposia become the vehicle by which the triumphs of sound supplier–customer partnerships are conveyed to future potential suppliers in obtaining their commitment.

SUPPLIER AND PROJECT SELECTION AND PLANNING

Once the supplier policy deployment process is complete and symposia have been held to present the concept to the most important suppliers, the buying organization must then select those suppliers that are most closely aligned with the direction of the buying organization. The leaders are chosen according to how well they measure up in terms of the quality characteristics established, whether they are capable of supplying the products that are deemed of highest priority, and their willingness to work within the understanding of the new culture and the proposed relationship.

Once the suppliers have been lined up, the business of designing a process that produces the desired product or service features can proceed. Creating such processes requires the buying organization and each supplier to jointly identify a specific project for improvement. The quality project selected should focus on those processes that produce the priority quality characteristics.

A project plan and objectives are determined by the supplier in conjunction with the needs of the buying organization. Both organizations commit to improving the selected process for their mutual benefit. Review cycles are built into the project schedule so that both parties can assess their progress toward the joint goals and countermeasures can be taken to ensure attainment of those goals.

QUALITY IMPROVEMENT ACTIVITIES

A key factor concerning quality improvement projects is where along the total quality management road the supplier is. Beginners will obviously require more tutoring from the buying organization. On the other hand, supplier organizations that have more experience in total quality management can assist the buying organization with quality improvement and the buying organization can also help the supplier, which is an ideal situation.

A good way to strengthen the ties of the supplier–customer relationship is for the supplier and a commodity team to work together closely on establishing product or service standards and specifications (the criteria for acceptable and outstanding performance). This kind of teaming sets the stage for the type of open and honest communication that is the foundation for the coordinated efforts and cooperation to come (i.e., agreeing on measurement methods). What to measure is dictated by such factors as the type of product and/or service rendered, the voice of the customer, and the capabilities of the supplier in question.

Obviously, it is in the best interest of the buying organization to help its external suppliers of choice with implementing total quality management. The help comes principally in the form of establishing performance measures. Without measurements, a company has no means for assessing the progress of its suppliers along the path to continuous improvement. In addition, measurements empower people to pinpoint errors and fix them.

CONTINUOUS IMPROVEMENT

The supplier should understand the concepts of continuous improvement and the Systematic Improvement Method,[3] which can be used to improve the processes identified within the scope of the selected improvement projects. During the quality improvement pilot project phase, suppliers are asked to define realistic, measurable, continuous improvement goals, expressed in understandable language and tied to a deadline. The purpose is to reduce variation around these targets on an ongoing basis. The overall aim is to build on the success of an effective pilot project, in order to reproduce the activity elsewhere in the organization and make continuous improvement a way of life for the supplier. As the continuous improvement project continues, the supplier and the buying organization will realize various benefits:

- Learn to use the tools of continuous improvement
- Understand the results of following the Systematic Improvement Method[3]
- Improve the quality of the products and services for use by the buying organization
- Improved market share for the supplier, who will have a higher quality product or service to offer to other buyers

PROJECT RESULTS AND MONITORING

Over time, after the buying organization has sparked the quality improvement initiative, the supplier is expected to assume responsibility for it. This means that the supplier must put internal systems in place in an effort to meet or exceed customer expectations. To ensure an enduring win–win supplier–customer relationship, the buying organization augments the supplier's internal assessment with its own external assessment. This results in a two-dimensional performance feedback mechanism comprised of how the supplier sees itself and how others see it. The feedback enables the supplier organization to determine how well it is measuring up against the jointly defined objective criteria for adequate and exceptional performance.

Measurements are critical, because they enable a company to assess how effectively and efficiently it is meeting proposed goals. Given the importance of measurement, the buying organization and its suppliers of choice should be sure that they are speaking the same measurement language. Speaking the same measurement language requires, among other things, training operators to measure and test in the same way and using compatible, calibrated instruments.

Those product or service characteristics that directly impact priority performance should be submitted to statistical process control (SPC). The supplier and the buying organization should set up a system for controlling variance and determining process capability. SPC consists of erecting parameters for a process in order to take corrective action when variations fall outside of the established limits. Its purpose is to measure conformance to customer standards and eliminate unacceptable variance, thereby managing a process when the results fall outside of acceptable statistical control limits.

SPC also enables checking for trends. If trends are spotted, adjustments or remedial interventions can be made to the work process in order to prevent the process from getting out of control and outside specifications.

Initially, a supplier would apply SPC on a limited basis, focusing exclusively on major quality characteristics. Eventually, the use of SPC will proliferate, and all quality characteristics will be generated by statistically controlled, capable systems.

Some common measures of supplier performance are as follows:

- Process capability
- Cost of quality/cost of poor quality
- Product delivery to specification
- Product delivery on schedule
- Degree of customer satisfaction
- Customer complaints
- Repeat business
- Cycle time
- Quantity of product delivered
- Product safety
- Reliability
- Life cycle costs

This monitoring process fulfills most of the needs of the feedback subsystem of PSQM, but it is a bit limited. A more general and thorough feedback mechanism should be established in order to continuously assess the supplier's capability. A periodic review of the supplier's performance on all products and services provided should also be done. This can start with the criteria associated with the original projects selected and then be expanded to include all priority products and services supplied.

CERTIFICATION

At this juncture, the buying organization sets out to verify whether or not the suppliers of choice are indeed able to systematically meet its needs. Those suppliers that share the greatest similarity with the buying organization's corporate quality objectives, score well on customer satisfaction ratings, have implemented a total quality management system, and have demonstrated trustworthiness and a desire to establish a long-term customer–supplier relationship are awarded certification.

There can be different levels of supplier certification. An introductory level of total quality management awareness might consist of a commitment to total quality on the part of the supplier's leadership, the formation of quality improvement teams, and the use of basic problem-solving methods and tools. An intermediate level could involve a commitment to measurement (i.e., SPC). The highest level of certification could be when a total quality management system has been implemented and deployed throughout the supplier organization. That is when a company's vision, mission, and goals have been communicated throughout the organization and people have been educated and trained to work in concert to attain quality results at the best cost. In effect, the organization's major business systems show process capability.

REVIEW OF CERTIFICATION

Few suppliers have the wherewithal to endure the demands of continuous improvement. Those that have what it takes to make the grade are viable candidates for a long-term relationship. Partnership with one or a few suppliers is more manageable and facilitates communication, coordination, and cooperation, which is highly desirable. A limited number of suppliers is ultimately better, especially if the suppliers selected can reliably meet the needs of the buying organization in the long term.

It is important to periodically assess the certification level of all suppliers to ensure that they continue to maintain or improve their levels of quality, delivery, and commitment to a quality improvement process that were the original basis for their certification. Management changes or other circumstances may sometimes cause a supplier to change its philosophy so that it is no longer as aligned as it once was with the buying organization.

Using mutually agreed upon objective criteria as a yardstick, the process capability of key internal systems is evaluated and the management commitment to total quality is also assessed. This assessment is then discussed at a PSQMC meeting to determine if the supplier has the right to continue with the current certification level or whether the level should be changed.

REVIEW OF THE PSQM SYSTEM

PSQM is a system that is initially designed by the buying organization as a model that will work best for the organization in attaining its quality objectives. After the PSQM system has been implemented, it should be reviewed periodically to determine if changes are warranted. The PSQMC should perform this review with the purpose of determining the status of the overall objectives of the PSQM system, identifying any problems that have been found in attaining the objectives, and implementing countermeasures to ensure that the objectives are met.

These countermeasures may include the need to change some of the PSQM subsystems as originally designed. What is most important is to recognize that the same concepts that apply to any process within the organization also apply to the PSQM system. This process should continue to be improved over time. In order to do so, a periodic review is necessary, in which problems and their causes are identified, countermeasures are implemented, and monitoring processes are established to assess progress.

ENDNOTES

1. Mizuno, Shigeru (1988). *Management for Quality Improvement—The 7 New QC Tools*. Cambridge, Mass.: Productivity Press.
2. Blanchard, Kenneth and Johnson, Spencer (1982). *The One Minute Manager*. New York: William Morrow.
3. Fernandez, Ricardo R. (1993). *Process Management and Improvement*. Miami, Advent Group, Inc.
4. Figures 10.1 to 10.4 ©Advent Group, Inc.

ABSTRACTS

ABSTRACT 10.1
SUPPLIER QUALITY MANAGEMENT:
A MATTER OF RELATIONSHIPS, NOT MANDATES

Schermerhorn, Michele
Quality Digest, December 1992, pp. 44–46

Mandating that one's suppliers adopt a focus on quality neglects an important TQM principle, says the author: the focus for improvement should be upon processes, not people. She offers a four-step plan to lead suppliers to a quality approach:

1. **Developing a supplier quality management strategy:** Senior managers must define the relationship they wish to pursue with suppliers, communicate that vision to the rest of the business, and ensure that all supporting systems can contribute to the strategy's success. A supplier quality management team then identifies key suppliers and develops an action plan.
2. **Sharing the vision with suppliers:** Senior management communicates the vision of a mutually beneficial customer–supplier relationship to every employee and to senior executives of key supplier organizations. Next, representatives of production, sales, and purchasing visit the supplier site to help the supplier understand how their product or service is used.
3. **Educating suppliers:** The education begins with a common philosophy and language of quality, and it continues with (a) measuring work processes, (b) tying measurement to identification and prioritization of process problems, and (c) identifying root causes of problems and undertaking corrective action.
4. **Coordinating improvement efforts:** Four systems need to be jointly developed and implemented: (a) measurement, (b) corrective action, (c) problem-solving, and (d) recognition systems. *(©Quality Abstracts)*

CHAPTER 11

CONCLUSIONS AND FUTURE EXPECTATIONS

Throughout this book, the need for total quality management and, more specifically, the need to integrate suppliers into the overall organizational processes and systems has been discussed. A PSQM system was proposed as one successful approach to accomplish this integration. In addition to the systematic approach itself, implementation of this approach was also discussed. The question now is what conclusions can be drawn from the information presented and what changes in the future will be affected by and will affect the PSQM system.

ORGANIZATIONAL SUCCESS FACTORS

Today's customer is a more educated consumer who demands reasonably priced, high-quality, personalized products and services. It thus follows that niche marketing strategies have proliferated. In the new approach, companies target a specific customer base with tailored, superior goods and services. Naturally, organizations that want to succeed in this high-pressure, competitive climate must continuously increase their time to market capability if they want to stay in the ball game. No wonder Kanter[1] suggests that the organization of today must be focused, fast, flexible, and friendly if it is to see tomorrow. Let's take a closer look at these and other success factors as they pertain to the PSQM system today and in the future.

Customer driven: In the past, some organizations held such a large share of the market that they could enjoy the ability to shape customer demand for their products and services. This is no longer viable. With higher customer expectations and increased competition, organizations must identify and sometimes predict their customer needs and adopt a strategy that links their suppliers in assisting them to do so more effectively in the long term.

Focus: Focus is the ability to zero in on what it is you want. Focus is primordial, for without it, organizations drift aimlessly. Think of an organization as a camera. First, it must have a clear picture of its objectives. Once the targets are in sharp relief, then and only then can it take aim and shoot. A camera with auto-focus has great difficulty in focusing on a group. It can only focus on one person in a group. If all others in the group are to be in focus, they must be on the same plane as that one person or they will be out of focus. Focusing on just a few objectives is analogous to this.

Speed: Speed is a critical factor in the American free-enterprise system. An organization must have the ability to get where it wants to go quickly. Speed translates into efficiency. Given so many are in the running, getting there first often makes a big difference. By integrating suppliers deeply into the organization, and with the advent of communication technologies that even further assist in the integration, the supplier can more quickly respond to and sometimes get ahead of the buying organization's needs, even to the point of suggesting directions for improvements.

Flexibility: The capability to adjust to an agreed-upon course of action in light of new, relevant information is a survival skill that many industries are finding difficult to assimilate. The current business environment changes by the minute, largely due to technological advances. Flexibility affords an organization a way to redirect energies in order to capitalize on new opportunities. Good customer–supplier relationships furnish flexibility because they are built on complementary needs. In other words, the needs and characteristics of the respective parties mesh. One partner's strengths fill in for the other's weakness and vice versa.

Learning/adapting: In addition to being flexible, an organization also needs to be able to learn from itself and others and to adapt those lessons into the very fiber of the organization. This is sometimes called benchmarking and extended benchmarking, as referred to by Camp.[2] An organization must have its radar on, constantly searching for opportunities. As is true of most radar, however, the information collected becomes much more accurate and comprehensive with additional antennas. The suppliers in an organization's supplier base whose interests are directly associated with the success of the organization can be these additional antennas that identify additional opportunities for improvement, which one organization alone cannot do.

Friendship: Because the pace of change in business is dizzying, no one can go it alone in the corporate jungle and expect to survive. This dynamic and competitive reality calls for building friendships. An organization needs to befriend all groups in its environment on whom the company depends, so that the entire network wins together. Friendly partnerships within and outside of the organization are the foundation of healthy supplier–customer relationships.

Management commitment: This is probably the most crucial factor, because without it, all others just crumble. Management must buy into the long-term aspects of this philosophy and be patient because the results are not realized overnight. Management must be willing to allow the system to prove itself and must actively be part of and support the process. If suppliers do not see that management within the buying organization is committed to the process, they will not become true partners and the system will fail.

Long-term: The relationships that need to be built must be long-term in nature. A significant investment will be made on both sides in establishing the relationship. This investment needs time to pay off, similar to a long-term capital investment with an internal rate of return. It may take time to recover the investment, but once it is recovered, there are usually significant financial rewards. Taylorism once taught that work must be simplified and standardized to create interchangeable parts. This has since been expanded to include interchangeable workers, interchangeable customers, and interchangeable suppliers. This mentality will hurt the organization in the long run.

Instead, establishing and maintaining long-term mutually beneficial relationships will pay off over time.

Teamwork: This is one of the factors that has the greatest effect not only the external customer–supplier relationships but also their internal cousins. Teamwork and cross-functional objectives and projects are essential to the success of an organization. The organization must understand that each department or business unit does not work in a vacuum. They all work toward common goals and objectives, many of which cannot be met without the cooperation of all involved. Similarly, suppliers must be a part of these efforts when their products/services are integral to the process in question.

Innovation: Because of the ever-increasing rate of technological changes, organizations must be willing to discover and use technology to improve their products and services for their customers. Suppliers can perform a critical function in this aspect because they are often the developers of new technology that they then offer to their buying organizations.

In summary, survival and prosperity in the existing corporate climate require focus, speed, flexibility, and friendliness. Organizations should focus on what they do well and avoid being distracted by trying to do too much. A company cannot be all things to all customers. A fast response is vital because of the ever-growing number of competitors. An organization that is always playing catch-up is as good as dead. A premium is placed on flexibility because out of it arises innovation, which requires teamwork and cooperation. Last but not least is friendliness, which is at the very heart of sound supplier–customer relationships. In the final analysis, internal and external suppliers and customers must coexist in a friendly climate; otherwise, the entire process may falter.

At the very heart of the supplier–customer relationship is the issue of make versus buy decisions. There are diametric views regarding this pressing question. On the one side is the position that the secret to success in business is to manufacture everything possible from within. The opposing point of view attributes business success to purchasing almost everything from subcontractors. Whatever an organization's strategy may be regarding make versus buy decisions, the pivotal issue is meeting and/or exceeding customer expectations in the most effective and efficient manner.

THE BUSINESS ENVIRONMENT TODAY AND TOMORROW

Organizations that want to survive in the future must prepare themselves today for the environment in which they will be conducting business. This environment seems to be changing in ways that are very significant and that support the need for implementing a PSQM system. Some of these factors, as well as the importance of a PSQM system in order to deal with them effectively, are addressed here.

Win–Win

Organizations are finding that an adversarial relationship often does not lead to success in the current business environment. Business relationships seem to be headed toward a much friendlier and more cooperative environment. Yet a typical approach toward procurement is still for the buying organization to relentlessly chip away at the supplier's price, even if it means putting the supplier out of business. This scenario is commonplace and a win–lose reality. Win–lose thinking produces adversarial relationships. The parties involved can be consumed by a feverish "winner take all" mentality, resulting in a disservice to the end user. A more principled approach to sound customer–supplier relations consists of keeping an eye on the long view, with separate and distinct entities working in concert for their mutual benefit. This win–win arrangement enhances the long-term economic viability of both sides while simultaneously keeping the end user satisfied.

The Extended and Virtual Organizations

The extended organization conveys to suppliers and other significant stakeholders (i.e., customers, employees) the role of partners in the corporation's future. It calls for everyone involved to commit to communicating, cooperating, coordinating, and synergizing, in a word—teamwork. The central thesis of this book is that companies of all shapes and sizes must link up with their suppliers in order to achieve total quality. Integrating the supplier into the organization will mean higher quality and lower costs, which was previously thought to be impossible. Consider that the organization of the 21st century will generate instantaneous products and/or services, called *virtual product*. This will require a completely new kind of company, made up of adaptive temporary systems that will, for instance, evolve in response to a pressing need or a vexing problem. Davidow and Malone[3] call this new organizational structure a virtual corporation. What is being suggested is nothing short of a complete reinvention of how business should work. In their thought-provoking book, Hammer and Champy[4] call this procedure of radical organizational redesign *business reengineering*. Essentially, reengineering deals with redesigning the basic tasks of a corporation into coherent business processes. By *process* Hammer and Champy mean any given set of activities that, as a whole, produce a result of value to a customer. Clearly, the new corporation taking shape is more customer driven and customer managed. Thus, the customer–supplier relationship becomes of paramount importance, and an effective PSQM system becomes a key to business success.

Education

Businesses will be depending more and more on a knowledge-based worker who is able to handle the increasingly technical positions that will become available once all the reengineering has taken place. The SCANS report[5] entitled "What Work Requires of Schools" explains that employees of the future will need to be competent in the following areas:

Workplace competencies	Foundation skills
Information	Three R's
Interpersonal systems	Speaking
Resource allocation	Listening
Technology	Problem solving
	Creativity
	Reasoning
	Responsibility
	High self-esteem
	Self-management
	Sociability
	Integrity

Our educational institutions are now preparing for this eventuality. They are changing the way they address the needs of students in order to better prepare them for this future. It will still be incumbent upon industry to help in the area of education. Organizations will be asked to be partners in the educational effort. They will be asked for input as to their needs in particular sectors and localities. They will also be asked to participate in the educational experience through involvement in such programs as student visits to plants.

PSQM needs to consider the educational system as a supplier also. Even though organizations do not directly pay for the educational service, they pay indirectly through taxes. They should assist in improving the educational system so that the outcome will be members of the work force who will be adequately prepared to take on the new challenges.

Educational programs need to be improved internally to include not only classroom time but also one-on-one training and follow-up, so that the information and skills that were learned in the classroom are properly applied. This reinforces the learning experience and opens the door to future creative applications.

For additional information, see Abstract 11.1 at the end of this chapter.

ISO 9000 and Supplier Certification

The current trend toward requiring ISO 9000 registration will indeed continue well into the future. As time goes on, the registration requirements will probably become better defined and possibly even more stringent than they are today. The key, however, is that registration will become a requirement. Many companies in the future will not even consider doing business with an organization that is not ISO registered. Registration may be a competitive advantage now, but in the future it will simply be a business requirement. It is also logical to conclude that if this type of registration becomes a requirement, then organization-specific certification will become less of a necessity. Companies that are currently performing continuous audits to certify their suppliers will be able to reduce the frequency and extent of the audits if the supplier is ISO capable. Companies may still want to assure themselves that certain specific needs are being met, but the scope of the certification process can be reduced.

This benefits both the supplier and the buying organization, because both will be able to spend their time more productively than in an audit mode.

Electronic Data Interchange and Telecommunications

With the advent of the INTERNET and the future expected improvements in all areas of telecommunications, many changes will take place in the way that customers and suppliers interface in their everyday business transactions. Electronic data interchange (EDI) is currently proving to be tremendously successful in many different industries, including automotive, transportation, retail, and utilities. The ANSI X-12 standards are becoming more encompassing, i.e., they are incorporating more types of transactions. New encryption methods and electronic signatures are allowing business transactions to become seamless and many magnitudes faster and more accurate. Huge investments in fiber-optic networks and digital cellular technology will greatly expand the capabilities for business communications. In the not-too-distant future, it is very likely that the great majority of business transactions will take place in an electronic environment. This technology will provide a great means for partners to get closer together by integrating their information systems. A future criterion for the selection of long-term partners may include the capability to perform business transactions in an EDI environment.

Information Systems

We are moving very quickly into the information age. Whereas in the past products were passed from hand to hand and later services were provided to customers, in the future the major commodity will probably be information. Data that provide analytical assistance will pass from the supplier to the customer and back, but more importantly, information will be the actual commodity for which customers will be paying. This is evident from the tremendous growth in information systems and technologies that is taking place today. These same systems and technology are allowing the great revolution of reengineering to occur at such a rapid rate of deployment. Processes that in the past were considered impossible are run-of-the-mill today—everybody is doing it. There are fewer impossibilities. Now the question is not whether or not it can be done, but instead what is the best and most cost-efficient way that it can be done. Information systems amplify the capabilities of both the supplier and the buying organization. This holds true in all areas, from manufacturing and R&D to administrative services. All areas benefit, as do their partners.

Transportation

Our transportation infrastructure has not had a major overhaul in many years. Many a documentary has focused on the dangerous conditions that exist on some of the main bridges and traffic arteries in the United States. As the economy grows and more products are manufactured, they must be moved along this infrastructure to the eventual customers. Therefore, a tremendous expenditure will be needed to meet this increased traffic pattern. Another alternative that many partners in a customer–supplier relationship will take advantage of is locating their plants in the vicinity of the buying organization. This would decrease transportation costs and increase the reliability of delivery times, which in turn would allow both parties to become more active in a just-in-time environment. Location then becomes very important in the selection of partners for long-term customer–supplier relationships.

Empowerment of the Supplier as a Partner

Some companies still assume that total quality management is limited to team activities and statistical process control. Although these are very important components of the system, they do not comprise the whole. Without all the pieces working together in an integrated fashion, the organization will not make great strides in its total quality management efforts. Improvements will be slow in coming and frustration will build. This frustration will in turn help to further disintegrate the total quality management efforts and lead to a spiral of failure. Integration is one of the keys to success. The entire organization must be headed in the same direction or else the organization will be weakened. Its efforts will be scattered and the results hit or miss. Suppliers should be brought into the inner folds of the buying organization as part of the extended enterprise. Integration of suppliers will provide countless benefits to both partners.

Legal Considerations

With so many changes taking place today in the relationships between business trading partners, it is difficult to predict how the courts will react to the many creative ways business transactions are being handled. Disputes may become more difficult for one side or the other to prove. Contracts may become more difficult to enforce. For example, precedent has not yet been clearly set on the effect of not having hard copy signatures and transactions that spell out the complete contract each time a product or service is purchased. The purpose of EDI is to eliminate as much paperwork as possible, yet it is the paper that historically has provided the evidence that the transaction indeed took place or was intended to take place. Encryption is another issue that is now being reviewed by the federal government. There is no problem with using it, but the government wants easy access to all information, even that which is encrypted.

GETTING ON WITH IT

One of Deming's fourteen points (#14) is to accomplish the transformation. PSQM is also a transformation that needs to take place. The longer it takes to get started, the longer it will take to start realizing the benefits. The change is inevitable, and those who procrastinate will be overrun by those who act. Deming also talked about the "wildfires of quality" that will take hold and fan out quickly as more organizations implement a total quality management system. As part of this system, suppliers must be brought into the fold. The process of integrating suppliers will multiply from company to company, and the total quality management philosophy will spread quickly, like wildfire. The question is whether an organization will be caught by surprise and get burned by the "wildfire" or will use the fire to energize its activities in new and rich areas that offer the potential for significant improvement and success.

ENDNOTES

1. Kanter (1989). *When Giants Learn to Dance.* New York: Simon & Schuster.
2. Camp, Robert C. (1989). *Benchmarking—The Search for Industry Best Practices that Lead to Superior Performance.* Milwaukee: ASQC Quality Press.
3. Davidow, William H. and Malone, Michael S., *The Virtual Corporation—Structuring and Revitalizing the Corporation for the 21st Century.* New York: Harper Business.
4. Hammer, Michael and Champy, James (1993). *Reengineering the Corporation.* New York: Harper Business.
5. SCANS, Secretary's Commission on Achieving Necessary Skills (1991). "What Work Requires of Schools." A SCANS Report for America 2000, U.S. Department of Labor, June 1991.
6. Figures 10.1 to 10.4 ©Advent Group, Inc.

ABSTRACTS

ABSTRACT 11.1
BREAK YOUR BARRIERS AND BE A BETTER PRESENTER

Louw, Antoni A.
Training & Development, February 1992, pp. 17–22

Business people dread speaking in front of groups more than practically anything else, says the author. He believes most speaking difficulties stem from the speaker personally and can be avoided with a few simple techniques. Consequently, he examines several common barriers to public speaking and offers advice to help with each of them: (1) an inability to create an appropriate, enthusiastic "presence" for public speaking, (2) the assumption that audience members won't listen to you because they automatically disagree with your ideas, (3) the self-imposed pressure that can come with presentations for VIPs, and (4) a fear of making mistakes. A sidebar elaborates on various tricks of the speaking "trade":

- Practice and practice some more.
- Use different words in each rehearsal to find the most effective ones for communicating your ideas.
- "Embrace" your audience by taking ownership of the room.
- Accompany key points with analogies or real-life examples.
- Vary your pace.
- Be committed to your topic.
- Place presentation aids a few feet away from you, forcing you to walk over to them and back, thus giving some movement to your presentation.
- Pay attention to negative or quizzical reactions, but without putting the trainee on the spot.
- Pause periodically, but at appropriate places.
- Value your audience's points of view.

(©*Quality Abstracts*)

MICHIGAN CONSOLIDATED GAS COMPANY

Benson Manlove and Sherryl Love

APPLYING THE QUALITY PROCESS TO AN MRO ENVIRONMENT*

When a natural gas utility company begins focusing on the quality process, it challenges its departments to provide opportunities for change and make improvements. This is how Material Management stepped up to that challenge.

*The introductory portion of this chapter was written by Benson Manlove, Vice President, Administration, and Sherryl Love, Manager of Purchasing, Michigan Consolidated Gas Company (MichCon), Detroit, Michigan. The material in this chapter is the property of MichCon, and we are indebted to them for permission to use it.

Background

Michigan Consolidated Gas Company (MichCon) is a natural gas distribution, transmission, and storage company. It serves 1.1 million customers in more than 500 Michigan communities. In 1991, MichCon launched "The Power of You...Build the Future," a corporate philosophy aimed at making MichCon a premier gas distribution company. The cornerstone of the program is employee empowerment. The corporate philosophy also focuses on quality service by adopting the Malcolm Baldrige criteria.

"The Power of You...Build the Future" gives MichCon employees the freedom to identify ways to improve customer service while simultaneously enhancing corporate performance and adding shareholder value.

Along with this new corporate philosophy, MichCon developed a Vision Statement:

> We, the employees of MichCon, acknowledge our unique responsibility in providing services critical to the quality of life in the communities we serve.

> Therefore, we are dedicated to being a premier organization, and the best natural gas company, by continuously improving value to our customers and shareholders.

MichCon is aligning its core business processes and will begin reengineering in July 1994.

Why Change

As a utility, MichCon relied mostly on regulation and never considered itself a true player in the competitive arena. As MichCon looked to the future, however, it realized various forces were going to introduce the gas industry to competition. MichCon could not continue to do business in the same old way. It had to prepare for the future. It had to become competitive.

MichCon decided it was better to prepare for change while in a position of strength than to do so under pressure. To make this change, MichCon declared a bold strategy. Part of the strategy is to achieve

100 percent customer/client satisfaction and 100 percent employee satisfaction.

Material Management developed a strategy to move the company closer to 100 percent client satisfaction. It did so by streamlining the procurement process through "state of the art" technology and improved processes.

Streamlining the Procurement Process

The procurement process in the past was labor intensive. In some cases, it took up to 60 days to process a purchase order. The process was full of unnecessary tasks and generated tons of paperwork. The supplier's quality and on-time delivery were poor and the internal client was dissatisfied with the service. The material tracking system software did not work properly. The procurement staff was frustrated and overworked. Material Management was working harder, but not smarter.

The new system eliminates paper and reduces cycle time, unneeded tasks, and manual steps while it improves quality and controls and reduces direct and indirect costs.

The system is divided into two key processes: the Procurement Cycle and Supplier Quality. This system allows the internal client to handle the procurement process online. Clients can make the requisition, get it approved, direct it to a buyer and/or supplier, and pay for the material upon receipt via a wire transfer. This process reduces paperwork, eliminates errors through online validation, and enables online budgetary controls while reducing cycle time. It enforces approval controls, eliminates control tasks, expedites requisitions to the correct buyer, eliminates manual distribution steps, and enables quick and efficient sourcing.

Supplier Quality Process

The purpose of MichCon's Quality Supplier Program is to extend MichCon's philosophy of customer satisfaction and quality to its suppliers and manufacturers who provide goods and/or services to MichCon.

MichCon's Quality Supplier Program consists of three classifications: Approved, Certified, and Preferred quality levels. The levels were designed to promote continuous growth in the areas of quality, delivery, service, and pricing.

MichCon improved its on-time delivery from January 1992 to November 1993 from 58 percent to 75 percent and improved its Material Acceptance level from 97.9 percent to 98.25 percent.

Each quality level has specific performance criteria which must be met before a supplier can progress to the next level. Suppliers will receive awards for performance growth. To reach the Preferred Level means a supplier has reached MichCon's highest quality performance level. This level warrants that supplier special preference.

Two methods are used to determine a supplier's performance:

1. **Supplier Rating System:** Measures a supplier's quality, delivery, pricing, and service.
2. **Supplier Evaluation Audit:** Evaluates a supplier's facility, capabilities, management practices, and its efforts in quality.

Supplier Quality Computation Process

A baseline performance rating is established for the supplier. MichCon measures ongoing improved performance or nonperformance.

Example

		Weight	Weight adjusted score
12-month cumulative	Quality	= 90% × 0.35	= 31.5
12-month cumulative	On-time delivery (OTD)	= 85% × 0.30	= 25.5
Annual or as-needed assessment	Service	= 87% × 0.25	= 22
Annual or as-needed assessment	Price	= 98% ×.0.10	= 9.8
			88.6% Baseline

Percentage of Conformance

Deviations noted in the areas of Quality and On-Time Delivery are monitored on an ongoing basis and compared to the total number of shipments in a given period of time. Conformance to Quality means that the requirements of the Contract, Purchase Order (quantity, part number, size, etc.), and applicable MichCon Material Standard(s) and/or industry standard(s) have been met. On-Time Delivery means that a shipment has arrived at the agreed upon location or work has been completed on or by the promised date.

Example

Line items receipted during the month	= 10
Deviation from Quality or OTD = 1 or 1/10	= 10%
Therefore,	
The current month's percentage of conformance	= **90%**

Adjusted Percentage of Conformance

This percentage is derived by comparing the current month to the baseline rating for the first month only. Subsequent monthly percentages of conformance will be compared to the previous month's percentage.

- Add one percentage point if current month's percentage is greater than last month's percentage.
- Add zero percentage points if current month's percentage is the same as last month's percentage.
- Deduct two percentage points if current month's percentage is less than last month's percentage.

Example

Current month's performance of conformance	= 90%
Is greater than	
Baseline Performance Rating (or previous month's rating)	= 88.6%
Therefore, one point adjustment	+ 1
Adjusted Percentage of Conformance	= **89.6%**

Conclusion

For MichCon to become competitive, it had to move away from "business as usual" to "breakthrough" improvements. Performing in maintenance mode is not the way competitive companies do business. Material Management is now helping MichCon move forward by working smarter, but not harder. The new online procurement process and quality supplier system are "breakthrough" improvements that have made a positive impact on client satisfaction along with significant reductions in cycle time.

MichCon
QUALITY SUPPLIER'S MANUAL
(GOODS AND SERVICES)

QUALITY PROGRAMS FOR MichCon SUPPLIERS:
A LETTER FROM THE PRESIDENT

We at MichCon have challenged ourselves to turn our company into the premier natural gas provider in the country. Together, we've developed a set of values appropriate to that task that we will proudly carry into the future. Today, we are breathing life into those values by transforming words into actions.

We invite you, our suppliers, to enthusiastically accept the same challenge. Together, we will enable MichCon to remain competitive by forming long-term partnerships, which is one of our Supplier Program goals. Our other goal is to be provided with the highest quality supplies at the lowest cost.

I know our Quality Programs for Suppliers will provide a foundation upon which our mutual success can be built.

Stephen E. Ewing
President and Chief Operating Officer
MichCon

INTRODUCTION

The purpose of MichCon's Quality Program is to extend MichCon's philosophy of customer satisfaction and quality to its suppliers and manufacturers who provide goods and/or services to MichCon.

Our Quality Supplier Program consists of three classifications: Approved, Certified, and Preferred quality levels. The quality levels were designed to promote continuous growth in the areas of quality, delivery, service, and pricing.

Each quality level has specific performance criteria which must be met before a supplier can progress to the next level. Suppliers will receive awards for performance growth. To reach the Preferred Level means a supplier has reached MichCon's highest quality performance level, which warrants that supplier special preference. The classification levels and awards are further defined in the following sections.

Two methods are used to determine a supplier's performance.

1. A Supplier Rating System which measures a supplier's quality, delivery, pricing, and service
2. A Supplier Evaluation Audit which evaluates a supplier's facility and its capabilities, its management practices, and its efforts in quality (see Exhibit B)

These methods are further defined in the Rating System section.

MICHCON'S QUALITY CLASSIFICATION LEVELS

Level I: Approved Supplier

Supplier Audit

Suppliers must be audited by Purchasing and/or Quality Assurance/Lab before they may become Approved Suppliers. This audit can be done two ways, by telephone and/or on-site, depending on the type and quantity of material being considered for use. All suppliers must complete a Supplier Evaluation Audit Form and return it to MichCon. The type and date of audit conducted will be determined by Purchasing and the Lab.

Financial Stability

To do business with MichCon, a supplier must have an accounting rating of satisfactory or better.

Quality Program

Suppliers must have a formal quality program in place. This includes a quality manual and a formalized quality training program for employees.

Rejection Rate

Supplier's acceptance level must not drop below 96% acceptance for 12 consecutive months.

On-Time Delivery

Supplier's On-Time Delivery rate must be greater than 70% for 12 consecutive months. (On-Time Delivery = the date mutually agreed upon by the buyer and supplier that material will arrive or the date the service will begin.)

New Suppliers

Any supplier that either introduces a new product or supplies an approved product(s) will be given six months to establish a performance history. Upon completion of the six months, the supplier will be evaluated against the previously mentioned criteria. If all the criteria are met, they will be added to MichCon's Approved Supplier list.

Level II: Certified Supplier

Supplier Audit

Before a supplier can become a Certified Supplier for MichCon, all the criteria of Level I, Approved Supplier, must be met and the following improvements demonstrated.

Rejection Rate

Supplier's acceptance level must not drop below 98% acceptance for 12 consecutive months.

On-Time Delivery

Supplier's On-Time Delivery rate must be greater than 85% for 12 consecutive months.

New Suppliers

A supplier must have 12 months documented history with MichCon and meet all the above criteria before being considered for this level.

Level III: Preferred Supplier

Supplier Audit

Before a supplier can become a Preferred Supplier for MichCon, all the criteria of Level II, Certified Supplier, must be met with the following improvements.

Rejection Rate

Supplier's acceptance level must not drop below 99% acceptance for 12 consecutive months.

On-Time Delivery

Supplier's On-Time Delivery rate must be greater than 95% for 12 consecutive months.

New Suppliers

A supplier must have 12 months documented performance history with MichCon before being considered for the Preferred Level.

MICHCON'S QUALITY SUPPLIER RATING SYSTEM

Introduction

MichCon's Quality Supplier Rating System was developed to:

- Rate supplier's overall performance in the areas of quality, delivery, price, and service and to identify opportunity areas for improvements
- Coach and help supplier's quality for the Preferred Supplier quality level
- Reward suppliers who demonstrate continuous growth
- Share supplier's performance both within the company and outside the company

The information in this section should provide for you a clearer understanding of our rating system and how we compute your overall performance rating.

Suppliers are measured by the following quality elements: On-Time Delivery, Material Acceptance Percent, and Service. These elements are defined as follows.

Quality Elements Measurement

A. On-Time Delivery

On-Time Delivery is the date that the supplier and the buyer mutually agree that the material will arrive at MichCon's receiving dock and/or the date the supplier agrees the service will begin.

Purchasing generates a monthly report which depicts your Delivery/Service Statistics.

Your rate of performance is measured by the date material was actually received against the date the material was promised and/or the date you actually start the service against the date that was mutually agreed upon.

Material on-time parameters consist of 2 days late or 5 days early. Material will not be considered late if it is received two days after the promise date. The two days are the period of grace allowed for shipping delays. Early shipments are measured the same as nonconformance. Shipments received five days prior to the Purchase Order promise date are acceptable as on-time shipments. Shipments six days or earlier are considered nonconformance to the "On-Time Delivery" element.

There are no special parameters for services; they must start the date they were mutually agreed upon.

B. Acceptance Percentage

Our Material Acceptance Percentage (in a given period) = lots of material received/lots of material rejected.

I. Material Acceptance Percentage

Inspections are performed by the end users. End users may visually and/or functionally inspect the material before acceptance. If the material is rejected, it will be returned to the receiving dock for proper processing.

2. Contractor's Service Acceptance

Service acceptance levels will be determined based upon the following factors:

A. Does the material meet all of MichCon's specifications?
B. Was the service performed in accordance with the contract and scope of work?
C. Number of reworks/deficiencies.

Note: Either one or both of the above may be used to determine a supplier's overall Acceptance Percentage.

C. Service

Your service level is measured based upon input from the user(s) and buyer(s). All users and buyers fill out a quantitative survey. Exhibit A also evaluates the supplier's accessibility, responsiveness, price, and quality.

Computation of Total Rating

The total rating is compiled and stated on the Quality Evaluation/ Rating Computation Form #6305 (Exhibit A). The computation consists of:

On-Time Delivery & Price + Acceptance Level
+ Service Level + Extra credit points

The total rating of a supplier will be expressed in the rating score. That score will be calculated and the supplier will be placed in the appropriate classification.

After preparing the rating form, the Supplier Performance Evaluation/Appraisal Review (SPEAR) Team will review the data to determine which quality classification level you meet. After the review, a formal letter will be sent to you, notifying you of your classification level.

The supplier rating information will be retained on file for one year and will be made available to any activity and/or supplier upon request.

Performance Monitoring

Any time a supplier's performance deteriorates and its rating drops below the appropriate level for each performance element, a brief description of the underlying deficiency must be recorded on the rating form.

When a significant change occurs, such as a major decrease in the supplier's rating score, the SPEAR Team must review the details of the deterioration with the supplier and the buyer. The supplier must provide to the SPEAR Team a written plan of steps taken to correct the problem within 30 days from the date the meeting took place.

Frequency of Review

A. Approved/Certified Suppliers

All ratings (except those for Preferred Suppliers) will be calculated and sent to you at least twice a year unless you are on performance monitoring. Suppliers on performance monitoring will receive monthly rating reports until their performance reaches an acceptable level or they are disapproved by MichCon.

Adjustments to Supplier Rating

The following conditions will warrant the re-rating of suppliers:

- You are exhibiting serious quality concerns.
- Major changes have been made in your organizational structure (i.e., manufacturing, quality processes, safety, change in services provided, etc.).
- Your quality level falls below satisfactory or below the classification it has been approved for by MichCon.
- When you submit a written request for a re-rating to Purchasing in an effort to demonstrate that significant improvements have taken place in your product and/or service performance.

B. Preferred Quality Suppliers

Preferred Suppliers will be re-assessed if deterioration occurs for more than three consecutive months in any of the performance elements. The SPEAR Team will meet with you, the Preferred Supplier, to identify what has caused the change in performance and assist you in developing an improvement plan. If your performance level is corrected within six months and you consecutively maintain the Preferred Level for three of the six months, you will maintain the Preferred classification. If you cannot maintain a Preferred Level for three consecutive months within the six-month period, the SPEAR Team may choose to place you back at the Certified Level and monitor your performance for a year.

C. New Suppliers

New suppliers will be evaluated within three to six months after a sample/first production shipment is approved. Subsequent reviews will be in accordance with the terms mentioned above.

D. Low-Volume Suppliers

Low-volume suppliers or "one-time buy" suppliers will be rated at the discretion of the SPEAR Team.

Rating Criteria

The rating criteria will be explained to you prior to your rating period in order to give you performance targets. Data will be collected for six months and evaluations will follow shortly after.

Each supplier will be advised of their rating and how it was computed. Good performance will be commended and less than satisfactory performance will be noted. As suppliers attain their goals, new goals will be set for the next evaluation period.

MichCon's QUALITY SUPPLIER COMPUTATION PROCESS

This document provides a reference to the guidelines used by MichCon in determining your total performance rating. Areas responsible for rating each category are listed in parenthesis next to the category. These areas will collaborate to submit one performance rating. Only the categories with sufficient information will be rated. Supporting documentation for each rating is encouraged.

CATEGORIES

QUALITY   40 Points Possible
(Project Manager, End User and/or Quality Assurance/Laboratory)

1. **Conformance to specifications:** Material and/or services should meet all of MichCon's specifications in accordance with the Purchase Order, Contract, and/or scope of work. All material data sheets and/or quality assurance information must accompany each shipment as specified by MichCon. Points range as follows:

   [ ] Very satisfied   (10 points)
   [ ] Satisfied   (7 points)
   [ ] Partially satisfied   (3 points)
   [ ] Unsatisfied   (0 points)

2. **Zero returns due to defects:** To achieve the best rating, a supplier must have NO record of returns due to defects since the last evaluation. Any rework history on the supplier's product and/or service will decrease the rating accordingly. This area requires the appropriate documentation.

[ ] No shipment returned and/or no reworks
performed since the last evaluation   (10 points)
[ ] Partial shipment returned and/or small
amount of reworks performed   (5 points)
[ ] One or more total shipments returned and/or
a high amount of reworks performed   (0 points)

3. **Internal Quality Control —Quality Manual:** QA should obtain a quality manual (where available) and rate its content as follows:

[ ] Manual exceeds MichCon's requirements   (5 points)
[ ] Manual meets MichCon's requirements   (3 points)
[ ] Manual exists and partially meets MichCon's
specifications   (2 points)
[ ] Manual exists but does not meet MichCon's
specifications   (1 point)
[ ] No manual exits   (0 points)

4. **Internal Quality Control—use of SPC (Statistical Process Control):**

[ ] Appropriate use of SPC   (5 points)
[ ] Implementing SPC   (3 points)
[ ] No use of SPC   (0 points)

5. **Safety Program:** Supplier has a safety program in place with a designated safety representative and appropriate measurement tools.

[ ] Employee safety training program in place,
monitored, and reported   (8 points)
[ ] Safety manual available to employees at time
of employment   (6 points)
[ ] Safety program in place without regular training   (2 points)
[ ] No safety program in place   (0 points)

6. **Quality Culture:**

[ ] Employee quality training program   (2 points)
[ ] No employee quality training program in place   (0 points)

TOTAL _____/40 points

Additional comments: _____

_____

_____

DELIVERY & PRICE   **40 Points Possible**
(Purchasing and Stock only)

1. **Degree of reasonableness of quoted lead time:** Rate in relation to other suppliers quoting the same item, or previous quotations from this supplier.

   [ ] Better than other suppliers   (5 points)
   [ ] Same as other suppliers   (4 points)
   [ ] Within 2 weeks of other suppliers   (3 points)
   [ ] Within 4 weeks of other suppliers   (2 points)
   [ ] Within 5–8 weeks of other suppliers   (1 point)
   [ ] Exceptionally long lead time   (0 points)

2. **Actual delivery compared to requested delivery (quantity):** This rating is based on actual delivery history of promise quantities compared to receipt quantities, with data pulled from the MM/AP (Material Management/Accounts Payable) system for the item in question. Allowable window is 5% of the requested quantity. Points are awarded based on the following scale:

   [ ] 90–100% of total deliveries   (5 points)
   [ ] 80–89% of total deliveries   (4 points)
   [ ] 70–79% of total deliveries   (3 points)
   [ ] 60–69% of total deliveries   (2 points)
   [ ] Below 59% of total deliveries   (0 points)

3. **Actual delivery compared to quoted delivery (timeliness for goods or services):** This rating is based on actual delivery history of promise dates compared to receipt dates, with data pulled from the MM/AP system for the item in question. The allowable window is 2 days late or 5 days early from the scheduled delivery date. Points are awarded based on the following scale:

   [ ] 100% of total deliveries/services   (10 points)
   [ ] 90–99% of total deliveries/services   (9 points)
   [ ] 80–89% of total deliveries/services   (8 points)
   [ ] 70–79% of total deliveries/services   (7 points)
   [ ] 60–69% of total deliveries/services   (6 points)
   [ ] 50–59% of total deliveries/services   (5 points)
   [ ] 49% of total deliveries/services   (0 points)

   Note: Reduce score by half if any delivery is more than 30 days late.

4. **Adequate packaging to avoid damage in shipment, manageable quantities, and form:** To be rated by storeroom personnel or the Project Manager, this category is to encourage improvements in these areas where needed.

[ ] Packaging to specs   (2 points)
[ ] Packaging sometimes to specs   (1 point)
[ ] Packaging not to specs   (0 points)

5. **Quoted net price "in line" with competition (plus or minus 5%):**

[ ] Plus or minus 5%   (3 points)
[ ] Not in line with competition   (0 points)

6. **Quoted net price "in line" with previous quotations (plus or minus 5%):**

[ ] Plus or minus 5%   (3 points)
[ ] Not in line with competition   (0 points)

7. **Low bidder (net price): 3 points possible**

[ ] Low bidder   (3 points)
[ ] Not low bidder   (0 points)

8. **Lowest maximum escalation for successive years:** Quoted maximum percent escalation for successive years of agreement should be evaluated in relation to quote price versus any competitor's quote and versus inflation.

[ ] Lowest maximum percent escalation   (3 points)
[ ] Second lowest percent escalation   (2 points)
[ ] Third lowest percent escalation   (1 point)
[ ] Highest percent escalation   (0 points)

9. **Offering of special payment terms:**

[ ] 2% or higher 10, net 30   (3 points)
[ ] 1% 10, net 30   (2 points)
[ ] 1/2% 10, net 30   (1 point)
[ ] Net 30   (0 points)

10. **Service—Regularity of conversation with Buyer:**

[ ] Frequently communicates with buyer   (3 points)
[ ] Sometimes communicates with buyer   (2 points)
[ ] Never communicates with buyer   (0 points)

TOTAL _____/40 points

Additional comments: _____

_____

_____

SERVICE   20 Points Possible
(Users, Engineering Laboratory, Purchasing, and Accounting)

1. **Communication, responsiveness to problems, availability for field assistance:** Ratings should be a collaboration of all those employees in a department who have contact with suppliers. This includes such activities as calls regarding incoming shipments and/or services, availability for training, direct involvement in problem solving, etc.

   [ ] Very responsive   (5 points)
   [ ] Somewhat responsive   (3 points)
   [ ] Not responsive   (0 points)

2. **Job performance: (to be rated by project leader, manager, and/or user).** Job was performed in a timely manner in accordance with agreed-upon start and completion dates.

   [ ] Project started on time or early   (5 points)
   [ ] Project not started on time   (0 points)
   [ ] Project completed on time or early   (5 points)
   [ ] Project completed late   (0 points)

3. **Compliance with billing requirements (to be rated by Accounts Payable):** To include such criteria as inclusion of Purchase Order Number on invoices, ease of matching invoice to Purchase Order, etc.

   [ ] Invoice legible with all pertinent data, i.e.,
       P.O. number, line item, price, etc.   (5 points)
   [ ] Invoices sometimes correct   (1 point)
   [ ] Invoices always missing data   (0 points)

TOTAL _____/20 points

Additional comments: _____

_____

_____

_____

_____

FINANCIAL STABILITY (Accounting/Purchasing)

Rate S for Satisfactory or U for Unsatisfactory

1. **Credit check:** No point value. Rate S or U only. Approved, Certified, and Preferred status cannot be awarded without a score of S here.

2. **Review of annual report (where available):** No point value. Rate S or U only. (Not a mandatory category.)

EXTRA CREDIT (Purchasing only)   15 Points Possible

1. **Attendance at Quality Briefings (add 2 points for each attended):** Briefings will serve as "mini" Quality courses for suppliers. Purchasing will document attendance dates and who attended. This is an opportunity to earn "extra credit."

2. **Involvement on Quality Team (if yes, add 5 points):** If a supplier is represented on a Quality Team, 5 additional points are earned. "Guest" appearances, such as attending one team meeting, are worth 1/2 point each.

3. **Monthly supplier awards (add 3 points for each award):** This program is not fully developed. It will be based on exceptional performance by a supplier in any one month. The supplier can be nominated (with documentation) by anyone in the company (to be approved by the SPEAR Team).

4. **Product innovation, research and development (5 points possible):** To be rated by the Laboratory and Engineering only. Suppliers will receive extra points for developing and presenting new products. Range of points is 0–5.

5. **No extra expenses incurred:** If no extra expenses were incurred, 3 extra points are to be given. If MichCon incurs any extra expenses due to a contractor's inappropriate bidding of the job, 0 points are to be given.

6. **Minority supplier participation: (2 points possible):** Supplier will receive two extra points for each Minority supplier it utilizes in reference to our contract.

TOTAL _____/20 points

TOTAL POINTS _____/120 possible points

Additional comments: _____

_____

_____

COMPUTATION SUMMARY

120 total possible points: 100 + 20 extra credit points

120 points are possible, including extra credit points. For a supplier to qualify for our Quality Classification levels, the overall computation rating must be as follows:

[ ] 90–120   Preferred Level
[ ] 80–89   Certified Level
[ ] 70–79   Approved Level

Having an overall computation rating of any of the above points only qualifies a supplier for that level. The supplier must also meet the balance of the criteria of each level before awarded the level status. (See the previous section entitled Quality Classification Levels.)

EXHIBIT A
SUPPLIER'S OVERALL QUALITY
EVALUATION/RATING COMPUTATION

This evaluation/rating computation form will be utilized by the Supplier Performance Evaluation/Appraisal Review (SPEAR) Team to determine the overall quality rating and classification of a supplier. The team should only rate the appropriate categories. Inappropriate categories should be left blank. Any supporting documentation for the ratings should be attached to this form. The final score will be the total of all categories. Points shown are the most possible in each category; the highest score is the most favorable rating, and zero is the least favorable.

QUALITY   40 Possible Points
(Project Manager, End User, and/or Quality Assurance (QA/Laboratory)

Conformance to MichCon's specifications (0–10 pts)   _____
Zero returns due to defects (0–10 pts)   _____
Internal quality control: Quality Manual (0–5 pts)   _____
Internal quality control: Use of SPC (0–5 pts)   _____
Internal Safety Program (0–8 pts)   _____
Quality Culture (0–2 pts)   _____
                    TOTAL SCORE   _____

DELIVERY & PRICE (Purchasing & Stock)   40 Possible Points

Reasonableness of quoted lead time (0–5 pts)   _____

Actual delivery compared to requested delivery:
Quantity (0–5 pts)   _____

Actual delivery compared to quoted delivery:
On-time deliveries (0–10 pts)   _____

Adequate packaging to avoid damages in shipment,
manageable quantities, and form (0–2 pts)   _____

PRICE "in line" with competition (plus or minus 5%)
(0–3 pts)   _____

PRICE "in line" with previous quotations (plus or
minus 5%) (0–3 pts)   _____

Low bidder (0–3 pts)   _____

Lowest maximum escalation for successive years
(0–3 pts)   _____

Offering of special payment terms (0–3 pts)   _____

Service—Regularity of conversation with buyer
(0–3 pts)   _____

TOTAL SCORE   _____

SERVICE   20 Possible Points
(Users, Engineering/Lab, Purchasing & Accounting)

Responsiveness to problems, availability for field
assistance (0–5 pts)   _____

JOB PERFORMANCE
- Project started on time (0–5 pts)   _____
- Project completed on time (0–5 pts)   _____
- Compliance with billing requirements (0–5 pts)   _____

TOTAL SCORE   _____

FINANCIAL STABILITY   No point value
(Accounting/Purchasing) S = Satisfactory or U = Unsatisfactory

Credit checks   _____

Review of Annual Report   _____

EXTRA CREDIT (Purchasing Only)

Attendance of Quality Briefings (add 2 pts for
each attended)   _____

Involvement on Quality Team (if yes, add 5 pts)   _____

Monthly Supplier Award (0–3 pts)   _____

Product innovations, research and development (5 pts)   _____

No extra expense incurred (3 pts)   _____

Minority supplier participation (add 2 pts for each
participant)   _____

RATING SCORES

Quality   _____

Delivery/price   _____

Service   _____

Financial stability   _____

SUBTOTAL   _____

*Extra credit   _____

GRAND TOTAL   _____

RATING PERFORMED BY

Name _____   Department _____   Date _____

Name _____   Department _____   Date _____

Name _____   Department _____   Date _____

MichCon's QUALITY SUPPLIER AWARDS

Introduction

MichCon's Supplier Recognition program was developed to recognize suppliers who have demonstrated continuous growth performance in the areas of quality, delivery, price, and service. The type of recognition depends upon a supplier's improvement factors. As a supplier reaches each level of MichCon's Quality Supplier classification—Approved, Certified, or Preferred—the award increases in value and status. The awards follow.

Level I (Approved Supplier)

Approved Suppliers will receive a congratulatory letter from MichCon stating that they are an Approved Supplier for particular products, materials, and/or services.

Level II (Certified Supplier)

Suppliers who meet the criteria of Certified will receive a Certificate which demonstrates MichCon's appreciation for their continuous improvement. (See sample certificate on next page.)

This Certifies that MichCon Recognizes

as a valued supplier who meets the standards

of a

Certified Quality Supplier

By reaching the Certified Level, you have demonstrated your dedication
to MichCon's quality efforts to become a premier natural gas distribution company.
Your achievements also prove that you value our partnership.
Thank you for your continuous improvement. We look forward to your
becoming one of our Preferred Suppliers in the near future.

Sherryl Love
Purchasing Manager

Purna Pai
Quality Assurance Manager

Date Award Issued

michcon

Steve Ewing
President & Chief Operating Officer, MichCon

Level III (Preferred Supplier)

The Preferred Level is MichCon's highest quality level and should be rewarded accordingly. When a supplier reaches this level, it truly demonstrates a commitment to providing quality to its customers.

Suppliers who reach the Preferred Level will receive the following:

- Single-source procurement—this includes preference over Approved and Certified suppliers
- Multi-year/partnership agreements
- A plaque to display in their business office
- Announcement to local newspaper(s)
- Company's name and date they became Preferred will appear on MichCon's lobby plaque
- Lunch or dinner with an officer from MichCon
- Mention in MichCon's internal publication (space permitting)

MichCon's QUALITY SUPPLIER AUDIT

Introduction

MichCon's Supplier Evaluation Audit (Exhibit B, #6303), Audit Questionnaire/Checklist (Exhibit C, #6301), and Supplier Evaluation Determination (Exhibit D, #6302) forms were developed to provide a consistent method to evaluate a supplier's facility and its capabilities, its management practices, and its efforts in quality. These audit forms are usually sent to a supplier prior to an on-site visit or may be given to the supplier at the time of the visit.

EXHIBIT B
SUPPLIER EVALUATION AUDIT

Date:

Supplier name:

Supplier address:
City: State: Zip code:

Sales representative's name:

Name of person completing questionnaire:
Title: Phone number:

Name of person to contact for site audit:

Number of employees:
    Union _____   Non-union _____
    If union, contract expiration date_____

List any other scheduled plant shutdown periods: _____

Is your company minority or women owned?   ❏ Yes   ❏ No
If yes, check the proper ownership   ❏ Minority   ❏ Women
and submit a copy of certification

Major source of financial backing (lending bank, etc.):

Does any type of supplier performance program exist at your company?
❏ Yes   ❏ No

How do you evaluate and measure suppliers? _____

Do you manufacture to any JIT requirement?   ❏ Yes   ❏ No

What is your on-time delivery ratio to your customers? _____

Do you have statistical process control (SPC)?   ❏ Yes   ❏ No
    If no, are you planning on implementing SPC?   ❏ Yes   ❏ No

Does a formal quality control program exist in your plant with written QC
manuals and a quality control training program?   ❏ Yes   ❏ No

How are inspection samples determined? _____

Is material issued on a first-in, first-out (FIFO) basis?   ❏ Yes   ❏ No

What is your scrap rate? (Figure should be based on % to annual purchases)

EXHIBIT C
SUPPLIER AUDIT QUESTIONNAIRE/CHECKLIST

DOCUMENTATION CHECKLIST	YES	NO
1. Quality assurance manual	_____	_____
2. Statistical process control (SPC)	_____	_____
3. Test procedures	_____	_____
Receiving	_____	_____
In-process	_____	_____
4. Inspection procedures	_____	_____
Receiving	_____	_____
In-process	_____	_____
5. Workmanship standards	_____	_____
6. Equipment maintenance	_____	_____
7. Organizational chart	_____	_____
8. Process procedures	_____	_____
9. In-process travelers	_____	_____
10. Inspection material tags	_____	_____
11. Rejected or nonconforming material tags	_____	_____
12. Pre-audit questionnaire complete	_____	_____
13. Team approach	_____	_____

TOPIC CHECKLIST		
1. Order entry processing	_____	_____
2. Material procurement control	_____	_____
3. Manufacturing procedures/process	_____	_____
4. Inspection	_____	_____
5. Segregation of discrepant materials	_____	_____
6. Certification process	_____	_____
7. Documentation control	_____	_____
8. Quality improvement process	_____	_____
9. Susceptibility of process to loss of key personnel	_____	_____
10. Housekeeping/safety	_____	_____
11. In-house training	_____	_____
12. New product development	_____	_____

Comments/concerns: _____

_____

_____

EXHIBIT D
SUPPLIER EVALUATION DETERMINATION

Supplier name:

Supplier address:

City: State: Zip code:

Phone number: Contact person:

Date audit conducted:

MichCon's Quality Assurance representative:

MichCon's Purchasing representative:

DETERMINATION:

SUPPLIER ACCEPTED	**SUPPLIER ACCEPTED CONDITIONALLY**	**SUPPLIER NOT ACCEPTED**

REASON(S) FOR NOT ACCEPTING SUPPLIER OR ACCEPTING CONDITIONALLY:

1.

2.

3.

MichCon SUPPLIER QUALITY AUDIT SURVEY

Company name:_____

Div./subsidiary of: _____

Address: _____   Phone:_____

_____

_____

Manufacturer _____   Distributor _____

COMPANY PERSONNEL

Chief Executive Officer   _____

Plant Manager   _____

Sales Manager   _____

Quality Manager   _____

Engineering Manager   _____

Order Entry Contact(s)   _____

Person responsible for   _____
MichCon specs

Person(s) responsible for _____
corrective action on
quality nonconformance

COMPANY INFORMATION

Established in: _____

Number of personnel: _____ Manufacturing: _____

Administrative: _____

QA/QC: _____

Number of shifts: _____

Overall size of facility: _____ft²

Age of building: _____

Age of equipment: _____

Present production level is at _____ % of capacity.

Percent of capacity/volume devoted to MichCon production: _____%

Operation(s) that supplier subcontracts: _____

_____

Union shop?   YES _____   NO_____

Contract expiration date: _____

Gross annual sales: $_____

Recognized as certified/approved by: _____

Approved product(s) supplied to MichCon (use additional sheet if necessary):

MichCon Spec/Product   **Internal Name/Product Code**

_____

_____

_____

Other products produced or supplied at this location which may be of benefit
to MichCon:

_____

_____

_____

Are any MichCon purchase order or specification requirements in conflict with supplier's standards or methods which could be reviewed for our mutual benefit? If so, list below:

Product requirements:

Testing requirements:

Documentation/certification:

Packaging requirements:

Shipping/delivery requirements:

Other:

The scoring system is 0–5 with 5 being the highest score and 0 the lowest. N/A means not applicable.

A. QUALITY MANAGEMENT

An ongoing effort demonstrated by all levels of management through words and actions to the principles of continuous improvement and a dedication to excellence.

1. Is there a formal company program/process to bring about improvements in quality and productivity?   5 4 3 2 1 0 N/A

2. If scored greater than or equal to 3 in A.1, is the emphasis on satisfying the customer's needs and requirements, doing things right the first time, and continuous improvement?   5 4 3 2 1 0 N/A

3. Is there evidence of top management commitment to and support of the program/process?   5 4 3 2 1 0 N/A

4. Is a Quality Policy published, posted, accessible to all employees?   5 4 3 2 1 0 N/A

5. Is the Quality Policy well-known by all employees?   5 4 3 2 1 0 N/A

6. Is there formal training/education for all employees? If so, describe.   5 4 3 2 1 0 N/A

7. Are there formal training or employee certification programs in use for testing equipment and/or high-skill operations? If yes, are records kept?   5 4 3 2 1 0 N/A

8. Are you using statistical methods and techniques on processes to guide action to more consistently meet customer product and service requirements?   5 4 3 2 1 0 N/A

9. Is the team approach utilized to bring about improvements in quality and process?   5 4 3 2 1 0 N/A

10. Is there evidence of good housekeeping and safe practices/environment?   5 4 3 2 1 0 N/A

B. QUALITY ASSURANCE

Those planned, systematic, and preventative actions which are necessary to ensure that materials, product, and processes conform to specified requirements.

1. Does a Quality Control Manual exist? If so, is it current and accessible? **5 4 3 2 1 0 N/A**

2. Are there formalized procedures/work instructions? If so are they: _____ **Yes** _____ **No**

   a. Aligned with the Quality Manual? **3 2 1 0 N/A**

   b. Current and up-to-date? **3 2 1 0 N/A**

   c. Accessible to pertinent personnel? **3 2 1 0 N/A**

   d. Properly adhered to? **3 2 1 0 N/A**

   e. Support and/or satisfy MichCon's quality needs? **3 2 1 0 N/A**

3. Is there a documented system for controlling material/equipment through all stages of production such that identification status and traceability are maintained? **5 4 3 2 1 0 N/A**

4. Briefly describe what gauges or test/measuring equipment are utilized in each of the following areas:

   Incoming materials   **In-process materials**   **Final materials**

   a. Is there a written schedule for the calibration of testing/measuring equipment and is it adhered to? **3 2 1 0 N/A**

   b. Are there standards used for calibration traceable to recognized reference sources? **3 2 1 0 N/A**

   c. Are calibration records kept and for how long? **3 2 1 0 N/A**

   d. Are gauges and test/measure equipment well maintained? **3 2 1 0 N/A**

5. Are there written process monitoring and con-   5 4 3 2 1 0 N/A
trol procedures to ensure quality of finished
products?

6. Is there a written policy for the disposition of   5 4 3 2 1 0 N/A
nonconforming finished product?

7. Is there a system in place to ensure that all   5 4 3 2 1 0 N/A
nonconforming materials are isolated from ap-
proved materials?

8. Is there a defined, closed-looped "corrective   5 4 3 2 1 0 N/A
action system" which focuses on nonconfor-
mance and prevention of failure?

9. Is there a procedure to perform internal audits   5 4 3 2 1 0 N/A
on your Quality Process? If so, at what fre-
quency?

C. MATERIAL CONTROL

An established documented system to ensure the quality of incoming
materials and services.

1. Is there a formal Supplier Quality Manage-   5 4 3 2 1 0 N/A
ment evaluation, selection, and rating system?

2. Is supplier certification or approval required   5 4 3 2 1 0 N/A
prior to the purchase of critical materials?

3. Are suppliers of critical materials required to   5 4 3 2 1 0 N/A
demonstrate that their processes are in statis-
tical control?

4. Do you monitor your suppliers? If so, how?   5 4 3 2 1 0 N/A

5. Are there specifications for all purchased   5 4 3 2 1 0 N/A
materials?

6. Are incoming materials inspected, docu-   5 4 3 2 1 0 N/A
mented, and monitored prior to use in pro-
duction and are accurate records maintained?

7. Is there a sampling and testing procedure for   5 4 3 2 1 0 N/A
materials? If so, what formal sampling plan is
utilized?

8. Are materials identified and traceable to Test and/or Certification Reports?   5 4 3 2 1 0 N/A

9. Is there a formal procedure for the disposition of nonconforming materials? If so, how are these materials handled?   5 4 3 2 1 0 N/A

10. Are rejected incoming materials identified and physically segregated to prevent use?   5 4 3 2 1 0 N/A

11. Do you subcontract work to external sources? If so, are there adequate controls to assure quality of the subcontracted work?   5 4 3 2 1 0 N/A

D. PROCESS CONTROL

The system which consistently provides and controls the tools, methods, and machines for the production and delivery of products or services in a stable environment.

1. Is there a written sequence or flow diagram detailing the manufacturing/administrative sequence/process?   5 4 3 2 1 0 N/A

2. Are statistical control measurements and methods utilized in all critical process areas to determine process stability and reduction of product concerns?   5 4 3 2 1 0 N/A

3. Are the processes in continuous control and capable of meeting MichCon's quality requirements?   5 4 3 2 1 0 N/A

4. Is there an effective system of which the process and/or inspection status of the product is indicated throughout the manufacturing sequence?   5 4 3 2 1 0 N/A

5. How are changes in the process documented?   5 4 3 2 1 0 N/A

6. How are these changes transmitted internally?   5 4 3 2 1 0 N/A

7. Are changes which may affect the product communicated to the customer?   5 4 3 2 1 0 N/A

E. CUSTOMER SERVICE

All those activities performed to satisfy and/or exceed the customer's needs or expectations.

1. Do you have EDI capability? If so, what type of system do you have?
   5 4 3 2 1 0 N/A

2. Are there records maintained that show compliance with MichCon's shipping and handling requirements?
   5 4 3 2 1 0 N/A

3. Is outgoing product inspected prior to packaging or shipping? If so, what formal sampling plan is utilized?
   3 2 1 0 N/A

4. Is there verification prior to shipping that ensures all purchase order requirements and shipping instructions have been met?
   5 4 3 2 1 0 N/A

5. Do/will you provide certification of product conformance?
   5 4 3 2 1 0 N/A

6. Do you have a system for monitoring your delivery performance? If so, how?
   5 4 3 2 1 0 N/A

7. Are you continually working to improve delivery performance? If so, how?
   5 4 3 2 1 0 N/A

8. Indicate whether there is documented evidence for each of the following:
   a. Reduced set-up times   3 2 1 0 N/A

   b. Reduced start-up scrap   3 2 1 0 N/A

   c. Reduced lead times   3 2 1 0 N/A

9. Is there an effective system in place for addressing customer concerns?
   5 4 3 2 1 0 N/A

SUPPLIER AUDIT RATING

	Actual points	Total possible points
A. Quality Management	_____	50
B. Quality Assurance	_____	62
C. Raw Material Control	_____	55
D. Process Control	_____	35
E. Customer Service	_____	47
Actual Total	_____	

Total Possible _____249_____

Minus NA's _____

Total Adjusted _____
Points

% attained equals the Actual Total/Total Possible or Adjusted = _____ %

70%–84% qualifies supplier for Approved Status

85%–94% qualifies supplier for Certified Status

95%–100% qualifies supplier for Preferred Status

Facilities should provide improvement plans within an agreed upon time for each section (A through E) that falls below 70% attainment for that section.

Evaluation conducted by: _____

_____

_____

Date of evaluation: _____

Date survey completed: _____

MichCon
GLOSSARY OF TERMS
FOR SUPPLIER QUALITY

Consistent performance: The proven ability to meet or exceed a specification or requirement on a continuous basis.

Continuous improvements: An ongoing effort which reflects positive results brought about by changes in the way things are done.

Documented quality system: The development, implementation, and maintenance of written procedures or instruction to establish processes that are capable of ensuring continuous conformance and exceeding agreed upon specification(s) or requirements.

DOT: Department of Transportation.

EDI (Electronic Data Interchange): Direct computer-to-computer exchange business information between organizations in a standard format.

Inspection: The physical act of verifying whether service or work, as provided by the contractor, conforms to the applicable specification(s) and/or requirement(s).

Management commitment: A dedicated ongoing effort demonstrated by all levels of management through words, plans, and actions, to the principles of total quality (i.e., continuous improvement, customer satisfaction, teamwork, employee involvement, training and education, etc.).

Nonconformance: Any deviation from a standardized work process, specification, or requirement.

Policy: A documented predetermined decision on how specified actions will be handled.

Procedures: Documented steps that will be followed to complete a task.

Quality service: The customer's perception that what was received meets, satisfies, or exceeds the requirement(s) of the contract.

Self-assessment questionnaire: A questionnaire that is completed by a Contractor that does business with MichCon.

Team: Share and build on one another's ideas, coordinate efforts, and understand how actions impact others.

Team approach: A process in which employees are allowed to solve their own problems together and are educated, trained, and able to make decisions with regard to work improvements.

Workmanship: The level of quality work to complete a job.

FILLING in the GAPS with a HISTORY of TOTAL QUALITY

Frank Voehl

In order to prepare for the future, we must also look to the past. The history of total quality holds many valuable lessons as keys to creating a better world of today.

IN THE BEGINNING

About the year one million B.C., give or take a few centuries, man first began to fashion stone tools for hunting and survival.[1] Up until 8000 B.C., however, very little progress was made in the quality control of these tools. It was at this time that man began assembling instruments with fitting holes, which suggests the use of interchangeable parts on a very limited basis. Throughout this long period, each man made his own tools. The evidence of quality control was measured to some extent by how long he stayed alive. If the tools were well made, his chances of survival increased. A broken axe handle usually spelled doom.

INTRODUCTION OF INTERCHANGEABLE PARTS AND DIVISION OF LABOR

A little over 200 years ago, in 1787, the concepts of interchangeable parts and division of labor were first introduced in the United States. Eli Whitney, inventor of the cotton gin, applied these concepts to the production of 10,000 flintlock rifles for the U.S. military arsenal. However, Whitney had considerable difficulty in making all the parts exactly the same. It took him ten years to complete the 10,000 muskets that he promised to deliver in two years.

Three factors impacted Whitney's inability to deliver the 10,000 muskets in two years as promised. First, there was a dramatic shortage of qualified craftsmen needed to build the muskets. Consequently, Whitney correctly identified the solution to the problem—machines must do what men previously did. If individual machines were assembled to create each individual part needed, then men could be taught to operate these machines. Thus, Whitney's application of division of labor to a highly technical process was born. Whitney called this a *manufactory*.

Next, it took almost one full year to build the manufactory, rather than two months as Whitney originally thought. Not only did the weather inflict havoc on the schedule, but epidemics of yellow fever slowed progress considerably.

Third, obtaining the raw materials in a timely, usable manner was a hit-or-miss proposition. The metal ore used was often defective, flawed, and pitted. In addition, training the workers to perform the actual assembly took much longer than Whitney imagined and required a considerable amount of his personal attention, often fifteen to twenty hours a day. Also, once the men were trained, some left to work for competing armories.[2]

To compound these factors, his ongoing cotton gin patent lawsuits consumed a considerable amount of his highly leveraged attention and time. Fortunately for Whitney, his credibility in Washington granted him considerable laxity in letting target dates slip. War with France was no longer imminent. Thus, a quality product and the associated manufacturing expertise were deemed more important than schedule. What was promised in 28 months took almost 120 months to deliver.

Luckily for Whitney, the requirement of "on time and within budget" was not yet in vogue. What happened to Whitney was a classic study in the problems of trying to achieve a real breakthrough in operations. Out of this experience, Whitney and others realized that creating parts exactly the same was not possible and, if tried, would prove to be very expensive. This concept of interchangeable parts would eventually lead to statistical methods of control, while division of labor would lead to the factory assembly line.

THE FIRST CONTROL LIMITS

The experiences of Whitney and others who followed led to a relaxation of the requirements for exactness and the use of tolerances. This allowed for a less-than-perfect fit between two (or more) parts, and the concept of the "go–no-go" tolerance was introduced between 1840 and 1870.[3]

This idea was a major advancement in that it created the concept of upper and lower tolerance limits, thus allowing the production worker more freedom to do his job with an accompanying lowering of cost. All he had to do was stay within the tolerance limits, instead of trying to achieve unnecessary or unattainable perfection.

DEFECTIVE PARTS INSPECTION

The next advancement centered around expanding the notion of tolerance and using specifications, where variation is classified as either meeting or not meeting requirements. For those pieces of product that every now and then fell outside the specified tolerance range (or limits), the question arose as to what to do with them. To discard or modify these pieces added significantly to the cost of production.

However, to search for the unknown causes of defects and then eliminate them also cost money. The heart of the problem was as follows: how to reduce the percentage of defects to the point where (1) the rate of increase in the *cost of control* equals the rate of *increase* in *savings*, which is (2) brought about by *decreasing the number of parts rejected.*

In other words, inspection/prevention had to be cost effective. Minimizing the percent of defects in a cost-effective manner was not the only problem to be solved. Tests for many quality characteristics require destructive testing, such as tests for strength, chemical composition, fuse blowing time, etc. Because not every piece can be tested, use of the statistical sample was initiated around the turn of the century.

STATISTICAL THEORY

During the early part of the twentieth century, a tremendous increase in quality consciousness occurred. What were the forces at work that caused this sudden acceleration of interest in the application of statistical quality control? There were at least three key factors.

The first was a rapid growth in standardization, beginning in 1900. Until 1915, Great Britain was the only country in the world with some type of national standardization movement. The rate of growth in the number of industrial standardization organizations throughout the world, especially between 1916 and 1932, rose dramatically.[4] During that fifteen-year period, the movement grew from one country (Great Britain) to twenty-five, with the United States coming on line about 1917, just at the time of World War I.

The second major factor ushering in the new era was a radical shift in ideology which occurred in about 1900. This ideological shift was away from the notion of exactness of science (which existed in 1787 when interchangeability of parts was introduced) to probability and statistical concepts, which developed in almost every field of science around 1900.

The third factor was the evolution of division of labor into the factory system and the first assembly line systems of the early twentieth century. These systems proved to be ideal for employing an immigrant workforce quickly.

SCIENTIFIC MANAGEMENT AND TAYLORISM

Frederick Winslow Taylor was born in 1856 and entered industry as an apprentice in the Enterprise Hydraulics Shop in 1874. According to popular legend, the old-timers in the shop told him: "Now young man, here's about how much work you should do each morning and each afternoon. Don't do any more than that—that's the limit."[5]

It was obvious to Taylor that the men were producing below their capacity, and he soon found out why. The short-sighted management of that day would set standards, often paying per piece rates for the work. Then, when a worker discovered how to produce more, management cut the rate. In turn, management realized that the workers were deliberately restricting output but could not do anything about it.

It was Taylor's viewpoint that the whole system was wrong. Having studied the writings and innovations of Whitney, he came to realize that the concept of division of labor had to be revamped if greater productivity and efficiency were to be realized. His vision included a super-efficient assembly line as part of a management system of operations. He, more than anyone at the time, understood the inability of management to increase individual productivity, and he understood the reluctance of the workers to produce at a high rate. Because he had been a working man, it was apparent to him that there was a tremendous difference between *actual* output and *potential* output. Taylor thought that if such practices applied throughout the world and throughout all industry, the potential production capacity was at least three or four times what was actually being produced. When he became a foreman, Taylor set out to find ways to eliminate this waste and increase production.

For more than twenty-five years, Taylor and his associates explored ways to increase productivity and build the model factory of the future. The techniques they developed were finally formalized in writing and communicated to other people. During the early years of this experimentation, most who knew about it were associated with Taylor at the Midvale Steel Company and Bethlehem Steel.

Other famous names began to enter the picture and contribute to the body of science of the new management thinking. Among them were Carl G. L. Barth, a mathematician and statistician who assisted Taylor in analytical work, and Henry L. Gantt (famous for the Gantt chart), who invented the slide rule. Another associate of Taylor's, Sanford E. Thompson, developed the first decimal stopwatch.[5] Finally, there was young Walter Shewhart, who was to transform industry with his statistical concepts and thinking and his ability to bridge technical tools with a management system.

At the turn of the century, Taylor wrote a collection of reports and papers that were published by the American Society of Mechanical Engineers. One of the most famous was *On the Art of Cutting Metals*, which had worldwide impact. With Maunsel White, Taylor developed the first high-speed steel. Taylor was also instrumental in the development of one of the first industrial cost accounting systems, even though, according to legend, he previously knew nothing about accounting.

Frank G. and Lillian Gilbreth, aware of Taylor's work in measurement and analysis, turned their attention to mechanizing and commercializing Taylorism. For their experimental model, they chose the ancient craft of bricklaying. It had been assumed that production in bricklaying certainly should have reached its zenith thousands of years ago, with nothing more to be done to increase production. Yet Frank Gilbreth was able to show that, by following his techniques and with proper management planning, production could be raised from an average of 120 bricks per hour to 350 bricks per hour, and the worker would be less tired than he had been under the old system.

The Gilbreths refined some of the studies and techniques developed by Taylor. They used the motion picture camera to record work steps for analyses and broke them down into minute elements called "therbligs" (Gilbreth spelled backwards). Their results were eventually codified into the use of predetermined motion–time measures which were used by industrial engineers and efficiency experts of the day.

By 1912, the efficiency movement was gaining momentum. Taylor was called before a special committee of the House of Representatives which was investigating scientific management and its impact on the railroad industry. He tried to explain scientific management to the somewhat hostile railroad hearings committee, whose members regarded it as "speeding up" work. He said:

> Scientific management involves a complete mental revolution on the part of the *working man* engaged in any particular establishment or industry…a complete mental revolution on the part of these men as to their duties toward their work, toward their fellowman, and toward their employers.

And scientific management involves an equally complete mental revolution on the part of those on *management's side*...the foreman, the superintendent, the owner of the business, and the board of directors. Here we must have a mental revolution on their part as to their duties toward their fellow workers in management, toward their workmen, and toward all of their daily problems. Without this complete mental revolution on both sides, scientific management does not exist!

I want to sweep the deck, sweep away a good deal of the rubbish first by pointing out what scientific management is not—it is not an efficiency device, nor is it any bunch or group of efficiency devices. It is not a new system of figuring costs. It is not a new scheme of paying men. It is not holding a stopwatch on a man and writing things down about him. It is not time study. It is not motion study, nor an analysis of the movements of a man. Nor is scientific management the printing and ruling and unloading of a ton or two of blank forms on a set of men and saying, "Here's your system—go to it."

It is not divided foremanship, nor functional foremanship. It is not any of these devices which the average man calls to mind when he hears the words "scientific management." I am not sneering at cost-keeping systems—at time-study, at functional foremanship, nor at any of the new and improved schemes of paying men. Nor am I sneering at efficiency devices, if they are really devices which make for efficiency. I believe in them. What I am emphasizing is that these devices in whole or part are *not* scientific management; they are useful adjuncts to scientific management, but they are also useful adjuncts to other systems of management.[5]

Taylor found out, the hard way, the importance of the cooperative spirit. He was strictly the engineer at first. Only after painful experiences did he realize that the human factor, the social system, and mental attitude of people in both management and labor had to be adjusted and changed completely before greater productivity could result.

Referring to his early experiences in seeking greater output, Taylor described the strained feelings between himself and his workmen as "miserable." Yet he was determined to improve production. He continued his experiments until three years before his death in 1915, when he found that human motivation, not just engineered improvements, could alone increase output.

Unfortunately, the human factor was ignored by many. Shortly after the railroad hearings, self-proclaimed "efficiency experts" did untold damage to scientific management. Time studies and the new efficiency techniques were used by incompetent "consultants" who sold managers on the idea of increasing profit by "speeding up" employees. Consequently, many labor unions, just beginning to feel their strength, worked against the new science and all efficiency approaches. With the passing of Taylor in 1915, the scientific management movement lost, for the moment, any chance of reaching its true potential as the catalyst for the future total quality management system. Still, the foundation was laid for the management system that was soon to become a key ingredient of organizations of the future.

WALTER SHEWHART—THE FOUNDING FATHER

Walter Shewhart was an engineer, scientist, and philosopher. He was a very deep thinker, and his ideas, although profound and technically perfect, were difficult to fathom. His style of writing followed his style of thinking—very obtuse. Still, he was brilliant, and his works on variation and sampling, coupled with his teachings on the need for documentation, influenced forever the course of industrial history.

Shewhart was familiar with the scientific management movement and its evolution from Whitney's innovation of division of labor. Although he was concerned about its evolution into sweatshop factory environments, his major focus was on the other of Whitney's great innovations—interchangeable parts—for this encompassed variation, rejects, and waste.

To deal with the issue of variation, Shewhart developed the control chart in 1924. He realized that the traditional use of tolerance limits was short-sighted, because they only provided a method for judging the quality of a product that had already been made.[6]

The control limits on Shewhart's control charts, however, provided a ready guide for acting on the process in order to eliminate what he called *assignable causes*[8] of variation, thus preventing inferior products from being produced in the future. This allowed management to focus on the future, through the use of statistical probability—a prediction of future production based upon historical data. Thus, the emphasis shifted from costly correction of problems to prevention of problems and improvement of processes.[7]

Like Taylor, Shewhart's focus shifted from individual parts to a systems approach. The notion of zero defects of individual parts was replaced with zero variability of system operations.

Shewhart's Control System

Shewhart identified the traditional act of control as consisting of three elements: the act of specifying what is required, the act of producing what is specified, and the act of judging whether the requirements have been met. This simple picture of the control of quality would work well if production could be viewed in the context of an exact science, where all products are made exactly the same. Shewhart knew, however, that because variation is pervasive, the control of quality characteristics must be a matter of probability. He envisioned a statistician helping an engineer to understanding variation and arriving at the economic control of quality.[8]

Shewhart's Concept of Variation

Determining the *state of statistical control* in terms of degree of variation is the first step in the Shewhart control system. Rather than specifying what is required in terms of tolerance requirements, Shewhart viewed variation as being present in everything and identified two types of variation: *controlled* and *uncontrolled.*

This is fundamentally different from the traditional way of classifying variation as either acceptable or unacceptable (go–no-go tolerance). Viewing variation as controlled or uncontrolled enables one to focus on the causes of variation in order to improve a process (before the fact) as opposed to focusing on the output of a process in order to judge whether or not the product is acceptable (after the fact).

Shewhart taught that controlled variation is a consistent pattern of variation over time that is due to random or *chance causes*. He recognized that there may be many chance causes of variation, but the effect of any one of these is relatively small; therefore, which cause or causes are responsible for observed variation is a matter of chance. Shewhart stated that a process that is being affected only by *chance* causes of variation is said to be *in a state of statistical control*.

All processes contain chance causes of variation, and Shewhart taught that it is possible to reduce the chance causes of variation, but it is not realistic or cost effective to try to remove them all. The control limits on Shewhart's control charts represent the boundaries of the occurrence of chance causes of variation operating within the system.

The second type of variation—uncontrolled variation—is an inconsistent or changing pattern of variation that occurs over time and is due to what Shewhart classified as *assignable causes*. Because the effects of assignable causes of variation are relatively major compared to chance causes, they can and must be identified and removed.[9] According to Shewhart, a process is *out of statistical control* when it is being affected by assignable causes.

One of Shewhart's main problems was how to communicate this newfound theory without overwhelming the average businessman or engineer. The answer came in the form of staged experiments using models which demonstrated variation. His *ideal bowl experiment*[10] with poker chips was modeled by his protege, W. Edwards Deming, some twenty years later with his famous *red bead experiment*.

Another major contribution of Shewhart's first principle of control was recognition of the need for operational definitions that can be communicated to operators, inspectors, and scientists alike. He was fond of asking, "How can an operator carry out his job tasks if he does not understand what the job is? And how can he know what the job is if what was produced yesterday was O.K., but today the same product is wrong?" He believed that inspection, whether the operator inspects his own work or relies on someone else to do it for him, must have operational definitions. Extending specifications beyond product and into the realm of operator performance was the first attempt to define the "extended system of operations" which would greatly facilitate the production process.

The Shewhart System of Production

Shewhart's second principle—the act of producing what is specified—consists of five important steps (Shewhart's teachings are in italics):

1. Outline the data collection framework: *Specify in a general way how an observed sequence of data is to be examined for clues as to the existence of assignable causes of variability.*

2. Develop the sampling plan: *Specify how the original data are to be taken and how they are to be broken up into subsamples upon the basis of human judgments about whether the conditions under which the data were taken were essentially the same or not.*

3. Identify the formulas and control limits for each sample: *Specify the criterion of control that is to be used, indicating what statistics are to be computed for each subsample and how these are to be used in computing action or control limits for each statistic for which the control criterion is to be constructed.*

4. Outline the corrective actions/improvement thesis: *Specify the action that is to be taken when an observed statistic falls outside its control limits.*

5. Determine the size of the database: *Specify the quantity of data that must be available and found to satisfy the criterion of control before the engineer is to act as though he had attained a state of statistical control.*[1]

The Shewhart system became a key component of the technical system of total quality. The works of Deming, Juran, Feigenbaum, Sarasohn, Ishikawa, and others who followed would amplify Shewhart's concept of quality as a *technical system* into its many dimensions, which eventually led to the body of knowledge known as total quality.

The Shewhart Cycle: When Control Meets Scientific Management

From the "exact science" days of the 1800s to the 1920s, *specification, production,* and *inspection* were considered to be independent of each other when viewed in a straight line manner. They take on an entirely different picture in an inexact science. When the production process is viewed from the standpoint of the control of quality as a matter of probability, then specification, production, and inspection are linked together as represented in a circular diagram or wheel. *Specification and production* are linked because it is important to know how well the tolerance limits are being satisfied by the existing process and what improvements are necessary. Shewhart compared this process (which he called the Scientific Method) to the dynamic process of acquiring knowledge, which is similar to an experiment. Step 1 was formulating the hypothesis. Step 2 was conducting the experiment. Step 3 was testing the hypothesis.[11] In the Shewhart wheel, the successful completion of each interlocking component led to a cycle of continuous improvement. (Years later Deming was to popularize this cycle of improvement in his famous Deming wheel.)

Shewhart Meets Deming

It was at the Bell Laboratories in New Jersey where Shewhart, who was leading the telephone reliability efforts during the 1930s, first met Deming. Shewhart, as discussed earlier, was developing his system for improving worker performance and productivity by measuring variation using control charts and statistical methods. Deming was impressed and liked what he saw, especially Shewhart's intellect and the *wheel*—the Shewhart cycle of control. He realized that with training, workers could retain control over their work processes by monitoring the quality of the items produced. Deming also believed that once workers were trained and educated and were empowered to manage their work processes, quality would be increased and costly inspections could once and for all be eliminated. He presented the idea that higher quality would cost less, not more. Deming studied Shewhart's teachings and techniques and learned well, even if at times he was lost and said that his genius was in knowing when to act and when to leave a process alone. At times he was frustrated by Shewhart's obtuse style of thinking and writing.[12]

In 1938, Shewhart delivered four lectures to the U.S. Department of Agriculture (USDA) Graduate School at the invitation of Deming. In addition to being in charge of the mathematics and statistics courses at the USDA Graduate School, Deming was responsible for inviting guest lecturers. He invited Shewhart to present a series of lectures on how statistical methods of control were being used in industry to economically control the quality of manufactured products. Shewhart spent an entire year developing the lectures, titled them *Statistical Method from the Viewpoint of Quality Control*, and delivered them in March of 1938. They were subsequently edited into book format by Deming and published in 1939.

In a couple of years both Deming and Shewhart were called upon by the U.S. government to aid the war effort. As David Halberstam recounted, the War Department, impressed by Shewhart's theories and work, brought together a small group of experts on statistical process control (SPC) to establish better quality guidelines for defense contractors.[13] Deming was a member of that group and he came to love the work.

ORIGINS OF DEMING

Who was Dr. W. Edwards Deming, the man who was to take Shewhart's teachings, popularize them, and even go beyond? He was born on October 14, 1900 and earned his Ph.D. in physics at Yale University in the summer of 1927, which is where he learned to use statistical theory. As a graduate student in the late 1920s, he did part-time summer work at the famous Western Electric Hawthorne plant in Chicago. It was at this plant that Elton Mayo some ten years later would perform his experiments later known as the Hawthorne Experiments. While working at Hawthorne, Deming could not help noticing the poor working conditions of this sweatshop environment, which employed predominantly female laborers to produce telephones. Deming was both fascinated and appalled by what he saw and learned. It was at Hawthorne where he saw the full effects of the abuses of the Taylor system of scientific management. He also saw the full effect of Whitney's second great innovation—division of labor—when carried to extreme by ivory tower management uncaring about the state of the social system of the organization. So what if the work environment was a sweatshop—the workers were paid well enough! "The women should be happy just to have a job" seemed to be the unspoken attitude.

When Deming Met Taylor(ism)

A couple of years before meeting Shewhart, when Deming encountered Taylorism at Hawthorne, he found a scientific management system with the following objectives:

- Develop a science for each element of work.
- Scientifically select a workman and train and develop him.
- Secure whole-hearted cooperation between management and labor to ensure that all work is done in accordance with the principles developed.
- Divide the work between management and labor. The manager takes over all work for which he is better suited than the workman.

It was the fourth point, which evolved out of the division of labor concept, that Deming found to be the real villain. In practice, this meant removing from the worker basic responsibility for the quality of the work. What Deming disliked was that workers should not be hired to think about their work. That was management's job. Errors will occur, but the worker need not worry—the inspector will catch any mistakes *before* they leave the plant. In addition, management could always reduce the per-piece pay to reflect scrap and rework. Any worker who produced too many inferior quality pieces would be fired.

The problem with Taylorism is that it views the production process mechanistically, instead of holistically, as a system which includes the human elements of motivation and respect. Taylorism taught American industry to view the worker as "a cog in the giant industrial machine, whose job could be defined and directed by educated managers administering a set of rules."[14] Work on the assembly lines of America and at Hawthorne was simple, repetitive, and boring. Management was top-down. Pay per piece meant that higher output equals higher take-home pay. Quality of work for the most part was not a factor for the average, everyday worker.

This system found a friend in the assembly line process developed by Henry Ford and was widely incorporated into America's private and public sectors. Taylor's management system made it possible for waves of immigrants, many of whom could not read, write, or speak English (and at times not even communicate with one another), to find employment in American factories. Taylor's ideas were even introduced into the nation's schools.[15]

Edwards Deming had various colleagues at the time, one of whom was Joseph Juran, another famous quality "guru." They rebelled at the scientific management movement. They felt that the authoritarian Taylorism method of management was degrading to the human spirit and counterproductive to the interests of employees, management, the company, and society as a whole.[16] Mayo and his Hawthorne research team confirmed these feelings with their findings: good leadership leads to high morale and motivation, which in turn leads to higher production. Good leadership was defined as democratic, rather than autocratic, and people centered, as opposed to production centered. Thus began the human relations era.

POST-WORLD WAR II

When the war ended, American industry converted to peacetime production of goods and services. People were hungry for possessions and an appetite developed worldwide for products "made in the U.S.A." The focus in the United States returned to quantity over quality, and a gradual deterioration of market share occurred, with billions of dollars in international business lost to Japanese and European competitors. These were the modern-day phoenixes rising from the ashes of war. America became preoccupied with the mechanics of mass production and its role as world provider to a hungry people. What followed was an imbalance between satisfying the needs of the worker and a lack of appreciation for and recognition of the external customer. America moved away from what had made it great!

The Japanese Resurrection

Japan first began to apply statistical control concepts in the early 1920s, but moved away from them when the war began.[17] In 1946, under General Douglas MacArthur's leadership, the Supreme Command for the Allied Powers (SCAP) established quality control tools and techniques as the approach to affect the turnaround of Japanese industry. Japan had sacrificed its industry, and eventually its food supply, to support its war effort. Subsequently, there was little left in post-war Japan to occupy. The country was a shambles. Only one major city, Kyoto, had escaped wide-scale destruction; food was scarce and industry was negligible.[17]

Against a backdrop of devastation and military defeat, a group of Japanese scientists and engineers—organized appropriately as the Union of Japanese Scientists and Engineers (JUSE)—dedicated themselves to working with American and Allied experts to help rebuild the country. Reconstruction was a daunting and monumental task. With few natural resources available or any immediate means of producing them, export of manufactured goods was essential. However, Japanese industry—or what was left of it—was producing inferior goods, a fact which was recognized worldwide. JUSE was faced with the task of drastically improving the quality of Japan's industrial output as an essential exchange commodity for survival.

W. S. Magill and Homer Sarasohn, among others, assisted with the dramatic transformation of the electronics industry and telecommunications. Magill is regarded by some as the father of statistical quality control in Japan. He was the first to advocate its use in a 1945 lecture series and successfully applied SPC techniques to vacuum tube production in 1946 at NEC.[18]

Sarasohn worked with supervisors and managers to improve reliability and yields in the electronics field from 40 percent in 1946 to 80–90 percent in 1949; he documented his findings for SCAP, and MacArthur took notice. He ordered Sarasohn to instruct Japanese businessmen how to get things done. The Japanese listened, but the Americans forgot. In 1950, Sarasohn's attention was directed toward Korea, and Walter Shewhart was asked to come to Japan. He was unable to at the time, and Deming was eventually tapped to direct the transformation.

In July 1950, Deming began a series of day-long lectures to Japanese management in which he taught the basic "Elementary Principles of Statistical Control of Quality." The Japanese embraced the man and his principles and named their most prestigious award for quality The Deming Prize. During the 1970s, Deming turned his attention back to the United States and at 93 years old (at the time of this writing) is still going strong. His Fourteen Points go far beyond statistical methods and address the management system as well as the social system or culture of the organization. In many ways, he began to sound more and more like Frederick Taylor, whose major emphasis in later years was on the need for a *mental revolution*—a transformation. Deming's Theory of Profound Knowledge brings together all three systems of total quality.

THE OTHER "GURUS" ARRIVE

What began in Japan in the 1950s became a worldwide quality movement, albeit on a limited basis, within twenty years. During this period the era of the "gurus" evolved (Deming, Juran, Ishikawa, Feigenbaum, and Crosby). Beginning with Deming in 1948 and Juran in 1954, the movement was eventually carried back to the United States by Feigenbaum in the 1960s and Crosby in the 1970s. Meanwhile, Ishikawa and his associates at JUSE kept the movement alive in Japan. By 1980, the bell began to toll loud and clear in the West with the NBC White Paper entitled "If Japan Can Do It, Why Can't We?" The following are thumbnail sketches of the teachings of the other gurus.

Joseph Juran

Joseph Juran was the son of an immigrant shoemaker from Romania and began his industrial career at Western Electric's Hawthorne plant before World War II. He later worked at Bell Laboratories in the area of quality assurance. He worked as a government administrator, university professor, labor arbitrator, and corporate director before establishing his own consulting firm, the Juran Institute, in Wilton, Connecticut. In the 1950s, he was invited to Japan by JUSE to help rebuilding Japanese corporations develop management concepts. Juran based some of his principles on the work of Walter Shewhart and, like Deming and the other quality gurus, believed that management and the system are responsible for quality. Juran is the creator of statistical quality control and the author of a book entitled *The Quality Control Handbook.* This book has become an international standard reference for the quality movement.

Juran's definition of quality is described as "fitness for use as perceived by the customer." If a product is produced and the customer perceives it as fit for use, then the quality mission has been accomplished. Juran also believed that every person in the organization must be involved in the effort to make products or services that are fit for use.

Juran described a perpetual spiral of progress or continuous striving toward quality. Steps on this spiral are, in ascending order, research, development, design, specification, planning, purchasing, instrumentation, production, process control, inspection, testing, sale, service, and then back to research again. The idea behind the spiral is that each time the steps are completed, products or services would increase in quality. Juran explained that chronic problems should be solved by following this spiral; he formulated a break-through sequence to increase the standard of performance so that problems are eliminated. To alleviate sporadic problems, which he finds are often solved with temporary solutions, he suggests care-fully examining the system causing the problem and adjusting it to solve the difficulty. Once operating at this improved standard of performance, with the sporadic problem solved, the process of ana-lyzing chronic and sporadic problems should start over again.

Juran pointed out that companies often overlook the cost of pro-ducing low-quality products. He suggested that by implementing his theories of quality improvement, not only would higher quality prod-ucts be produced, but the actual costs would be lower. His Cost of Quality principle was known as "Gold in the Mine."

Juran is known for his work with statistics, and he relied on the quantification of standards and statistical quality control techniques. He is credited with implementing use of the Pareto diagram to im-prove business systems as well.

Juran's concept of quality included the managerial dimensions of planning, organizing, and controlling (known as the Juran Tril-ogy) and focused on the responsibility of management to achieve quality and the need to set goals. His ten steps to quality are as follows:

1. Build awareness of opportunities to improve.
2. Set goals for improvement.
3. Organize to reach goals.
4. Provide training.
5. Carry out projects to solve problems.
6. Report progress.
7. Give recognition.
8. Communicate results.
9. Keep score.
10. Maintain momentum by making annual improvement part of the regular systems and processes of the company.

Ishikawa and the Japanese Experts

Kaoru Ishikawa studied under both Homer Sarasohn and Edwards Deming during the late 1940s and early 1950s. As President of JUSE, he was instrumental in developing a unique Japanese strategy for total quality: the broad involvement of the entire organization in its *total* sense—every worker, every process, and every job. This also included the complete life cycle of the product, from start to finish.

Some of his accomplishments include the success of the quality circle in Japan, in part due to innovative tools such as the cause-and-effect diagram (often called the Ishikawa fishbone diagram because it resembles a fish skeleton). His approach was to provide easy-to-use analytical tools that could be used by all workers, including those on the line, to analyze and solve problems.

Ishikawa identified seven critical success factors that were essential for the success of total quality control in Japan:

1. Company-wide total quality control (CWTQC) and participation by *all* members of the organization
2. Education and training in all aspects of total quality, which often amounts to thirty days per year per employee
3. Use of quality circles to update standards and regulations, which are in constant need of improvement
4. Quality audits by the president and quality council members (senior executives) twice a year
5. Widespread use of statistical methods and a focus on problem prevention
6. Nationwide quality control promotion activities, with the national imperative of keeping Japanese quality number one in the world
7. Revolutionary *mental* attitude on the part of both management and workers toward one another and toward the customer, including welcoming complaints, encouraging risk, and a wider span of control

Ishikawa believed that Japanese management practices should be democratic, with management providing the guidelines. Mission statements were used extensively and operating policies derived from them. Top management, he taught, must assume a leadership position to implement the policies so that they are followed by all.

The impact on Japanese industry was startling. In seven to ten years, the electronics and telecommunications industries were transformed, with the entire nation revitalized by the end of the 1960s.

Armand Feigenbaum

Unlike Deming and Juran, Feigenbaum did not work with the Japanese. He was Vice President of Worldwide Quality for General Electric until the last 1960s, when he set up his own consulting firm, General Systems, Inc. He is best known for coining the term *total quality control* and for his 850-page book on the subject. His teachings center around the integration of people–machine–information structures in order to economically and effectively control quality and achieve full customer satisfaction.

Feigenbaum taught that there are two requirements to establishing quality as a business strategy: establishing customer satisfaction must be central and quality/cost objectives must drive the total quality system. His systems theory of total quality control includes four fundamental principles:

- Total quality is a continuous work process, starting with customer requirements and ending with customer satisfaction.
- Documentation allows visualization and communication of work assignments.
- The quality system provides for greater flexibility because of a greater use of alternatives provided.
- Systematic re-engineering of major quality activities leads to greater levels of continuous improvement.

Like Juran and Deming, Feigenbaum used a visual concept to capture the idea of waste and rework—the so-called Hidden Plant. Based upon studies, he taught that this "Hidden Plant" can account for between 15 and 40 percent of the production capacity of a company. In his book, he used the concept of the "9 M's" to describe the factors which affect quality: (1) markets, (2) money, (3) management, (4) men, (5) motivation, (6) materials, (7) machines and mechanization, (8) modern information methods, and (9) mounting product requirements.

According to Andrea Gabor in "The Man Who Discovered Quality," Feigenbaum took a nut-and-bolts approach to quality, while

Deming is often viewed as a visionary. Nuts and bolts led him to focus on the benefits and outcomes of total quality, rather than only the process to follow. His methods led to increased quantification of total quality program improvements during the 1970s and 1980s.

Philip Crosby

Unlike the other quality gurus, who were scientists, engineers, and statisticians, Philip Crosby is known for his motivational talks and style of presentation. His emergence began in 1961, when he first developed the concept of zero defects while working as a quality manager at Martin Marietta Corporation in Orlando, Florida. He believed that "zero defects" motivated line workers to turn out perfect products. He soon joined ITT, where he quickly moved up the ranks to Vice President of Quality Control Operations, covering 192 manufacturing facilities in 46 countries. He held the position until 1979, when he opened his own consulting company, which became one of the largest of its kind with over 250 people worldwide.

He established the Quality College in 1980 and used that concept to promote his teachings and writings in eighteen languages. It has been estimated that over five million people have attended its courses, and his trilogy of books are popular and easy to read. It is in these works where he introduces the four absolutes of his total quality management philosophy:

1. The definition of quality is conformance to requirements.
2. The system of quality is prevention of problems.
3. The performance standard of quality is zero defects.
4. The measurement of quality is the price of nonconformance, or the cost of quality.

The fourth principle, the Cost of Quality, is similar to Feigenbaum's Hidden Plant and Juran's Gold in the Mine. Like Deming, he has fourteen steps to quality improvement. Also like Deming, he has been very critical of the Malcolm Baldrige National Quality Award, although his influence (like Deming's) can be seen in virtually all seven categories.

He departs from the other gurus in his emphasis on performance standards instead of statistical data to achieve zero defects. He believes that identifying goals to be achieved, setting standards for the final product, removing all error-causing situations, and complete organizational commitment comprise the foundation for excellence.

ISO 9000 AND THE QUALITY MOVEMENT

At the turn of the century, England was the most advanced nation in the world in terms of quality standards. During World War I, England led the charge and during World War II was at least the equal of the United States—with one exception. England did not have Shewhart, Deming, and the other American quality gurus. It was not until the Common Market accepted the firm touch of Prime Minister Margaret Thatcher that the European movement was galvanized in 1979 with the forerunner of ISO 9000. It was Thatcher who orchestrated the transformance of the British ISO 9000 series for the European community. In less than 20 years, it has become the worldwide quality standard.

ENDNOTES

1. Shewhart, W. A. (1931). *Economic Control of Quality of Manufactured Product*. New York: Van Nostrand.
2. Olmstead, Denison (1972). *Memoir of Eli Whitney, Esq.* New York: Arno Press.
3. Walter Shewhart on the "go–no-go" concept: If, for example, a design involving the use of a cylindrical shaft in a bearing is examined, interchangeability might be ensured simply by using a suitable "go" plug gauge on the bearing and a suitable "go" ring gauge on the shaft. In this case, the difference between the dimensions of the two "go" gauges gives the minimum clearance. Such a method of gauging, however, does not fix the maximum clearance. The production worker soon realized that a slack fit between a part and its "go" gauge might result in enough play between the shaft and its bearing to cause the product to be rejected; therefore, he tried to keep the fit between the part and its "go" gauge as close as possible, thus encountering some of the difficulties that had been experienced in trying to make the parts exactly alike.
4. Walter Shewhart was the first to realize that, with the development of the atomic structure of matter and electricity, it became necessary to

regard laws as being statistical in nature. According to Shewhart, the importance of the law of large numbers in the interpretation of physical phenomena will become apparent to anyone who even hastily surveys any one or more of the following works: Darrow, K. K. (1929). "Statistical Theories of Matter, Radiation, and Electricity." *The Physical Review Supplement*, Vol. I, No. I, July 1929 (also published in the series of Bell Telephone Laboratories reprints, No. 435); Rice, J. (1930). *Introduction to Statistical Mechanics for Students of Physics and Physical Chemistry*. London: Constable & Company; Tolman, R. E. (1927). *Statistical Mechanics with Applications to Physics and Chemistry*. New York: Chemical Catalog Company; Loeb, L. B. (1927). *Kinetic Theory of Gases*. New York: McGraw-Hill; Bloch, E. (1924). *The Kinetic Theory of Bases*. London: Methuen & Company; Richtmeyer, F. K. (1928). *Introduction to Modern Physics*. New York: McGraw-Hill; Wilson, H. A. (1928). *Modern Physics*. London: Blackie & Son; Darrow, K. K. (1926). *Introduction to Contemporary Physics*. New York: D. Van Nostrand; Ruark, A. E. and Urey, H. C. (1930). *Atoms, Molecules and Quanta*. New York: McGraw-Hill.

5. Matthies, Leslie (1960). "The Beginning of Modern Scientific Management." *The Office*, April 1960.

6. Walter Shewhart on the use of the control chart: Whereas the concept of mass production of 1787 was born of an *exact* science, the concept underlying the quality control chart technique of 1924 was born of a *probable* science, which has empirically derived control limits. These limits are to be set so that when the observed quality of a piece of product falls outside of them, even though the observation is still within the limits L_1 and L_2 (tolerance limits), it is desirable to look at the manufacturing process in order to discover and remove, if possible, one or more causes of variation that need not be left to chance.

7. Shewhart noted that it is essential, however, in industry and in science to understand the distinction between a stable system and an unstable system and how to plot points and conclude by rational methods whether they indicate a stable system. To quote Shewhart, "This conclusion is consistent with that so admirably presented in a recent paper by S. L. Andrew in the *Bell Telephone Quarterly*, Jan., 1931, and also with conclusions set forth in the recent book *Business Adrift*, by W. B. Donham, Dean of the Harvard Business School. Such reading cannot do other than strengthen our belief in the fact that control of quality will come only through the weeding out of assignable causes of variation—particularly those that introduce lack of constancy in the chance cause system."

8. As the statistician enters the scene, the three traditional elements of control take on a new meaning, as Shewhart summarized: "Corresponding to these three steps there are three senses in which statistical control may play an important part in attaining uniformity in the

quality of a manufactured product: (a) as a concept of a statistical state constituting a limit to which one may hope to go in improving the uniformity of quality; (b) as an operation or technique of attaining uniformity; and (c) as a judgment."

9. Deming refers to assignable causes as being "specific to some ephemeral (brief) event that can usually be discovered to the satisfaction of the expert on the job, and removed."

10. Shewhart used what he called the *Ideal Bowl Experiment* to physically characterize a state of statistical control. A number of physically similar poker chips with numbers written on them are placed in a bowl. Successive samples (Shewhart seems to prefer a sample size of four) are taken from the bowl, each time mixing the remaining chips. The chips removed from the bowl are drawn by chance—there are only chance causes of variation. In speaking of chance causes of variation, Shewhart proves, contrary to popular belief, that the statistician can have a sense of humor. "If someone were shooting at a mark and failed to hit the bull's-eye and was then asked why, the answer would likely be *chance*. Had someone asked the same question of one of man's earliest known ancestors, he might have attributed his lack of success to the dictates of fate or to the will of the gods. I am inclined to think that in many ways one of these excuses is about as good as another. The Ideal Bowl Experiment is an abstract means of characterizing the physical state of statistical control." A sequence of samples of any process can be compared mathematically to the bowl experiment and, if found similar, the process can be said to be affected only by random or chance causes of variation or can be characterized as being in a *state of statistical control*. Shewhart states: "It seems to me that it is far safer to take some one physical operation such as drawing from a bowl as a physical model for an act that may be repeated at random, and then to require that any other repetitive operation believed to be random shall in addition produce results similar in certain respects to the results of drawing from a bowl before we act as though the operation in question were random."

11. It may be helpful to think of the three steps in the mass production process as steps in the scientific method. In this sense, specification, production, and inspection correspond, respectively, to formulating a hypothesis, conducting an experiment, and testing the hypothesis. The three steps constitute the dynamic scientific process of acquiring knowledge.

12. The following story was related at one of Deming's now-famous four-day quality seminars: I remember him (Shewhart) pacing the floor in his room at the Hotel Washington before the third lecture. He was explaining something to me. I remarked that these great thoughts should be in his lectures. He said that they were already written up in his third and fourth lectures. I remarked that if he wrote up these

lectures in the same way that he had just explained them to me, they would be clearer. He said that his writing had to be foolproof. I thereupon remarked that he had written his thoughts to be so darn foolproof that no one could understand them.

13. Halberstam, David (1960). The War Effort during WWII, Lectures, Articles and Interview Notes.

14. This is a general consensus feeling among many historians and writers as to the inherent "evil" of Taylorism—machine over man. Walter Shewhart, to his credit and genius, tries to marry quality control and scientific management. In the foreword to his 1931 master work referred to in Endnote 8, he writes, "Broadly speaking, the object of industry is to set up economic ways and means of satisfying human wants and in so doing to reduce everything possible to routines requiring a minimum amount of human effort. Through the use of the scientific method, extended to take account of modern statistical concepts, it has been found possible to set up limits within which the results of routine efforts must lie if they are to be economical. Deviations in the results of a routine process outside such limits indicate that the routine has broken down and will no longer be economical until the cause of trouble is removed."

15. Bonstingal, John Jay (1992). *Schools of Quality*. New York: Free Press.

16. The Hawthorne Experiments, Elton Mayo, 1938.

17. Voehl, F. W. (1990). "The Deming Prize." *South Carolina Business Journal*, 1990 edition, pp. 33–38.

18. This was first pointed out by Robert Chadman Wood in an article about Homer Sarasohn, published in *Forbes* in 1990.

GLOSSARY

Abnormal variation: Changes in process performance that cannot be accounted for by typical day-to-day variation. Also referred to as nonrandom variation.

Acceptable quality (AQL): The maximum number of parts that do not comply with quality standards.

Activity: The tasks performed to change inputs into outputs.

Adaptable: An adaptable process is designed to maintain effectiveness and efficiency as requirements change. The process is deemed adaptable when there is agreement among suppliers, owners, and customers that the process will meet requirements throughout the strategic period.

Appraisal cost: The cost incurred to determine defects.

Benchmarking: A tool used to improve products, services, or management processes by analyzing the best practices of other companies to determine standards of performance and how to achieve them in order to increase customer satisfaction.

Business objectives: Specific objectives which, if achieved, will ensure that the operating objectives of the organization are in alignment with the vision, values, and strategic direction. They are generally high level and timeless.

Business process: Organization of people, equipment, energy, procedures, and material into measurable, value-added activities needed to produce a specified end result.

Business process analysis (BPA): Review and documentation (mapping) of a key business process to understand how it currently functions and to establish measures.

Competitive: A process is considered to be competitive when its overall performance is judged to be as good as that of comparable processes. Competitiveness is based on a set of performance characteristics (defects, costs, inventory turnaround, etc.) that are monitored and tracked against comparable processes within the corporation, the industry, and/or the general business community.

Competitive benchmarking: Comparing and rating the practices, processes, and products of an organization against the competition. Comparisons are confined to the same industry.

Conformance: Affirmative indication or judgment that a product or service

311

has met specified requirements, contracts, or regulations. The state of meeting the requirements.

Continuous improvement: This is a principle used by W. Edwards Deming to examine improvement of product and service. It involves searching unceasingly for ever-higher levels of quality by isolating sources of defects. It is called *kaizen* in Japan, where the goal is zero defects. Quality management and improvement is a never-ending activity.

Control: The state of stability, or normal variation and predictability. It is the process of regulating and guiding operations and processes using quantitative data. Control mechanisms are also used to detect and avoid potential adverse effects of change.

Control charts: Statistical plots derived from measuring a process. Control charts help detect and determine deviations before a defect results. Inherent variations in manufacturing and nonmanufacturing processes can be spotted and accounted for by designers.

Corrective action: The implementation of effective solutions that result in the elimination of identified product, service, and process problems.

Cost of quality: The sum of prevention, appraisal, and failure costs, usually expressed as a percentage of total cost or revenue.

Critical success factors (CSFs): Areas in which results, if satisfactory, will ensure successful corporate performance. They ensure that the company will meet its business objectives. CSFs are focused, fluctuate, and are conducive to short-term plans.

Cross-functional: A term used to describe individuals from different business units or functions who are part of a team to solve problems, plan, and develop solutions for process-related actions affecting the organization as a system.

Cross-functional focus: The effort to define the flow of work products in a business process as determined by their sequence of activities, rather than by functional or organizational boundaries.

Culture (also vision): The pattern of shared beliefs and values that provides members of an organization rules of behavior or accepted norms for conducting operational business.

Customer: The recipient or beneficiary of the outputs of work efforts or the purchaser of products and services. May be either internal or external to the company.

Customer, internal: Organizations have both external and internal customers. Many functions and activities are not directly involved with external customer satisfaction, but their outputs provide inputs to other functions and activities within the organization. Data processing, for example, must provide an acceptable quality level for many internal customers.

Customer requirements (also called valid requirements): The statement of needs or expectations that a product or service must satisfy. Requirements must be specific, measurable, negotiated, agreed to, documented, and communicated.

Customer/supplier model: The model is generally represented using three interconnected triangles to depict inputs flowing into a work process that, in turn, adds value and produces outputs that are delivered to a customer. Throughout the process, requirements and feedback are fed from the customer to the supplier to ensure that customer quality requirements are met.

Cycle time: The elapsed time between the commencement and completion of a task. In manufacturing, it is calculated as the number of units of work-in-process inventory divided by the number of units processed in a specific period. In order processing it can be the time between receipt and delivery of an order. Overall cycle time can mean the time from concept of a new product or service until it is brought to market.

Defect: Something that does not conform to requirements.

Document of understanding (DOU): A formal agreement defining the roles, responsibilities, and objectives of all the parties to that agreement. The degree of detail is dictated by the nature of the agreement, but it should always clearly address the requirements of the work product in question.

Effective: An effective process produces output that conforms to customer requirements. The lack of process effectiveness is measured by the degree to which the process output does not conform to customer requirements (that is, by the level of defect of the output).

Effectiveness: The state of having produced a decided or desired effect; the state of achieving customer satisfaction.

Efficiency: A measure of performance that compares output production with cost or resource utilization (as in number of units per employee per hour or per dollar).

Efficient: An efficient process produces the required output at the lowest possible (minimum) cost. That is, the process avoids waste or loss of resources in producing the required output. Process efficiency is measured by the ratio of required output to the cost of producing that output. This cost is expressed in units of applied resource (dollars, hours, energy, etc.).

Employee involvement (EI): Promotions and mechanisms to achieve employee contributions, individually and in groups, to quality and less company performance objectives. Cross-functional teams, task forces, quality circles, or other vehicles for involvement are used.

Employee well-being and morale: Maintenance of work environment conducive to well-being and growth of all employees. Factors include health, safety, satisfaction, work environment, training, and special services such as counseling assistance, recreational, or cultural.

Executive Quality Service Council (EQSC): Comprised of members of executive management and union leadership who oversee the quality effort from a corporate view and set strategic direction.

Facilitator: Responsible for guiding the team through analysis of the process. Also concerned with how well the team works together.

Failure cost: The cost resulting from the occurrence of defects (such as scrap, rework/redo, replacement, etc.).

Functional organization: An organization responsible for one of the major corporate business functions such as marketing, sales, design, manufacturing, or distribution.

Human resource management: Development of plans and practices that realize the full potential of the work force to pursue the quality and performance objectives of the organization. Includes (1) education and training, (2) recruitment, (3) involvement, (4) empowerment, and (5) recognition.

Implementer: An individual working within the process and who is responsible for carrying out specific job tasks.

Indicators: Benchmarks, targets, standards, or other measures used to evaluate how well quality values and programs are integrated.

Information system: A database of information used for planning day-to-day management and control of quality. Types of data should include (1) customer related, (2) internal operations, (3) company performance, and (4) cost and financial.

Inputs: Products or services obtained from others (suppliers) in order to perform job tasks. Material or information required to complete the activities necessary for a specified end result.

Involved managers: Managers who have responsibility for the day-to-day activities and tasks within the process.

Just-in-time (JIT): The delivery of parts and materials by a supplier at the moment a factory needs them, thus eliminating costly inventories. Quality is paramount because a faulty part delivered at the last moment will not be detected.

Kaizen: See Continuous improvement

Leadership: The category of the Baldrige Award that examines personal leadership and involvement of executives in creating and sustaining a customer focus and clear and visible quality values.

Management for quality: The translation of customer focus and quality values into implementation plans for all levels of management and supervision.

Measurable outcomes: Specific results that determine, corporately, how well critical success factors and business objectives are being achieved. They are concrete, specific, and measurable.

Measurement: The methods used to achieve and maintain conformance to customer requirements. Measurement determines the current status of the process and whether the process requires change or improvement.

Mission: The core purpose of being for an organization. Usually expressed in the form of a statement 25 to 50 words in length.

Operating plans: Specific, actionable plans which, if carried out successfully, ensure that critical success factors are met, which in turn ensures that corporate business objectives are met. They are tied to critical success factors, are detailed, and contain measurements of success.

Operating Quality Service Council (OQSC): Comprised of activity management and their direct reports, and many include union and staff representation. The council oversees the quality effort within an activity and ensures that quality strategies support the corporate strategic direction.

Organization for quality: Structuring organizational activities to effectively accomplish the company's objectives.

Outputs: The specified end result, materials, or information provided to others (internal or external customers).

Pareto analysis (or Pareto chart): A statistical method of measurement to identify the most important problems through different measuring scales (for example, frequency, cost, etc.). Usually displayed by a bar graph that ranks causes of process variation by the degree of impact on quality (sometimes called the 80/20 rule).

Prevention activity: Elements of prevention activity include (1) education in process quality management and (2) process management (ownership, documentation/analysis, requirements activity, measurements including statistical techniques, and corrective action on the process).

Prevention cost: Costs incurred to reduce the total cost of quality.

Process: The organization of people, equipment, energy, procedures, and material into the work activities needed to produce a specified end result (work product). A sequence of repeatable activities characterized as having measurable inputs, value-added activities, and measurable outputs. It is a set of interrelated work activities characterized by a set of specific inputs and value-added tasks that produce a set of specific outputs.

Process analysis: The systematic examination of a process model to establish a comprehensive understanding of the process itself. The intent of the examination should include consideration of simplification, elimination of unneeded or redundant elements, and improvement.

Process capability: The level of effectiveness and efficiency at which the process will perform. This level may be determined through the use of statistical control charts. Long-term performance level after the process has been brought under control.

Process control: The activity necessary to ensure that the process is performing as designed. Achieved through the use of statistical techniques, such as control charts, so that appropriate actions can be taken to achieve and maintain a state of statistical control.

Process elements: A process is comprised of activities and tasks. A process may also be referred to as a subprocess when it is subordinate to, but part of, a larger process. A subprocess can also be defined as a group of activities within a process that comprise a definable component.

Process management: The disciplined management approach of applying prevention methodologies to the implementation, improvement, and change of work processes to achieve effectiveness, efficiency, and adaptability. Critical to the success of process management is the concept of cross-functional focus.

Process model: A detailed representation of the process (graphic, textual, mathematical) as it currently exists.

Process owner: Coordinates the various functions and work activities at all levels of a process, has the authority or ability to make changes in the process as required, and manages the process end-to-end so as to ensure optimal overall performance.

Process performance quality: A measure of how effectively and efficiently a process satisfies customer requirements. The ability of a product or service to meet and exceed the expectations of customers.

Process review: An objective assessment of how well the methodology has been applied to the process. Emphasizes the potential for long-term process results rather than the actual results achieved.

Quality function deployment (QFD): A system that pays special attention to customer needs and integrates them into the marketing, design, manufacturing, and service processes. Activities that do not contribute to customer needs are considered wasteful.

Quality Improvement Team (QIT): A group of people brought together to resolve a specific problem or issue identified by a business process analysis, individual employees, or the Operating Quality Service Council. A group of individuals charged with the task of planning and implementing process quality improvement. The three major roles in this task force are the team leader, team facilitator, and team members.

Quality management: The management of a process to maximize customer satisfaction at the lowest overall cost to the company.

Quality management system: The collective plans, activities, and events established to ensure that a product, process, or service will satisfy given needs. The infrastructure supporting the operational process management and improvement methodology.

Quality planning: The process of developing the quality master to link together all of the planning systems of the organization. The objective is to follow all areas of achievement of the vision, mission, and business objectives and to operationalize the strategy by identifying the requirements to achieve leadership in the market segments chosen. Includes key requirements and performance indicators and the resources committed for these requirements.

Quality tool: Instrument or technique that supports the activities of process quality management and improvement.

Requirements: What is expected in providing a product or service. The *it* in "do it right the first time." Specific and measurable customer needs with an associated performance standard.

Resource allocation: A decision to allocate resources, capital, and people to support specific operating plans, tied to the budget process.

Results: Results are, quite simply, a measurement of how well corporate business objectives are being met. Results require that standards and goals for performance are set and the results of processes and performance tracked.

Robust design: Making product designs "production-proof" by building in tolerances for manufacturing variables that are known to be unavoidable.

Root cause: Original reason for nonconformance within a process. When the root cause is removed or corrected, the nonconformance will be eliminated.

Six-sigma: A statistical term that indicates a defect level. One-sigma means 68% of products are acceptable, three-sigma means 99.75, and six-sigma means 99.999997% perfect or 3.4 defects per million parts.

Sponsor: Advocate for the team who provides resources and helps define mission and scope to set limits.

Stakeholder: Individual or department who either has an effect on the process or is affected by it.

Statistical process control (SPC): The use of statistical techniques, such as control charts, to analyze a work process or its outputs. The data can be used to identify deviations so that appropriate action can be taken to maintain a state of statistical control (predetermined upper and lower limits) and to improve the capability of the process.

Statistical quality control (SQC): A method of analyzing measured deviations in manufactured materials, parts, and products.

Strategic quality planning: Development of strategic and operational plans that incorporate quality as product or service differentiation and the load bearing structure of the planning process. Includes (1) definition of customer requirements, (2) projections of the industry and competitive environment for identification of opportunities and risks, (3) comparison of opportunities and risks against company resources and capabilities, (4) employee involvement, and (5) supplier capabilities.

Subprocesses: The internal processes that make up a process.

Suppliers: Individuals or groups who provide input. Suppliers can be internal or external to a company, group, or organization.

Taguchi methods: Statistical techniques developed by Genichi Taguchi, a Japanese consultant, for optimizing design and production.

Task: The basic work element of a process activity.

Total quality management (TQM): The application of quality principles for the integration of all functions and processes of the organization. The ultimate goal is customer satisfaction. The way to achieve it is through continuous improvement.

Variation: The degree to which a product, service, or element deviates from the specification or requirements. Quality in service organizations deals with identifying, measuring, and adjusting to variability resulting from interactions with customers, while manufacturing organizations are focused on bringing product variability under control.

Vision: The long-term future desired state of an organization, usually expressed in a 7- to 20-year time frame. Often included in the vision statement are the areas that the organization needs to care about in order to succeed. The vision should inspire and motivate.

INDEX

A

ABC analysis, 108
Adaptability, 237
Advent Group, Inc., 171
Aleo, J.P., Jr., 124
American Society for Quality
    Control, 9, 34
American Supplier Institute, 113
Assessment, 128
Assignable causes, 293, 294
Assistance, 106
Attribute data, 193
Atttribute measure, 196, 197
Audit, 106–107
    case study, 253, 254 255, 270–282,
        303
    certification and, 128–131
    ISO 9000, 155–156
Automotive industry, 2–3, 11
Awards, 265, 268–270

B

Baldrige, M., 31
Baldrige Award, see Malcolm
    Baldrige National Quality
    Award
Barth, C.G.L., 289
Bell-shaped curve, 195
Benchmarking, 101, 121, 168, 226, 237
Black, S.P., 137

Bottom line, impact of procurement
    on, 7–9
Breakthrough improvement, 167–168,
    169
Broadhead, J.L., 36
Brown, P., 185
BS 5750, 141
Business reengineering, 170–171, 240
Buyer, see Customer

C

Calibration, 131
Camp, R.C., 168
Capability index, 199–202
Categorical method, 203
Caterpillar Tractor Co., 137–138
Cause-and-effect diagram, 303
Celebration, 12
Central tendency, 194
Certification, 107, 125, 127–138,
        231–233, 241–242
    ISO 9000, 159–160
    objectives of, 127–128
    paradigms, 128, 129
    supplier audit, 128–131
    supplier selection and, 135–136
    types of, 132–135
Champion, 214
Champy, J., 170, 240
Chance causes, 294
Change control, 130–131

Cherry-Burrell Corp., 12
Chrysler, 134
Classification levels, 253
Clifford, S., 35
Cobb, I., 76
Collaboration, 12
Collins, F.C., 31, 34, 35, 36, 40, 42
Commodities, 99
  prioritizing, 105
Commodity teams, 62, 105–107, 221,
  223–224
Common cause variation, 192
Communication, 83–84, 106, 113, 185
Company-wide total quality control,
  303
Competition, 123–124, 236
Concurrent engineering, 171
Constancy of purpose, 49, 147
Consultants, 41, 211
Contingencies, reducing the number
  of suppliers and, 112
Continuous improvement, 165–186,
  229–230
  benchmarking, 168
  quality function deployment, 170
  quality tools and, 177
  reengineering, 170–171
  strategies, 166–168
  Systematic Improvement Method,
    171–177, 178–183
  value analysis, 169
Continuous process improvement,
  96–97
Contracts, 71, 72, 244
  reducing the number of suppliers
    and, 112
Control, 18–19, 293–294
Control chart, 18, 199, 292, 293, 307
Controlled variation, 293
Control limits, 287
Control system, 293, 294
Cooperation, 12, 70
Corporate Measurement System, 208
Corrective action, 131, 144, 156
Cost, 66, 185
Cost of control, 288
Cost of quality, 302, 305

Cost ratio method, 204
Counselors, 41
Cousins, P., 185
Creativity, 21, 47
Critical functions, 154
Critical interface, 148
Critical success factors, 101
Crosby, P., 40, 80, 305–306
Cross-functional management, 47
Cultural transformation, 22
Culture, 21, 47, 59–61, 261, see also
  Social system
Cumming/Onon Corporation, 27
Customer, 52
Customer credibility, 89–91
Customer expectations, 27
  supplier's perceptions of, 87–88
Customer focus and orientation,
  65–66
Customer group, 101
Customer needs, 106, 236
  communication of, 84–86
  hierarchy of, 66–68
Customer satisfaction, 16, 17, 20, 21,
  23, 25, 101, 304
  Baldrige Award and, 35
Customer service, 281
Customer–supplier integration, 13
Customer–supplier relationship, 49,
  50, 65–94, 225
  customer focus and orientation,
    65–66
  hierarchy of customer needs, 66–68
  Japanese model, 68–74
  in TQM, 80–94
Cycle time, 99, 129

D

Dale, B.G., 80
Davidow, W.H., 240
DeCarlo, N., 36, 37
Defects, 18
Delivery, 66, 262–263, 267, 276
Deming, W.E., 20, 21, 31, 53, 80, 147,
  300, 308

Deming Prize, 25, 135, 141, 300
 application checklist, 38–39
 Baldrige Award vs., 30–43
Deming wheel, 296
DeRose, L., 80
Design and implementation team,
 215–217
Design control, 155
Design process, 129
Detection, 193
Dispersion, 194
Disputes, 72, 244
Distribution, 193
Distributors, 122–123
Division of labor, 286–287, 288, 297
Documentation, 146–149, 272, 276,
 304
Drucker, P.F., 226
Duncan, R.M., 207
Duffy, J.F., 30

E

EDI, see Electronic data interchange
Education, 224–226, 234, 240–241
Electronic data interchange, 96,
 190–191, 242, 244
Eli Lilly, 12
Empowerment, 22, 243–244
Encryption, 244
Environment, 52, 102
Evaluating suppliers, 138
Ewing, S.E., 252
Extended benchmarking, 237
Extended organization, 4–6, 47, 239

F

Factory system, 288
Feedback, 50, 51, 52, 56, 125, 226
 measurement and, 187–189, see also
 Measurement
 methods, 189–191
 policy deployment and, 97, 107
 poor, 83–84

Feigenbaum, A., 304–305
Financial stability, 254, 265, 267
Fitness for use, 301
Flexibility, 236–237
Florida Power & Light, 32, 35, 36, 37,
 40, 100, 132–133, 170, 171
Flowchart, 25
Focus, 236
Forbes, C., 122
Ford Motor Company, 107, 110, 113,
 134
Friendship, 237

G

Gabor, A., 304
Gantt, H.L., 289
Gantt chart, 220
GE Silicones, 207
General Electric, 169
General Motors, 133
Gilbreth, F.G., 290
Gilbreth, L., 290
Globalization, 139–140
Globe Metallurgical, 33, 34
Goals, 119, 120
"Gold in the Mine," 302
Golomski, W., 34, 37, 41
Go–no-go tolerance, 287, 293, 306
Gopalakrishnan, K.N., 204
Governor's Sterling Award for
 Quality and Productivity, 135

H

Hammer, M., 170, 240
Hammons, C., 12
Harris Corporation, 62
Healthcare, 3–4
Hoshin planning, see Policy
 deployment
Hospital system, 54
House of Quality, 47, 104, 204
Hutchins, G., 77

I

Ideal bowl experiment, 294, 308
Implementation, 213–234
  certification, 231–233
  continuous improvement, 229–230
  design and implementation team,
    215–218
  management commitment, 213–215
  planning for, 218–221
  project results and monitoring,
    230–231
  PSQM structure, 221–224
  quality improvement activities, 229
  supplier and project selection and
    planning, 228
  supplier policy deployment, 226–227
  supplier symposia, 227–228
  training internal staff, 224–226
Improvement, 49, 50, 55–56, 125, 128,
    234
Improvement strategies, 166–171
Incentives, 129
Incremental improvement, 166–167,
    169
Individual activity management, 25
Information and analysis, 46
Information systems, 242–243
Innovation, 47, 238, 265
Input, 52
Inspection, 287–288, 295
Inspection, testing, and examination,
    130
Integration, 13, 49, 239, see also
    Linking
Interchangeable parts, 286–287, 292
Interface, 148
Internal audit, 303
Internal customer, 148
Internal quality audit, 155–156, see
    also Audit
Internal quality control, 261
INTERNET, 242
Inventory, 122
Ishikawa, K., 68, 69, 70, 80, 303–304
ISO 9000, 25, 139–163, 241–242, 306
  certification, 134, 159–160

defined, 140
documentation, 146–149
history of, 140–141
implementing, 158–160
internal quality audits, 155–156
management responsibility,
    149–153, 157, 158
marketing, 155
QA and, 141–146
quality measurement system,
    208–212
quality records, 157
quality system, 153–155
TQM and, 160–161

J

Japan, 28, 206, 299
  concept of control in, 18–19
Japan Quality Control Prize, 42
Japanese model of customer–supplier
    relationships, 68–74
JIT, see Just-in-time
Johnson, J.G., 62
Juran, J., 21, 52, 301–302
JUSE, see Union of Japanese
    Scientists and Engineers
Just-in-time, 63–64, 66, 67, 76, 96

K

Kaizen, 167
Kano, N., 17, 18
Keiretsu, 11, 28–29
King, R., 166
Kinni, T.B., 28
Kivenko, K., 122
Kodak, 124–125
Kume, H., 171

L

Lab controls, 131
Lascelles, D.M., 80
Leach, K., 33, 34, 36, 40

Leadership, 47, 57, 226
Life cycle costs, 114
Linking, 49, 50, see also Integration
    objectives of, 95–97
    policy deployment and, see Policy
        deployment
Louw, A.A., 246

M

Magill, W.S., 300
Major business process, 101
Malcolm Baldrige National Quality
    Award, 25, 45, 46, 134–135, 305
    Deming Prize vs., 30–43
Malone, M.S., 240
Management commitment, 129,
    213–215, 237
Management quality, 206
Management responsibility, 149–153,
    157, 158–159
Management system, 17, 20, 21,
    23–25, 47, 48, 49
Managers, 20, 47
Manual, 252–282, 261
Manufactory, 286
Manufacturing resource planning
    system, 122
Manufacturing system, 53
Marketing, 155
Material acceptance, 257
Material control, 279–280
Materials management, 130
Maximum, 195
McGregor, D., 21
Mean, 194
Measurement, 22, 121, 144, 173, 226,
    230, see also specific topics
    ISO 9000 quality system, 208–212
    statistical process control, 191–202
    supplier report card, 202–203
    supplier scoring methods, 203–204
    supplier selection and, 205
Median, 194
Michigan Consolidated Gas Com-
    pany, 247–284

applying the quality process to an
    MRO environment, 247–252
quality supplier's manual, 252–284
    audit, 270–282
    awards, 268–270
    classification levels, 253–256
    computational process, 260–266
    glossary of terms, 283–284
    overall evaluation/rating,
        266–268
    rating system, 256–260
Minimum, 105
Mission, 6, 24, 115–116, 144, 146, 147
Mission statement, 25, 116
Mode, 194
Moody, P.E., 13
Motivation, 21, 47, 128
Motorola, 133
Mutual confidence, 69–70

N

National Accreditation Council for
    Certification Bodies, 160
Negotiation, 107
Noguchi, J., 42
Nonconforming material, 131
Non-value-added steps, 96
Normal distribution, 195

O

Objectives, 24, 49, 98, 119, 144, 147
Olian, J.D., 121
On-time delivery, 254, 255, 256–257
Operational results, 46–47
Ota, F., 11
Output, 51–52

P

Packaging, 276
Pang, V.K., 27
Pareto chart, 108

Partnership, 13, 62–63, 77
  reducing the number of suppliers
    and, 112
P-D-C-A, see Plan, Do, Check, Act
Peach, R., 33, 37, 42
Performance monitoring, 258
Perkins, C., 78
Perry, J., Jr., 78
Personal feedback, 190
Plan, Do, Check Act, 18–19
  Systematic Improvement Method
    and, 171–177
Policy deployment, 47, 95–125,
    226–227
  steps in, 100–114
    deployment of TQM to suppliers,
      112–113
    establishing commodity teams,
      105–107
    life cycle costs, 114
    prioritization, 100–105, 108–109
    reducing the number of suppliers,
      109–112
  supplier within, 97–99
Policy statement, 150, 154
Population, 193
Prevention, 193, 288
Price, 262–263, 267
  certification and, 129
  purchasing decisions and, 10, 12–13,
    185
  reducing the number of suppliers
    and, 111
Prioritization, 172
  concept of, 100–102
  matrix, 102–105, 108
Probability, 288
Problem solving, 25
Procedures, 150–151
Process, 20, 51, 98, 192
  prioritizing, 105
Process capability, 101, 129, 199–202
Process control, 180
Process management, 24–25, 47, 130
Process quality, management of, 46
Processor, 52
Processor team, 52

Procter & Gamble, 12
Procurement, 130
  impact on bottom line, 7–9
Procurement policy, 98
Procurement process, streamlining,
    249
Production, 295, 296
Products, 99
  prioritization of, 108–109
Project, 99
  prioritization of, 108–109
Project management, 25
  tools, 219–221
Project plan, 228
Project selection, 228
PSQM, see Purchasing/supplier
    quality management
Purchasing, 155
Purchasing decisions, factors
    affecting, 9–10
Purchasing department, responsibil-
    ity of, 88–89
Purchasing power, 91–92
Purchasing/supplier quality manage-
    ment, see also specific topics
  continuous improvement and,
    165–185
  customer–supplier relationship,
    65–94
  implementation, 213–234
  ISO 9000 and, see ISO 9000
  measurement and feedback,
    187–212
  model for, 45–56
  policy deployment, 95–125, 226–227
  supplier certification, 127–138

Q

QA, see Quality assurance
QFD, see Quality function deploy-
    ment
Quality, 66
Quality assurance, 130, 278–279
  audit, 124
  ISO 9000 and, 141–145

Quality audit, 155–156, 303, see also Audit
Quality characteristics, 66
Quality circles, 303
Quality College, 305
Quality council, 222
Quality culture, 261
Quality forecasting, 207
Quality function deployment, 170
Quality improvement, 229
  tools, 51, 177–178, 196, 219–221, 225
Quality information, 131
Quality journal, 25
Quality loop, 152–153
Quality management, 277
Quality management systems, 78
Quality manual, 261
Quality policy, 149–150
Quality program, 254
Quality readiness assessment, 58–59
Quality records, 156, 157
Quality review, 152
Quality system, 153–155
Quality tools, 51, 177–178, 196, 219–221, 225

R

Range, 195
Rating system, 256–260
Receipt inspection, 130
Recognition and rewards, 121
Red bead experiment, 294
Reducing the number of suppliers, 109–112, 137
Reengineering, 170–171, 240
Rejection rate, 254, 255
Relationship matrix, 108
Reliability, 129
Report card, 202–203
Respect for people, 20
Rework, 23
Risk taking, 21
Rockart, J., 208
Run chart, 191
Rynes, S.L., 121

S

Sadhwani, A.T., 63
Safety, 66, 261
Sample, 193
Sarasohn, H., 300
Sarhan, M., 63
Scherkenbach, W., 107, 110
Schermerhorn, M., 234
Scientific management, 289–292, 295, 296, 297, 298, 309
Scoring methods, 203–204
Selection, 107
Service, 257, 264, 267
Service acceptance, 257
Services, 3–4
  prioritization of, 108–109
Setup times, 96
Severson, D., 12
Shewhart, W., 290, 292–297, 300, 306, 307, 308, 309
Shewhart system of production, 295
Shipping, 276
Six Sigma, 121
Social system, 17, 20–22, 47, 48, 49, 291
SPC, see Statistical process control
Speaking with facts, 16, 20, 25
Spechler, J., 47
Special cause variation, 192
Specifications, 113, 129, 130–131, 287, 295
Speed, 236
Sprow, E., 140
SQC, see Statistical quality control
Stakeholder, 17, 121
Standard deviation, 195, 196
Standardization, 167–168, 169, 176
Standards, 146, 148–149
Statistical control, 101, 198–199, 294, 308
Statistical methods, 303
Statistical process control, 113, 191–202, 230–231, 261, 297, 300
  definitions, 192–193
  process status, 198–202
  statistics, 194–196

tools, 196, see also Quality tools
types of measures, 193
Statistical quality control, 31, 63, 302
Statistical techniques, 51
Statistical theory, 288
Storage, handling and shipping, 130
Strategic quality planning, 46, 47, 55
Strategy management, 24
Supplier, 53, 99, see also Purchasing/
    supplier quality management
audit, 128–131, see also Audit
certification, see Certification
evaluation, 138
policy deployment and, 97–125,
    226–227
prioritization of, 108–109
quality, defined, 27
reducing the number of, 109–112,
    137
selection of, 27, 135–136, 205
TQM and, 45–48
variation, 110–111
Supplier manual, 252–282
Supplier performance rating system,
    124
Supplier quality process, 249–250
Supplier rating system, 256–260
Supplier report card, 202–203
Supplier scoring methods, 203–204
Supplier survey, 13
Supplier team improvement process,
    124–125
Symposia, 112–113, 227–228
Systematic Improvement Method,
    171–177, 225
case study, 178–183

T

Targets, 109
Taylor, F.W., 289–292, 297–299, 300
Team building, 226
Teams, 22, 25
Teamwork, 21, 47, 122–123, 226, 238,
    239
Technical Committee 176, 140

Technical system, 17, 20, 21, 22–23,
    47, 48, 49, 50
Telecommunication, 242
Thompson, S.E., 289
Tolerance, 287, 293
Tolerance limits, 287, 292
Total integrated management, 206
Total quality
as a system, 20–26
defined, 15–19
history of, 285–309
    control limits, 287
    Crosby, 305–306
    defective parts inspection, 287–288
    Deming, 296–299
    division of labor, 286–287
    early, 285–286
    Feigenbaum, 304–305
    interchangeable parts, 286–287
    Ishikawa, 303–304
    ISO 9000, 306
    in Japan, 299–300, 303–304
    Juran, 301–302
    scientific management, 289–292
    Shewhart, 292–297
    statistical theory, 288
    Taylor, 289–292
Total quality control, 304
Total quality management, 225
buyer–supplier relationship in,
    80–94
communication of requirements,
    84–86
customer's credibility, 89—90
methodology, 81–83
misguided supplier improvement
    objectives, 90–91
poor communication and feed-
    back, 83–84
purchasing's power, 91–92
purchasing's role, 88–89
supplier's perceptions of customer
    expectations, 87–88
deployment of to suppliers, 112–113
ISO 9000 and, 160–161
PSQM vs., 50–51
supplier within, 45–48

Training, 121, 224–226, 303
Transportation, 243
Trend chart, 191
Trends, 102
Tribus, M., 20, 22, 47

U

Uncontrolled variation, 293, 294
Union of Japanese Scientists and
    Engineers, 18, 21, 31, 41, 100,
    140, 220, 300, 303
Utility system, 54

V

Value analysis, 169
Values, 6, 49, 147
Variability, reducing the number of
    suppliers and, 110–111
Variability reduction, 184
Variable data, 193
Variables measure, 196, 197
Variance, 195
Variation, 23, 110–111, 192, 293–294
Verification, 127–128
Virtual organization, 6, 240
Virtual product, 240
Vision, 6, 49, 98, 147, 234
    prioritization and, 100–101
Vision statement, 117, 118

Voehl, F., 32, 34, 35, 37, 40, 41, 47
Volume of business, reducing the
    number of suppliers and,
    111–112

W

Waste, 23, 96
Weighted point method, 204
Western Electric Hawthorne, 297,
    298, 301
White, M., 290
Whitney, E., 286, 292
Wind, J.F., 138
Work instructions, 151
Written periodic feedback report,
    190, 202

X

Xerox, 168

Y

Yahagi, S., 206
Yokogawa-Hewlett-Packard, 34

Z

Zero defects, 185, 293, 305

ABOUT THE AUTHOR

Mr. Fernandez is currently a principal of Advent Group, Inc., a consulting firm that specializes in Total Quality Management, Procurement/Material Management, and Information/Business Systems. He is also affiliated with other firms that provide similar services, such as W.A. Golomski and Associates and IQS Consulting Corp. He has over 20 years of business experience in the service, healthcare, education, manufacturing, utility, and publishing industries, where he has held various management, staff, and line positions.

Mr. Fernandez serves as a Senior Examiner for the State of Florida Quality Award, the Sterling Award, and was an Advisor for the Bahamas Quality Award. He previously served in The Productivity Center teaching quality and productivity methods to government agencies.

During his career at Florida Power & Light, the first non-Japanese company to win the coveted Deming International Quality Award, Mr. Fernandez was extensively involved in the preparation of audit materials for the Deming Quality Prize and was selected as one of the first presenters to the auditors from JUSE in the Procurement unit.

Mr. Fernandez received his Master's in Business, concentrating in Statistics and Operations Research, and a Bachelor of Science in Industrial Engineering from the University of Miami. He studied under Drs. Kano and Kondo from the Japanese Union of Scientists and Engineers and attended seminars under Dr. W. Edwards Deming. He has also been an adjunct professor at various universities in Statistics, Quality Process Improvement, Management Science, Computer Simulation, Computer Programming, and Maintenance Management. He is a registered Professional Engineer, a Certified Purchasing Manager, and a Certified Purchasing Professional. He is listed in *Who's Who of Business Leaders* and *Outstanding Young Men of America*. He has also published various articles on quality, statistics, materials management, electronic data interchange, production planning, productivity, operations research, and forecasting.